Rousseau's Theodicy of Self-

CW00959609

This book is the first comprehensive study
theory of the type of self-love (*amour propre*) that, for him, marks the central
difference between humans and the beasts. *Amour propre* is the passion
that drives human individuals to seek the esteem, approval, admiration,
or love—the *recognition*—of their fellow beings. Neuhouser reconstructs
Rousseau's understanding of what the drive for recognition is, why it is
so problematic, and how its presence opens up far-reaching developmental
possibilities for creatures that possess it. One of Rousseau's central theses
is that *amour propre* in its corrupted, manifestations—pride or vanity—is
the principal source of an array of evils so widespread that they can easily
appear to be necessary features of the human condition: enslavement,
conflict, vice, misery, and self-estrangement. Yet Rousseau also argues that
solving these problems depends not on suppressing or overcoming the
drive for recognition but on *cultivating* it so that it contributes positively
to the achievement of freedom, peace, virtue, happiness, and unalienated
selfhood. Indeed, Rousseau goes so far as to claim that, despite its many
dangers, the need for recognition is a condition of nearly everything that
makes human life valuable and that elevates it above mere animal existence:
rationality, morality, freedom—*subjectivity* itself—would be impossible for
humans if it were not for *amour propre* and the relations to others it impels
us to establish.

Frederick Neuhouser is Professor of Philosophy and Viola Manderfeld
Professor of German at Barnard College, Columbia University and Affiliate
Scholar at the Center for Psychoanalytic Training, Columbia University.

Rousseau's Theodicy of Self-Love

Evil, Rationality, and the Drive for Recognition

Frederick Neuhouser

OXFORD
UNIVERSITY PRESS

OXFORD
UNIVERSITY PRESS

Great Clarendon Street, Oxford OX2 6DP

Oxford University Press is a department of the University of Oxford.
It furthers the University's objective of excellence in research, scholarship,
and education by publishing worldwide in

Oxford New York

Auckland Cape Town Dar es Salaam Hong Kong Karachi
Kuala Lumpur Madrid Melbourne Mexico City Nairobi
New Delhi Shanghai Taipei Toronto

With offices in

Argentina Austria Brazil Chile Czech Republic France Greece
Guatemala Hungary Italy Japan Poland Portugal Singapore
South Korea Switzerland Thailand Turkey Ukraine Vietnam

Oxford is a registered trade mark of Oxford University Press
in the UK and in certain other countries

Published in the United States
by Oxford University Press Inc., New York

© Frederick Neuhouser 2008

British Library Cataloguing in Publication Data

Data available

Library of Congress Cataloging in Publication Data

Data available

Typeset by Laserwords Private Limited, Chennai, India
Printed in Great Britain
on acid-free paper by
the MPG Books Group, Bodmin and King's Lynn

ISBN 978–0–19–954267–3 (hbk); 978–0–19–959205–0 (pbk)

10 9 8 7 6 5 4 3 2 1

for Jason

Acknowledgments

So many individuals and institutions have helped me to write this book that it is impossible to acknowledge them and their contributions adequately. My largest debt is to the numerous graduate and undergraduate students— at Barnard College, Columbia University, Cornell University, and the J. W. Goethe-Universität, Frankfurt—who have endured my attempts to work out my thoughts on Rousseau in seminars and lectures and who, in many cases, have decisively improved them. Thanks are also due to my many colleagues at the same institutions who have discussed, criticized, and most of all, supported this project. The secondary work that has most significantly influenced my thinking on Rousseau is N. J. H. Dent's path-breaking *Rousseau*, which opened my eyes to both the complexity and the philosophical importance of the ideas I discuss here. Two other works that treat *amour-propre* with unusual clarity and insight and that deserve to be read in conjunction with this book are Andrew Chitty's doctoral dissertation, 'Needs in the Philosophy of History: Rousseau to Marx', and Laurence D. Cooper's *Rousseau, Nature, and the Problem of the Good Life*.

Oran Moked conscientiously checked the book's many footnotes, made helpful suggestions regarding my translations from the French, and, most important, significantly improved the book's philosophical content through his comments on an earlier draft. I am also indebted to the hundreds of individuals throughout the world who have heard various versions of these ideas in colloquia and lectures and responded to them with patience, persistence, and critical insight. I am especially grateful to audiences at Barnard College, Columbia University, Princeton University, the University of Cambridge, the University of Arizona, the University of North Carolina, the University of Illinois-Chicago, Reed College, the University of Toronto, Brown University, the Johns Hopkins University, Northwestern University, the University of Pennsylvania, Sarah Lawrence College, the Rockefeller Foundation in Bellagio, Italy, the Columbia University Seminar on Psychoanalysis and Philosophy, and, in Germany, the Universities of Frankfurt, Halle, and Gießen. I also received generous financial support, without which the book could not have been written, from Barnard College, Cornell University, the Cornell University Society for the Humanities, and the Rockefeller Foundation.

To Jason Hill I owe a debt that extends far beyond the intellectual contributions he made to this book. Countless tiny installments of it—usually the meager results of a day's work—were read aloud to him on an almost daily basis. The book has benefited immeasurably from his insight, criticism, and encouragement. Even more important, the happiness and well-being of its author—preconditions of the book's existence—depended in large measure on his presence and love throughout the eight years in which it was written.

Finally, I want to thank the administrators of Barnard College, as well as my colleagues there, for providing me with an intellectual and 'spiritual' home after many years in which I was without one. Among other things, they have taught me how sweet, beneficent, and stimulating—all at once—'rule by women' can be. Rousseau, for whom finding precisely this combination was a lifelong psychosexual problem, would surely have appreciated the value of this gift.

Contents

Abbreviations of Works Cited

Rousseau

Quotations in the text are based on the following English translations. I have made minor amendments where appropriate.

DI   *Discourse on Inequality* (*Discourse on the Origin and Foundations of Inequality among Men*), in *The 'Discourses' and Other Early Political Writings*, trans. Victor Gourevitch (Cambridge: Cambridge University Press, 1997), 111–222.

DSA   *Discourse on the Sciences and Arts*, in *The 'Discourses' and Other Early Political Writings*, trans. Victor Gourevitch (Cambridge: Cambridge University Press, 1997), 1–28.

E   *Emile, or on Education*, trans. Allan Bloom (New York: Basic Books, 1979).

GM   Geneva Manuscript, in *The Social Contract and Other Later Political Writings*, trans. Victor Gourevitch (Cambridge: Cambridge University Press, 1997), 153–61. Page numbers in square brackets indicate passages omitted from Gourevitch's translation; these numbers refer to pages of *On the Social Contract*, ed. Roger D. Masters, trans. Judith R. Masters (New York: St. Martin's Press, 1978).

GP   *Considerations on the Government of Poland*, in *The Social Contract and Other Later Political Writings*, trans. Victor Gourevitch (Cambridge: Cambridge University Press, 1997), 177–260.

J   *Julie, or the New Heloise*, in *The Collected Writings of Rousseau*, trans. Philip Stewart and Jean Vaché (Hanover, N. H.: University Press of New England, 1997), vol. 6.

LCB   Letter to Christophe Beaumont (1762), in *The Collected Writings of Rousseau*, trans. Judith R. Bush and Christopher Kelly (Hanover, N. H.: University Press of New England, 2001), vol. 9, 17–83.

LMA   *Letter to M. d'Alembert on the Theatre*, in *Politics and the Arts*, trans. Allan Bloom (Ithaca, N. Y.: Cornell University Press, 1968).

LV   Letter to Voltaire (1756), in *The 'Discourses' and Other Early Political Writings*, trans. Victor Gourevitch (Cambridge: Cambridge University Press, 1997), 232–46.

LWM   *Letters Written from the Mountain*, in *The Collected Writings of Rousseau*, trans. Judith R. Bush and Christopher Kelly (Hanover, N. H.: University Press of New England, 2001), vol. 9, 131–306.

MCB   'Idea of the Method in the Composition of a Book', in *The 'Discourses' and Other Early Political Writings*, trans. Victor Gourevitch (Cambridge: Cambridge University Press, 1997), 300–4.

OC   *Oeuvres Complètes*, ed. Bernard Gagnebin and Marcel Raymond (Paris: Gallimard, Bibliothèque de la Pléiade, 1959–69), 4 vols.

OL   *Essay on the Origin of Languages*, in *The 'Discourses' and Other Early Political Writings*, trans. Victor Gourevitch (Cambridge: Cambridge University Press, 1997), 247–99.

PCC   *Plan for a Constitution for Corsica*, in *The Collected Writings of Rousseau*, trans. Judith R. Bush and Christopher Kelly (Hanover, N. H.: University Press of New England, 2001), vol. 11, 123–55.

PE   *Discourse on Political Economy*, in *The Social Contract and Other Later Political Writings*, trans. Victor Gourevitch (Cambridge: Cambridge University Press, 1997), 3–38.

RJJ   *Rousseau, Judge of Jean-Jacques: Dialogues*, in *The Collected Writings of Rousseau*, trans. Judith R. Bush, Christopher Kelly, and Roger D. Masters (Hanover, N. H.: University Press of New England, 2001), vol. 1.

RSW   *The Reveries of the Solitary Walker*, in *The Collected Writings of Rousseau*, trans. Charles E. Butterworth (Hanover, N. H.: University Press of New England, 2001), vol. 8, 1–90.

SC   *On the Social Contract*, in *The Social Contract and Other Later Political Writings*, trans. Victor Gourevitch (Cambridge: Cambridge University Press, 1997), 39–152. '*SC*, I.4.vi' refers to book 1, chapter 4, paragraph 6.

Other texts

KPV   Immanuel Kant, *Critique of Practical Reason*, ed. Mary Gregor (Cambridge: Cambridge University Press, 1997). Cited by page numbers of the German Academy of Sciences edition of Kant's collected works.

L   Thomas Hobbes, *Leviathan*, ed. Edwin Curley (Indianapolis: Hackett, 1994). '*L*, xxvi.20–3' refers to chapter 26, paragraphs 20–3.

NE   Aristotle, *Nicomachean Ethics*, trans. Terence Irwin (Indianapolis: Hackett), 1999.

TMS   Adam Smith, *The Theory of Moral Sentiments*, ed. Knud Haakonssen (Cambridge: Cambridge University Press, 2002). 'VII.ii.4.9' refers to part IV, section ii, chapter 4, paragraph 9. Since some parts have no section divisions and some sections have no chapters, some references contain only three numbers. Thus, 'III.2.8' refers to part III, chapter 2, paragraph 8.

Introduction

The topic of this book is Rousseau's rich and complex theory of *amour-propre*, a form of self-love that drives human individuals to seek the esteem, approval, admiration, or love—in short, the *recognition*—of their fellow beings. It is no exaggeration to say that for Rousseau this distinctively human passion is the most consequential feature of our species and that without it human existence would be unrecognizable as such. It is, after all, precisely the absence of *amour-propre* that makes the 'original state of nature' depicted in Part I of the Second Discourse—*On the Origin and Foundations of Inequality among Men*—appear as such a distant and alien condition, one in which, as Rousseau says more than once, humans are hardly distinguishable from (other) beasts. In the following pages I attempt to reconstruct Rousseau's understanding of what *amour-propre* is, why it is so problematic, and how its presence opens up far-reaching developmental possibilities for creatures, like us, that possess it. A systematic, if sometimes obscurely presented, account of the nature and importance of the human drive for recognition stands at the very core of Rousseau's philosophical vision. More than any other aspect of his thought, the theory of *amour-propre* is the foundation on which his social, political, and moral philosophy rests. A comprehensive grasp of that theory—the aim of this book—is indispensable for gaining access to Rousseau's still timely and compelling understanding of the perils and promise of human existence.

Amour-propre and theodicy

The central thesis of Rousseau's Second Discourse is that *amour-propre* in its 'inflamed,' or corrupted, manifestations—what earlier thinkers called

pride or vanity—is the principal source of an array of evils so widespread
that they can easily appear to be necessary features of the human condition:
enslavement (or domination), conflict, vice, misery, and self-estrangement.
In making this claim Rousseau is following the lead of both Augustine, for
whom pride is the source of primal sin, and Hobbes, who regards 'glory'
as one of the three causes of the state of war that constitutes the natural
condition of humankind. Yet Rousseau's understanding of the role that
amour-propre plays in human affairs goes significantly beyond the views of
his predecessors: not only does he offer a more nuanced account of the
many guises an inflamed drive for recognition can take and of the diverse
problems it poses for human well-being, he also argues that solving these
problems—finding a way for humans to flourish that does not require
divine transformation of their nature—depends not on suppressing or
overcoming *amour-propre* but on *cultivating* it so that it contributes positively
to the achievement of freedom, peace, virtue, happiness, and unalienated
selfhood. The most innovative aspect of Rousseau's view is his claim
that, despite its many dangers, *amour-propre* is also a condition of nearly
everything that makes human existence valuable and of all that elevates it
above that of the beasts: it is 'to this ardor to be talked about, to this furor
to distinguish oneself, ... [that] we owe what is best and worst among men:
our virtues and our vices, our sciences and our errors, our conquerors and
our philosophers' (*DI*, 184/*OC* 3, 189). Indeed, so I shall argue, Rousseau
goes so far as to claim that rationality, morality, and freedom—*subjectivity*
itself—would be impossible for humans if it were not for *amour-propre*
and the relations to other subjects that it impels those who possess it to
establish.

Even this brief description of Rousseau's view makes clear why—as
Kant himself pointed out—his theory of *amour-propre* can be considered
a theodicy.[1] Despite its essentially secular and naturalistic presuppositions,
the structure of Rousseau's account mirrors that of the traditional Christian
conception of human history: an original harmony among humans, God,
and world is ruptured by a fall from grace—an effect of human freedom—that corrupts human nature and initiates an era of evil and misery

---

[1] Jean Starobinski, in his capacity as editor of the Second Discourse in the Pléiades edition of
Rousseau's *Oeuvres complètes*, agrees with this claim (*OC* 3, lix). Taking his cue from Kant, Ernst
Cassirer, in *The Question of Jean-Jacques Rousseau* (New Haven, Conn.: Yale University Press, 1989),
71–82, also emphasizes the theodicean character of Rousseau's project; see n. 8 below.

but that also brings with it the possibility of redemption and transcendence (or *Aufhebung*, as one of Rousseau's disciples will call it). Clearly, Rousseau's theory of *amour-propre* is part of the long tradition of Christian preoccupation with the problem of evil.[2] Like his theological predecessors, Rousseau undertakes to show where human evil comes from; what would be required to remedy it; how its presence in the world is compatible with the goodness and power of God (or Nature); and, closely related to this, why a world in which evil is possible is, all things considered, preferable to its alternative. That the Second Discourse addresses the first of these questions is widely recognized. Many interpreters, too, read the *Social Contract* and *Emile* as offering remedies for the very problems diagnosed in the Second Discourse. What commentators have for the most part failed to see,[3] however, is that Rousseau constructs an elaborate answer to the final two questions as well. For, most prominently in *Emile* but in his political writings too, he envisions a form of culture in which the principal source of human ills, *amour-propre*, is transfigured into a servant of virtue, reason, and freedom.[4] In demonstrating the potential of *amour-propre* to cure the very ills it causes, Rousseau pursues a familiar theodicean strategy: seeking in evil itself a promise of redemption—the glimpse of a hidden possibility, if not a guarantee, that the human race can be raised above its fallen condition through a process of cultivation that ends by recreating, on a higher plane and in full self-consciousness, the harmony among humans—and between humans and nature—that was their original, pre-lapsarian lot.

The most important respect in which Rousseau diverges from traditional theodicy is that he refuses to see the redemptive potential of *amour-propre* as evidence of a *divine purpose* in nature, or more precisely, of the world's having a providential design that makes the realization of such a purpose necessary. If for Rousseau the human passion responsible for the world's

---

[2] Susan Neiman, *Evil in Modern Thought* (Princeton, N. J.: Princeton University Press, 2004), 36–57.

[3] The most notable exception is Jean Starobinski, one of the few commentators to have noticed and taken seriously what I call 'the redemptive potential' of *amour-propre*; see especially *Le remède dans le mal* (Paris: Gallimard, 1989), 165–208.

[4] Rousseau is not the first to ascribe a role in theodicy to pride or love of glory. Malebranche, Mandeville, and others have pursued this strategy, too, although Rousseau's version of the claim, I would argue, is the philosophically richest. For a discussion of Rousseau's predecessors in this matter, see Pierre Force, *Self-Interest before Adam Smith* (Cambridge: Cambridge University Press, 2003), 78–84.

evils is also a necessary condition of its redemption, it is *not* the case that redemption is guaranteed, or even probable. What distinguishes Rousseau's secular theodicy from Hegel's—and makes it more palatable as well—is its refusal to posit a necessary, dialectically determined course of history that ends with the great promise of human existence being fully realized. This is in part a consequence of the fact that *amour-propre* for Rousseau, unlike the drive for recognition for Hegel, is not characterized by an internal dialectic in which repeated attempts at satisfaction necessarily result, over time, in the drive's rational *Bildung* and the eventual realization of what retrospection reveals as its 'inner telos'. For Rousseau, fallenness may well be all that humans will in fact ever know; there may, indeed, be no actual return out of the conditions depicted at the end of the Second Discourse, which is to say: no actual escape from our present circumstances.[5]

If Rousseau's account of the dangers and promise of *amour-propre* is compatible with a thoroughgoing pessimism regarding both our actual present and future, one might reasonably wonder what the point of theodicy could be, given that for him its traditional aim—reconciliation, the affirming acceptance of a world in which evil and suffering appear to prevail—seems to be precluded. Clearly, one aim of Rousseau's theodicy is to demonstrate that the source of evil lies not in God, nor in his creation (nature), but in the human will.[6] Locating the cause of the fall in human freedom is a standard move in Christian theology, and Rousseau's choosing this path, too, is no doubt motivated in part by the traditional theologian's desire to clear God of all responsibility for the evil that pervades his creation: if evil enters the world only as the work of human beings, then God's creation remains faultless.[7] (This is part of what Kant meant when he said, 'After Newton and Rousseau, God is justified.'[8]) Rousseau, however, gives this familiar idea an important new twist by making human corruption the cumulative and unforeseen result of an extended series

---

[5] See, e.g. n. 11 below.

[6] Thus, Book I of *Emile* begins with the premise, presumably established in the Second Discourse: 'Everything is good as it leaves the hands of the author of things; everything degenerates in the hands of man' (*E* I, 37/*OC* 4, 245); see also *E* IV, 281–2/*OC* 4, 587–8.

[7] 'All that [man] does freely does not enter into the ordered system of providence and cannot be imputed to it. Providence does not will the evil that man does in abusing the freedom it gives him' (*E* IV, 281/*OC* 4, 587).

[8] 'Rousseau was the first to discover...the deeply concealed nature of man and to observe the hidden law that justifies Providence....After Newton and Rousseau, God is justified' (quoted by Neiman, *Evil in Modern Thought*, 53; and Cassirer, 72).

of free choices (conjoined with contingent natural occurrences) that, in contrast to the Christian narrative, do not involve the conscious willing of evil. As Rousseau tells the story, neither God nor nature nor the human being bears *moral* blame for the world's corruption. The most for which humans can be reproached in his theodicy is a fateful ignorance of the eventual consequences of their ultimately disastrous though innocent choices.

Yet exonerating God (or lamenting human ignorance) is not Rousseau's principal aim in recounting the origin of evil. By offering a naturalistic explanation of fallenness that invokes neither a sinful will nor an innate disposition to evil, Rousseau allows for at least the possibility of a this-worldly remedy for human corruption, one that avoids positing a supernatural power (God's grace) or an other-worldly venue (the life beyond) in order to envisage evil's defeat. Redemption, if it is to occur, can (and must) be a wholly earthly affair, and the conditions under which such an outcome is possible are painstakingly investigated in the two most important of Rousseau's 'positive' philosophical works, *Emile* and the *Social Contract*, both of which could be described as undertaking to 'discover what it would be necessary to do in order to prevent [men] from becoming [evil]' (LCB, 29/OC 4, 937). Still, the highly unusual and demanding conditions that these solutions to the problem of evil presuppose—not merely a godlike legislator and an improbably wise tutor but also a complete wiping clean of the historical slate (in the case of politics) and total seclusion from the particular bonds of family (in the case of education)—must make us wonder exactly what kind of possibility Rousseau takes himself to be demonstrating.

On my reading, Rousseau's positive accounts of the good social order and of the free and healthy personalities that inhabit it demonstrate the possibility of human redemption in a quite specific sense. In both undertakings Rousseau attempts to construct a comprehensive remedy for the evils engendered (primarily) by *amour-propre* that is constrained only by the limits of human nature, on the one hand, and the basic features of the natural world, on the other. Thus, the *Social Contract*'s solution to the problem of political legitimacy begins by 'taking men as they are' (SC, 1.0.i/OC 3, 351), just as the first task of *Emile* is to get clear on 'the primitive dispositions' that constitute human nature and furnish the educator of human beings with the basic resources of his work

(*E* I, 39/*OC* 4, 248). By working out a systematic solution to the problems of human existence that is subject to these two broad constraints, Rousseau takes himself to show that whatever stands in the way, for us, of achieving the good life must be due not to defects of nature (either human or non-human)[9] but instead to contingencies of history that might have turned out differently[10] and are, in principle, susceptible to reform.

Clearly, the 'possibility' of redemption that Rousseau demonstrates with his theory of *amour-propre* is not possibility in any strong sense. It falls far short, for example, of showing that a remedy for human evils is 'really' possible in the sense of being actually achievable now, for us, given the particular place in history we happen to occupy today.[11] Hence, our earlier question remains unanswered: what, apart from exonerating God, is the point of demonstrating the 'possibility' of redemption if doing so neither reconciles us to our actual world nor gives us reason to expect a better one? Here, again, the traditional aims of theodicy are still partially at work in Rousseau's version of it. Even if his account of the redemptive potential of *amour-propre* cannot reconcile us to present reality—cannot guarantee that the promise of good that is hidden in the evils of our actual circumstances is or ever will be realized—there may still be a kind of reconciliation it offers: affirmation of *the world in its basic structure*. The realization that the world as set up by God is good—that the fundamental workings of nature are free of evil and compatible with happiness and freedom—brings with it an implicit acceptance of Creation as such and, at the same time, the overcoming of an otherwise understandable response to fallenness, namely, a posture of metaphysical defiance—a stubborn, unrelenting rejection of

---

[9] Rousseau locates the Second Discourse's chief accomplishment in its 'proof' that fallenness 'is not man's original [i.e. natural] state' (*DI*, 187/*OC* 3, 193).

[10] As Rousseau repeatedly insists, many of the phenomena that figure crucially in his narrative of corruption, including private property and the division of labor, are the results of 'fortuitous … circumstances … that could very well never have occurred' (*DI*, 139/*OC* 3, 140); inequality, too, 'required the fortuitous concatenation of several foreign causes that might never have arisen' (*DI*, 159/*OC* 3, 162).

[11] 'It is to the task of discovering what it would be necessary to do in order to prevent [men] from becoming [evil] that I dedicated my [*Emile*]. *I did not claim that such a thing was absolutely possible in the present order*' (LCB, 29/*OC* 4, 937; emphasis added). See also Rousseau's response to the king of Poland: 'there is no longer any remedy' (cited in Robert Derathé, 'L'unité de la Pensée de Jean-Jacques Rousseau', in *Jean-Jacques Rousseau* (Neuchâtel: Baconnière, 1962), 210). In this respect Rousseau's theory has affinities with Herbert Marcuse's project in *Eros and Civilization*, which, as one commentator puts it, 'demonstrat[es] the theoretical possibility of "a nonrepressive civilization"' without 'locat[ing] any empirical dynamics moving in that direction' (Joel Whitebook, *Perversion and Utopia* (Cambridge, Mass.: MIT Press, 1995), 25).

the world *in toto* that could also be theorized as a demonic, indeed, a Satanic, rebellion against God and his ways.

Rousseau himself points to another, less contemplative consequence of his proof that eradicating evil is compatible with human (and non-human) nature and that the resources necessary for doing so reside in the source of that evil itself. This further implication of his theory comes to light in a letter to Voltaire describing the accomplishments of the Second Discourse, in which Rousseau writes, 'I showed men how they bring their miseries upon themselves, and hence *how they might avoid them*' (LV, 234/OC 4, 1061; emphasis added). In other words, beyond whatever role it plays in reconciling human beings to a world in which evil exists, Rousseau's theodicy has a *practical* function that more orthodox versions of that project lack: by pinpointing the source of evil and showing how it can have radically different consequences from the ones we know, Rousseau's theory can serve as a guide for humans' attempts to transform the world so as to eliminate (or reduce) the evil effects of *amour-propre* in its corrupted forms. It is important, however, not to misconstrue the practical significance that Rousseau takes his theodicy to have. His central philosophical texts are clearly not to be read as how-to manuals for social or political revolution; they manifestly do not aim to lay out the concrete steps through which, given where we find ourselves now, a world free of evil could be constructed. For—to repeat—one message consistently conveyed by Rousseau's texts is that, even if philosophy can sketch the basic contours of a better world, it is far from clear that 'getting there from here' is a real possibility.

If Rousseau's theodicy has a practical function, it must be sought not in its capacity to furnish a blueprint for social reform but in something less concrete but no less important, namely, its power to 'orient' trans-formative praxis. That the vision of human flourishing developed in *Emile* and the *Social Contract* is in some way relevant to actual reform is evidenced by Rousseau's attempt in *Considerations on the Government of Poland* to devise concrete political and cultural measures that, by taking into account the specific circumstances of eighteenth-century Poland, aim to set that nation on a path that will bring it closer to realizing positive philosophy's ideals. Rousseau's account of evil and its possible remedy can orient transformative practice, first, by helping the social critic diagnose the problems of an actual society and, secondly, by supplying the general principles that, when supplemented by a thorough knowledge of particular circumstances, can guide the thinking of a real-world 'legislator' in figuring out, if not exactly how a given society can 'get there from here', then at least how it has the best chance of moving somewhat closer to that ideal.

There is a second sense in which Rousseau's theodicy offers practical orientation. By assuring the social reformer—as well as, perhaps, human agents more generally—that the goals of freedom and social harmony are not intrinsically contradictory nor in principle unachievable, Rousseau's account of evil shows that, if we can have no guarantee of there being a way out of our present fallenness, we can also not know a priori that no such path exists. In other words, Rousseau's theodicy implies a fundamental agnosticism with respect to the possibility of redemption in the here and now that, similarly to Kant's arguments concerning freedom in the *Critique of Pure Reason*, opens up and legitimizes a practical domain in which the ideals of reason can guide human action. In the absence of a contrary proof, Rousseau's demonstration of the possibility of redemption—even in the thin sense of possibility that it involves—gives actual human beings license to *believe* in the meaningfulness of transformative praxis and, so, encourages them both to cultivate a hope for humanity's future and to translate that hope into concrete action. In this respect the possibility of redemption envisaged by Rousseau's theodicy has a function analogous to the role the postulates of practical reason play for Kant in answering one of philosophy's three fundamental questions: what may the human being hope for?[12] Without losing sight of the daunting obstacles that in most times and places stand in the way of the human quest for freedom and happiness, Rousseau's theodicean impulse—his finding in *amour-propre* the potential both to cure the ills it produces and, in doing so, to elevate the species—functions as an antidote to a form of metaphysical despair that, as the most important of his successors realized, must somehow be conquered if engagement in the world is to appear to human beings as a meaningful possibility.

---

[12] Immanuel Kant, *Critique of Pure Reason*, trans. Paul Guyer and Allen W. Wood (Cambridge: Cambridge University Press, 1998), A805/B833. Joshua Cohen helpfully discusses this dimension of Rousseau's thought in 'The Natural Goodness of Humanity,' in *Reclaiming the History of Ethics*, ed. A. Reath, B. Herman, and C. M. Korsgaard (Cambridge: Cambridge University Press, 1997), 130–1.

The centrality of *amour-propre*

Even if it is granted that Rousseau's philosophical project can be fruitfully understood as a version of Christian theodicy, many readers will wonder why I focus so single-mindedly on the role that *amour-propre* plays in that narrative. The simplest answer is that Rousseau himself privileges *amour-propre* in his account of evil (and of the possibility of overcoming it) and that this crucial and distinctive feature of his view has gone largely unnoticed. To be sure, those who are skeptical of my interpretive approach can point to a number of considerations that appear to justify their hesitance. *Amour-propre* is, after all, only one of many phenomena the Second Discourse invokes in explaining the prevalence of war, domination, vice, and misery. Moreover, the apparent causal pluralism of the Second Discourse seems to be reinforced by *Emile*'s endorsement of an educational regimen that attends to the formation not only of *amour-propre* but also of pity, imagination, and love of self (*amour de soi*). Finally, the *Social Contract*—surely part of the solution Rousseau envisages to the evils depicted in the Second Discourse—appears to be wholly unconcerned with whatever significance the drive for recognition might have for politics and citizenship.

It is true that the *Social Contract* contains no explicit mention of *amour-propre* and that Emile's education has goals other than the proper cultivation of his passion for recognition. In the chapters that follow, however, I argue at length that the formation of *amour-propre* is the central, if not the exclusive, preoccupation of *Emile* and that, without mentioning that passion by name, the *Social Contract* can easily be understood as furnishing essential elements of the comprehensive response to the problematic consequences of *amour-propre* that Rousseau's thought as a whole aims to offer.[13] It is also the case—though this is often overlooked—that the Second Discourse explicitly accords a kind of explanatory primacy to *amour-propre* in its account of the 'origin and foundations' of inequality as well as of the other

---

[13] The second claim is nicely articulated by Cohen (109–11, 126–9), and I argue for it myself in the first half of Ch. 5. The first claim is implicit in the amount of attention Rousseau devotes to *amour-propre* in *Emile*, especially in Books I and IV, and I argue for it further in the second half of Ch. 5. The clearest textual evidence for the centrality of *amour-propre* to Emile's education is the statement: 'to decide whether … the dominant [passions] in his character will be humane and gentle or cruel and malignant, … we must know what position he will feel he has among men' (*E* IV, 235/*OC* 4, 523).

ills of human existence. Even though private property, material dependence, inequality of wealth, and the division of labor all play significant roles in Rousseau's explanation of war, domination, and vice, these economic phenomena are of secondary importance in relation to *amour-propre*. One manifestation of *amour-propre*'s fundamental status is that many of these supposedly distinct causes of human ills in fact depend on *amour-propre* for their existence and development. For, according to Rousseau's narrative, private property, material dependence, and the distinction between rich and poor both follow on and are made possible by the awakening of the passion to be recognized by others. As I argue in Chapter 4, even private property, the most plausible candidate for an independent cause of evil, is parasitic on *amour-propre* insofar as its rapid growth, and perhaps even its origin, is explained by the desire of individuals to establish external and publicly recognized signs of their worth for and in relation to others.[14]

Yet the claim that private property, material dependence, and social inequality cannot be explained independently of *amour-propre* is compatible with an understandably common reading of the Second Discourse, according to which no single element of Rousseau's account has causal primacy over the others. On such a reading there exists no one principal cause of evil but only a complex web of interconnected and equally consequential phenomena that together account for the origin and prevalence of 'artificial' (human-made) inequality. Though it would be wrong to deny the complexity of Rousseau's account and the existential independence of *some* of the phenomena it relies on, it is important to recognize that Rousseau himself does not endorse this reading of the Second Discourse. Even if some of the contributing causes of human fallenness arise independently of *amour-propre*—the invention of metallurgy and agriculture and the primitive division of labor that results from it seem not to depend on it—Rousseau explicitly and more than once ascribes causal primacy to the drive to acquire standing in the eyes of others. Although it is easy to overlook because of the work's complexity, the Second Discourse repeatedly describes its basic strategy for answering its guiding question—'What is the origin of inequality among men?' (*DI*, 130/*OC* 3, 129)—in terms of locating the *psychological* source of (non-natural)

---

[14] See Ch. 4, n. 7.

inequality: 'Having proved that inequality is hardly perceptible in the state of nature ..., it remains for me to show its origin and progress through the successive developments *of the human mind* [*esprit*]' (*DI*, 159/*OC* 3, 162; emphasis added).[15]

Rousseau's answer to his psychological question is unambiguous: the development of the human mind responsible for non-natural inequalities is the awakening and strengthening of *amour-propre*. Indeed, *amour-propre* is singled out as the principal cause of non-natural inequality in at least two senses: it is described not only as 'the *first step* towards inequality and vice' but also as the '*leavens*' whose 'fermentation ... produced compounds fatal to happiness and innocence'.[16] It is the latter claim that expresses the causal primacy of *amour-propre* in its most robust form: the drive to be recognized by others is the 'cause' of non-natural inequality in exactly the sense in which it is yeast that causes a loaf of bread to rise. To say that yeast is the cause of the bread's rising is not, of course, to claim that it can have that effect all by itself, in the absence of other conditions it needs—warmth, moisture, and flour—in order to do its work. In the same vein, the Second Discourse is clear in asserting that a variety of other, non-psychological conditions must obtain—leisure, the division of labor, private property, to name a few—if the awakening of *amour-propre* is to result eventually in widespread conflict, misery, and vice.[17] What nevertheless makes *amour-propre* the 'source' of non-natural inequality is that, like yeast in the making of bread, it supplies the 'force' (*DI*, 188/*OC* 3, 193), or power, that drives a certain process of growth or transformation. For, as I shall argue at length in Chapter 2, the passion to be recognized by others *fuels* the spread of inequality insofar as it alone among the elements of human psychology provides us with a motive to create inequalities beyond those that nature itself produces. In other words, *amour-propre* is the principal cause of inequality because it provides humans with a powerful incentive

---

[15] This strategy is also confirmed by the Discourse's conclusion: 'inequality, being almost nonexistent in the state of nature, owes its force and growth to the development of our faculties and the progress of the human mind [*esprit*]' (*DI*, 188/*OC* 3, 193).

[16] *DI*, 166/*OC* 3, 169–70; emphasis added. For further assertions of the causal primacy of *amour-propre*, see *DI*, 184, 188/*OC* 3, 189, 193. Elsewhere Rousseau calls *amour-propre* 'the principle of all wickedness' (*RJJ*, 100/*OC* 1, 790).

[17] Thus, the claim that *amour-propre* is the principal cause of non-natural inequality does not imply that it is a sufficient condition (though it does imply that it is a necessary condition) of that phenomenon.

to invent new forms of inequality, the purpose of which is to create a nearly unlimited range of opportunities to satisfy their need to acquire a valued standing in the eyes of, and in relation to, others. The Second Discourse's fundamental claim, then, is that it is only when the role of *amour-propre* in human affairs is acknowledged and sufficiently appreciated that it becomes possible to understand why inequality—and, by extension, human fallenness—is such a widespread and persistent feature of human society.

My reasons for focusing on *amour-propre* in this study do not rest entirely, however, on the consideration that Rousseau himself accorded it primacy in his understanding of the pitfalls and promise of human existence. There are also philosophical reasons for my approach, the most important of which is that, even apart from his claim that *amour-propre* is the *principal* cause of human ills (and the key to their cure), Rousseau offers an amazingly rich account of the place that the passion to be recognized by others occupies in human affairs. One indication of the magnitude of Rousseau's achievement is that many elements of his treatment of *amour-propre*—appropriated and further developed—play important roles in the thought of an impressively large number of later thinkers. The appropriators of Rousseau who figure most prominently in my interpretation are Adam Smith, Hegel, and Freud, although strains of thought developed by other philosophers—Kant, G. H. Mead, Sartre, Habermas, and Rawls—can be detected at various points as well. In response to the forward-looking stance that guides my interpretation, some readers of partial drafts of this book have accused me of transforming Rousseau into Hegel (or, sometimes, into Smith or Freud). While acknowledging a kernel of truth to these charges, I nevertheless plead 'not guilty' to them. My defense is that all of the doctrines of later thinkers that find their way into my interpretation of Rousseau—Smith's naturalistic account of the formation of moral character; Hegel's analysis of the dialectic of recognition as the very core of reason;[18] Freud's efforts to understand the roots of love and aggression as well as the nature and importance of narcissism—can plausibly be understood as the results of attempts to think through various aspects of the problems that Rousseau's theodicy of *amour-propre* addressed and to

---

[18] In Ch. 6 I argue that the view developed in the *Phenomenology of Spirit*—that the standpoint of reason is constituted by relations of reciprocal recognition among free and equal subjects—is implicit in Rousseau's account of 'public reason' in the *Social Contract*.

find solutions to them that make use of the philosophical resources he laid before us without having always seen precisely how to unite them into a satisfying position. As this defense of my approach should make clear, I pay more attention in this book to the subsequent development of Rousseau's ideas than to their antecedents because I am less interested in understanding the historical origins of his thought than in exploring its philosophical promise.

Preliminary remarks on my interpretation of *amour-propre*

There are several unusual or controversial aspects of my interpretation of Rousseau that should be noted at the outset. The most fundamental is my strict demarcation of *amour-propre* from the other type of self-love Rousseau is concerned with, *amour de soi*. More than most commentators, I insist on a sharp distinction between these two passions (or sentiments), which I articulate by specifying three necessary features of *amour-propre* that, taken together,[19] distinguish it from *amour de soi*. The three conditions that, on my reading, any instance of self-love must meet in order to be considered a form of *amour-propre* (and hence *not* a form of *amour de soi*) are: 1) that the good it seeks be *esteem* (or some other kind of judgment that one is worthy or valuable in some respect); 2) that the esteem or worth it desires be *defined comparatively* (in relation to the esteem or worth accorded to other individuals); and 3) that its goal be esteem or worth *in the eyes (judgment) of other subjects*. The last two of these conditions constitute what, following Rousseau, I call *amour-propre*'s 'relative' nature, a topic I discuss more thoroughly in Chapter 1.

---

[19] This qualification is important. It implies that *amour de soi* can also desire positive judgments of one's value as long as these judgments are not relative in the senses that characterize the aims of *amour-propre*. As N. J. H. Dent convincingly points out, 'self-estimating' *amour de soi* plays a (small) role in Rousseau's thought (*Rousseau* (Oxford: Basil Blackwell, 1988), 98–103). As long as the desired value judgments are not comparative in nature or the judgments of other subjects, *amour-propre* is not yet in play. As far as I can see, Rousseau does not consider the case where one desires judgments of one's worth that are relative in only one of the two senses distinguished here; for him, apparently, the two kinds of relativity always go hand in hand. At *RSW*, 73/*OC* I, 1079, Rousseau refers to 'being good in my own eyes' (*bon pour moi*) and explicitly associates it with *amour de soi*. In the same passage he makes clear that the two forms of relativity go together in *amour-propre* and that without them, *amour-propre* 'turns back into' *amour de soi*.

My way of defining *amour-propre* and of distinguishing it from *amour de soi* is not positively supported by—though it can be made consistent with—every utterance Rousseau makes on the matter. It can appear to be contradicted, for example, by the claim in *Emile* that *amour-propre* is but 'a modification' of *amour de soi* (*E* IV, 213/*OC* 4, 491).[20] Any interpreter of these texts must face up to the fact that, as Rousseau himself acknowledges, he does not always succeed in 'giving the same meanings to the same words' (*E* II, 108n/*OC* 4, 345n). This means that if we are to succeed in the end in ascribing a coherent position to Rousseau, we must be prepared at times to make distinctions he himself does not make and to privilege the 'spirit' of his texts over their 'letter'. Some degree of such interpretive judgment is necessary in reading any great philosopher; in the case of Rousseau somewhat more of it is called for than usual.

My way of defining *amour-propre* aims, above all, at doing justice to Rousseau's statement in the Second Discourse that 'one must not confuse *amour-propre* and *amour de soi-même*, two passions very different in their nature and effects' (*DI*, 218/*OC* 3, 219). Apart from a very few exceptions,[21] *Emile* repeatedly confirms this fundamental difference between the two forms of self-love, and, more important, it reinforces the Second Discourse's suggestion (*DI*, 218/*OC* 3, 219) that their principal difference lies in the *relativity* of *amour-propre* (in the two senses mentioned earlier).[22] But beyond these philological considerations, there are important philosophical reasons for distinguishing *amour-propre* from *amour de soi* as I do. One is that in the absence of a strict demarcation of the two it is impossible to understand the central genealogical claim of the Second Discourse, namely, that *amour-propre*, and not *amour de soi*, is the principal 'source,' or cause, of (non-natural) human inequality. It is only by distinguishing clearly

---

[20] The apparent conflict with my interpretation is easily resolved. The circumstance that *amour-propre* arises out of *amour de soi* does not imply that the former, once constituted, cannot differ from the latter in structure and aim in the ways I emphasize here. Rousseau appears to agree, for he says clearly that although *amour-propre* arises out of—results from a certain transformation of—*amour de soi*, it can nevertheless be distinguished from its source insofar as it has acquired a new object or direction. Another apparently problematic passage for my reading can be found at *E* II, 92/*OC* 4, 322, where Rousseau appears to equate *amour de soi* with *amour-propre*. This conflict, too, is easily resolved, for Rousseau clearly indicates that he is speaking of the latter 'in an extended sense' rather than in its standard meaning; see also *RSW*, 73/*OC* I, 1079.

[21] See the previous note.

[22] The most important passages are: *E* IV, 213–14, 235, 243/*OC* 4, 493, 523, 534; see also *RJJ*, 112/*OC* I, 805.

between the relative ends of *amour-propre* and the non-relative ends of *amour de soi* that Rousseau can argue that the former alone is responsible for the wide array of 'artificial' inequalities that characterize human society and account for its fallenness. Emphasizing the distinct natures and aims of the two forms of self-love is essential for understanding not only Rousseau's diagnosis of human ills but also his specific proposals for remedying them. For, as I show in Chapter 7, the distinctive resources *amour-propre* offers for ameliorating human existence reside in precisely the 'relative' features that distinguish it from *amour de soi*, namely, that it encourages us to accord weight to the normative judgments of other subjects and that it leads us to seek to achieve (a primitive version of) the comparative status—that of equal moral standing—on which the only possible solution to evil depends.

A further noteworthy feature of my interpretation is its absolute reliance on the premise that for Rousseau *amour-propre* is a 'neutral' feature of human beings, not intrinsically a force for good—this much is universally acknowledged—but also not only, or necessarily, bad in its consequences. The latter point has been noticed and emphasized by commentators before me,[23] yet the prevailing view among readers of Rousseau continues to be that *amour-propre* is a wholly negative phenomenon, always and only a source of havoc in human society.[24] My view, to repeat, is that Rousseau regards *amour-propre* as the principal source of the many evils that plague human beings but does not think that it leads to those evils necessarily, in all its possible forms. In addition, he believes it is possible for *amour-propre* to assume good forms that not only enrich and elevate human existence but also have the capacity to remedy the very ills the inflamed desire for recognition produces. The textual evidence for this more nuanced understanding of *amour-propre* is overwhelming and decisive. In *Emile*, for example, *amour-propre* is said to be 'a useful but dangerous instrument',

---

[23] Three important examples are Dent, Cohen, and Andrew Chitty, in 'Needs in the Philosophy of History: Rousseau to Marx' (Ph.D. thesis, Oxford University, 1994), 21. Extensive textual evidence for this claim is provided by Dent (21–5, 27–31, and throughout).

[24] Three notable examples are: Arthur O. Lovejoy, *Reflections on Human Nature* (Baltimore: Johns Hopkins Press, 1961), 227–8; Allan Bloom, *E*, 484, n. 17; and Cassirer, 75, who identifies *amour-propre* with 'selfish love, whose only satisfying pleasure is the oppression of others'. Although this view continues to be found in the secondary literature, my claim that it is the prevailing view is based mostly on the many conversations I have had with philosophers, political theorists, historians, and literary critics who may not have written on Rousseau but have read him attentively and regularly teach his texts.

one capable of producing both good and evil (*E* IV, 244/*OC* 4, 536), and many other passages in that text reinforce this assertion.[25] The distinction between the form *amour-propre* is capable of assuming in a well-educated human being and 'the [perverted or inflamed] form we believe natural to it' (*E* IV, 215/*OC* 4, 494) pervades *Emile*[26] and is a necessary premise of its pedagogical project. If it were not the case that *amour-propre*, properly educated, can be the source of 'humane and gentle' passions as well as of 'cruel and malignant' ones (*E* IV, 235/*OC* 4, 523),[27] the task set for Emile's tutor would be impossible from the outset. Although some earlier theorists of self-love did distinguish between a good or legitimate *amour de soi* and a sinful *amour-propre*,[28] Rousseau's innovation consists precisely in maintaining (a version of) their distinction between two *kinds* of self-love while acknowledging both the negative and positive potential of the latter variety.

If the textual evidence in support of my reading is so decisive, why is the dual nature of *amour-propre* so frequently overlooked? One reason is that *amour-propre*'s positive potential, though unmistakable in *Emile*, is almost entirely absent from the Second Discourse. That the drive for recognition appears there as an overwhelmingly negative phenomenon is easily explained by that text's diagnostic project and by the fact that its main

[25] e.g. *E* IV, 215, 246, 248, 252, 264/*OC* 4, 494, 538, 541, 547, 562; *E* V, 436, 439/*OC* 4, 806, 809. See also GM, 159/*OC* 3, 288; and *PE*, 16, 20/*OC* 3, 255, 260.

[26] e.g. *E* IV, 212, 244, 246, 252, 262–4, 265, 327/*OC* 4, 491, 536, 538, 547, 560–2, 564, 654. See also *DI*, 184/*OC* 3, 189; and *PCC*, 154/*OC* 3, 937. According to the latter, 'vanity … is but one of *amour-propre*'s two branches,' the other of which is pride, characterized here as a healthy form of *amour-propre*.

[27] Michael Rosen argues that this construal of Rousseau's claim rests on Allan Bloom's mistranslation of the passage in question (*On Voluntary Servitude* (Cambridge, Mass.: Harvard University Press, 1996), 85n. 77). With Rosen's correction taken into account, the passage should read: 'Since my Emile has until now looked only at himself, the first glance he casts on his fellows leads him to compare himself with them. And the first sentiment this comparison arouses in him is the desire to be in the first position. This is the point where *amour de soi* turns into *amour-propre* and where begin to arise all the passions that attach to the former passion (*qui tiennent à celle-là*) [i.e. to *amour de soi*]. But to decide whether among these passions those that will dominate his character will be humane and gentle or cruel and malignant, … we must know what position he will feel he has among men' (*E* IV, 235/*OC* 4, 523). Here Rousseau clearly says that 'among these passions' (those that 'attach to' *amour de soi*) there can be 'humane and gentle' passions. But the only passions 'attaching to' *amour de soi* that are under discussion here (or anywhere else in Rousseau) are various forms of *amour-propre*, the birth of which he is describing here ('the point where *amour de soi* turns into *amour-propre*').

[28] Force, 64n. Hans-Jürgen Fuchs painstakingly documents the changes in meanings of *amour-propre* prior to Rousseau in *Entfremdung und Narzißmus* (Stuttgart: J. B. Metzler, 1977). As Fuchs shows, most of Rousseau's contemporaries, too, read him as distinguishing an exclusively 'good' from an exclusively 'bad' form of self-love.

point is to find precisely in (inflamed, corrupted) *amour-propre* the principal cause of human ills. (Even here, however, Rousseau offers a glimpse of the more complex position he will espouse more explicitly in later texts when he ascribes to *amour-propre* 'what is best and worst among men, … that is to say, a multitude of bad things as against a small number of good ones' (*DI*, 184/*OC* 3, 189).) Moreover, though the idea of a healthy satisfaction of *amour-propre* plays an important role in the *Social Contract*—in its doctrine of equal political respect, a form of recognition provided by the republican rule of law—this is easily missed since the term *amour-propre* never appears there. If we add to these considerations the unfortunate circumstance that, at least among English-speaking philosophers, the Second Discourse and the *Social Contract* are much more widely read than *Emile*, much of the mystery surrounding the prevailing understanding of Rousseau dissolves.

A further problem, however, is that even *Emile* sometimes overstates the harmful potential of *amour-propre*, thereby encouraging the same misreading that the Second Discourse, when read by itself, tends to engender. When Rousseau says in *Emile* that '*amour-propre* … is never content and never could be' and then infers that 'the gentle and affectionate passions are born of *amour de soi*, and … the hateful and irascible passions are born of *amour-propre*' (*E* IV, 213–14/*OC* 4, 493), he unwittingly contributes to his readers' confusion and obscures his own true position.[29] (Here, too, it must be pointed out that these are the *only* two statements in *Emile* that unambiguously overstate the negative character of *amour-propre*; moreover, both appear in a single paragraph, just one page before the warning, cited above, that we not confuse *amour-propre* in all its possible manifestations with 'the [perverted or inflamed] form we believe natural to it' (*E* IV, 215/*OC* 4, 494).) These interpretive complications notwithstanding, when Rousseau's philosophical texts are read together with both care and sympathy, it is impossible, so my claim, to hold to the view that his distinction between *amour-propre* and *amour de soi*, in the words of one distinguished commentator, 'opposes two kinds of self-love, a good and bad form'.[30] If the basic approach of this book is correct, the failure to appreciate Rousseau's profound ambivalence about the powerful human

---

[29] *RJJ*, 112–13/*OC* 1; 805–6, also conveys the impression that *amour-propre* is exclusively bad.
[30] This is Allan Bloom's claim, *E*, 484, n. 17.

need to be recognized by others can only have the effect of rendering the deepest and most innovative features of his thought inaccessible.

Rousseau's 'system': The Second Discourse, *Emile*, and the *Social Contract*

Two features of this defense of my way of understanding *amour-propre* point to underlying presuppositions of my reading of Rousseau that will raise suspicion among some readers. First, the evidence I cite for the ethically neutral character of *amour-propre* comes exclusively from the three works—the Second Discourse, the *Social Contract*, and *Emile*—that, as will become even clearer in what follows, I regard as the principal texts of Rousseau's philosophical project. Second, in determining what does and does not count as evidence for my reading, I treat these texts as constituting a single, coherent system of thought, an implication of which is that my interpretive work is constantly guided by the goal of resolving, or at least reducing, any tensions that might appear to exist among them. In making the first of these interpretive choices, I am taking over a long-standing and widely accepted assumption among philosophers concerning where the philosophical substance of Rousseau's work is to be found.[31] Critics of this approach, often from academic disciplines other than philosophy, frequently, and with some justice, lament the fact that, by focusing on the three texts privileged here, philosophers typically fail to take account of other important works—the *Confessions, Julie, or the New Héloise*,[32] *Discourse on the Sciences and Arts, Essay on the Origin of Languages*, and *Rousseau, Judge of Jean-Jacques*, to name the most obvious—the inevitable result of which is a simplistic, distorted, or incomplete picture of Rousseau's achievements. My interpretation, though it does not ignore the latter group of texts, definitely accords only secondary importance to them, and in this respect it, too, will fail to satisfy those who think that all parts of Rousseau's *oeuvre* are deserving of equal attention or, alternatively, that his more literary

---

[31] Cassirer (47, 53−4) is an influential proponent of this view, though it goes as far back at least as Kant.

[32] I discuss some central philosophical themes of *Julie*—especially the conflict among culture, human nature, and morality—in an unpublished manuscript, 'Rousseau's *Julie*: Passion, Love, and the Price of Virtue'.

texts contain what is truly ground-breaking in his thought. My reason for proceeding as I do derives from the conviction that, probably more than those of any other figure in the modern era, Rousseau's works are too rich, too diverse and, if all are taken together at once, too full of contradictions to be comprehended *both* in their full depth and as parts of a single body of thought. Even if some of his later texts can be read as offering critiques or retractions of his earlier views—those I reconstruct here—there is a definite value to focusing intensely on a narrowly demarcated part of his intellectual work that by itself constitutes a well-defined yet comprehensive project of great philosophical interest. This book does not pretend to deliver the final word on Rousseau's intellectual achievement as a whole; it attempts instead to investigate in considerable detail—in a way that reveals the philosophical promise and limits of—the basic ideas behind a central aspect of Rousseau's first major intellectual project: the significance to human beings and society of the drive for recognition. In the end, the only criterion for judging the legitimacy of this approach is whether it succeeds in bringing into view a systematic account of *amour-propre* that both illuminates some of the fundamental conditions of human existence and provides a framework for systematic reflection on what a world might look like that is better suited to those conditions than our own.

The most controversial aspect of my taking Rousseau's three principal philosophical works to constitute a unitary project is my treatment of the *Social Contract* and *Emile* as complementary and compatible texts. On this matter, there seems to be a prevailing consensus, among political theorists at least,[33] that the two texts present competing rather than complementary responses to the problems diagnosed in the Second Discourse, each corresponding (perhaps) to a different set of socio-political conditions and possibilities: the despotic order of 1762 France (in the case of *Emile*) and conditions, such as those of Poland in 1772, that may allow the ideal of a legitimate political order to be approximated in reality (in the case of

[33] The *locus classicus* for this view is Judith N. Shklar, *Men and Citizens: A Study of Rousseau's Social Theory* (Cambridge: Cambridge University Press, 1969); see also Derathé, 215, 217–18. Two noteworthy exceptions to the prevailing consensus are: Maurizio Viroli, *Jean-Jacques Rousseau and the 'Well-Ordered Society'* (Cambridge: Cambridge University Press, 1988), 105; and Alessandro Ferrara, *Modernity and Authenticity: A Study of the Social and Ethical Thought of Jean-Jacques Rousseau* (Albany, N. Y.: State University of New York Press, 1993), 51–2. Pierre Burgelin (*OC* 4, xciv, cv–cvi) also suggests a reading similar to mine. My view of the relations among the three texts I focus on here is heavily influenced by Dent and Cassirer.

the *Social Contract*). (That the Second Discourse diagnoses the problems that the other two texts in some fashion attempt to solve appears to be generally accepted.) I believe, however, that this consensus is mistaken. It relies far too heavily on Rousseau's misleading remarks at the beginning of *Emile* concerning the need to choose between 'two contrary forms of instruction', each of which produces either men (*hommes*) or citizens (*citoyens*) but not both 'at the same time' (*E* I, 39/*OC* 4, 248), and it pays far too little attention to later passages in which this dichotomy is explicitly revoked (*E* I, 41/*OC* 4, 251; *E* IV, 328/*OC* 4, 655).

In Chapters 5 and 7 I go more deeply into the details of my interpretation, including the textual evidence supporting it, but since my view of the relation between *Emile* and the *Social Contract* informs my account of *amour-propre* from the very beginning, it will be helpful to indicate already here, very broadly, what I take that relation to be. One of the keys to understanding Rousseau's remark at the beginning of *Emile* that 'one must choose between making a man or a citizen' (*E*, 39/*OC* 4, 248) is to see that he has something very specific in mind there when referring to the education of citizens. As the passages that follow this much-cited remark clearly show, Rousseau is thinking of premodern models of citizenship—those of ancient Rome and Sparta, or citizenship as Plato depicts it in the *Republic*—the common characteristic of which he locates in the circumstance that members of the state think of themselves first as citizens—as Romans or Spartans—and only secondarily (or perhaps not at all) as individuals (*E* I, 40/*OC* 4, 249). Thus, when Rousseau denies that Emile can be educated both as man and citizen 'at the same time', he is asserting the incompatibility of Emile's education not with citizenship *tout court* but only with citizenship in its ancient form. On my reading, Rousseau alerts us to the existence of 'two contrary forms of instruction' not with the purpose of identifying *Emile* with one of the alternatives—an education that produces *hommes*—but in order instead to define its aim as the *overcoming* of that opposition (*E* I, 41/*OC* 4, 251). In this context, overcoming the opposition between man and citizen means devising an education that makes it possible for the goals implicit in each of these ideals to be realized for a single individual, and *Emile*'s solution to this problem consists in educating its charge in *two successive stages*: first in accordance with the ideal of man (in Books I–IV) and only later as a citizen (in Book V). The ultimate aim of Emile's education, in other words, is to produce a 'man-citizen', an individual who possesses the capacities required to embrace the general will of his polity as his own—the virtue essential to citizenship—while at the same time embodying *a certain version* of the ideal of self-sufficiency that defines men: the freedom to 'see with one's own eyes', to 'feel with one's own heart', to be governed only by 'one's own reason' (*E*, 255/*OC* 4, 551), rather than being compelled always to conduct oneself, or to judge, as others see fit.

The two-stage structure of Emile's education says something important about the relation between politics and domestic education (the forming of individual character independently of society's dictates and needs), though its message is *not* that the two should be regarded as self-sufficient and rival enterprises. Discovering what it does say about this relation requires understanding why Rousseau makes overcoming the opposition between man and citizen into *Emile*'s central goal. That it is Rousseau's intention for Emile to be formed as a citizen, even if only at the end of his education, is unmistakable (*E*, 327–8/*OC* 4, 654–5; *E* V, 458–67/*OC* 4, 836–49).[34] Equally clear is the reason this component of his education is necessary: the ideal of perfect self-sufficiency that guides the first stage of Emile's education cannot be realized by human beings, for, as Rousseau makes clear in Book IV, our passionate nature—our possession of both the sexual drive and *amour-propre*—means that, for beings like us, complete self-sufficiency is a false ideal. Moreover, this ideal is false not merely because it is impossible to achieve but also because it is *undesirable*; complete independence is incompatible not only with the deepest forms of happiness available to humans (*E* IV, 221/*OC* 4, 503; *DI*, 164/*OC* 3, 168) but also with the realization of the 'noblest' potential of the species (*SC*, I.8.i, iii; *DI*, 203/*OC* 3, 207). For these reasons neither familial nor political

---

[34] One common response to this obvious feature of *Emile* is to grant that Emile is to become a citizen *of some sort* but to insist that his attachment to the state cannot have the passionate character that Rousseau usually ascribes to citizenship, especially in the first book of *Emile*; (see, e.g. Laurence D. Cooper, *Rousseau, Nature, and the Problem of the Good Life* (University Park, Penn.: Penn. State University Press, 1999), 26, 52–5). While true, this implies only that Emile is not to become a citizen in the mode of Sparta or Rome. I see no reason to deny that Emile's education prevents him from having the kinds of attachments to his 'fatherland' (*E* V, 473–4/*OC* 4, 857–8) that taking up a position in a modern republic, one consistent with the principles of the *Social Contract*, requires. It is important to note that in these closing passages of the book, Emile's tutor explicitly rebuts his charge's cosmopolitanism and expressed indifference to which state he joins, asserting instead that the state in which a man was born has special claims on him. I am indebted to Alan Patten for encouraging me to take this objection to my view more seriously.

bonds can be avoided by Emile in adulthood (*E* V, 448/*OC* 4, 823), which means that if he is to be happy and free in his attachments to others, he must learn how to be not only a man but also a citizen. Therefore some form of education must be found that renders these ideals compatible.

The overall project of *Emile*, together with the place it occupies in Rousseau's thought as a whole, comes more clearly into view when one understands why Emile's education as a citizen must be preceded by his formation as a man. The reason for this sequence depends on the thought that being concerned *only* with realizing the former's aim—producing individuals who are able to embrace the general will as their own—is compatible with espousing a form of education—Sparta's, for example—that makes members of the state into bearers of the general will at the expense of their individual sovereignty, of their being governed only by their own independent reason. For, on Rousseau's view, political cohesion in Rome and Sparta rested on citizens' complete and mostly affective identification with their polity, an identification that was incompatible with their having any notion of their own interests or value as individuals and any sense of themselves as sovereign sources of moral authority and evaluation (*E* I, 39–40/*OC* 4, 249).

Modern citizens, on the other hand, are to differ from their ancient counterparts in that they conceive of and value themselves as individuals and, most important, submit to the general will only on the basis of their own rational insight into the goodness of the laws that obligate them. A central aim of Emile's formation is to make precisely this phenomenon possible by integrating the rational self-sufficiency of a man with the socially dependent disposition, or frame of mind, of the citizen. What Emile is to have learned by the end of his education is 'the most necessary art for a man and a citizen' (*E* IV, 327–8/*OC* 4, 654–5), namely, how to fulfill his duties to family and state without thereby sacrificing his sovereignty as a moral agent.[35] The essential difference, then, between Emile's education and that in a state like Sparta is not that one produces only men and the other only citizens but rather that whereas Sparta produces premodern citizens whose identities are completely exhausted by their membership

---

[35] More than most interpreters, Ferrara (69–86) emphasizes the formation of independent moral conscience as a principal aim of Emile's education.

in the state, Emile's domestic education produces individuals who in the end can assume the role of citizen *in a specific manner*, a manner consistent with achieving the goods most fundamental to being a man. The two-stage structure of this education—educating Emile first as a man and only after that as a citizen—is crucial to achieving this aim, for the main task of its first stage (as I shall explain in Chapter 5) is to equip Emile with the very resources he will need—self-affirmation that does not require the approval of others and confidence in his own judgments of what is good—if his inevitable loss of self-sufficiency in adulthood, once his *amour-propre* is fully awakened, is not to result in enslavement to the opinions of others and the complete absorption of his identity into his social roles, including that of citizen.

This line of thought implies not that *Emile* and political philosophy represent independent and conflicting projects, as many have asserted, but instead that each of the projects—via the ideals implicit in them—imposes constraints on the other. As I have just suggested, *Emile* is subject to constraints imposed on it by the ideal of the citizen in the sense that Emile's status as a man may not be purchased as the expense of his substantive ties to others, including those of citizenship. Thus, one condition of a successful education is that it form human individuals into beings who are able to assume their place in the state as citizens (as persons who are able to affirm the general will of their polity since they regard its good as their own). By the same token, Rousseau's political project in the *Social Contract* can be understood as constrained by the moral ideal 'man' that figures so prominently in *Emile*. For the *Social Contract* can be seen as an attempt to figure out not just how the ideal of the good of all can come to rule the life of a polity but also how the individuals who participate in that life can remain free, or autonomous (governed only by their own reason), in their allegiance to such an ideal. In other words, the *Social Contract* implicitly rejects certain possible solutions to the problem of political life (how citizens can be brought to care about the good of their polity) because they are incompatible with citizens remaining (ethically and rationally) sovereign individuals.

Finally, this system of mutual constraints finds its rationale in the thought that if individuals were to realize one of these ideals but not the other, they would miss out on some of the fundamental goods that human existence offers, *all* of which ought to be pursued insofar as achieving them jointly is possible. Rousseau's insistence that Emile's education be domestic rather than public, then, is in effect a declaration that there are ideals that ought to govern human lives beyond those implicit in political philosophy alone. The full measure of human excellence, in other words, is not exhausted by what political philosophy demands of human beings if *its* goal—bringing citizens to will the good of the polity as their own—is to be achieved. If individuals are fully to realize the promise of the modern world—if they are to be more than dependent and unindividuated vehicles of the general will of their respective polities—they must also be socialized as men, which is to say: educated in accordance with the ideal of a sovereign moral subject, a subject that exercises its own reason and is bound only by laws it itself recognizes as good.

Many readers will have already noticed my potentially confusing use of both gendered and non-gendered terms in this introduction. In discussing Emile's education and its relation to political philosophy, for example, I have used 'man' (when citing Rousseau or directly referring to his distinction between *homme* and *citoyen*) as well as 'human' (when speaking in my own voice, as the sympathetic reconstructor of Rousseau's position). In later chapters, in those contexts in which I mean to be discussing human beings and human nature in general, I regularly alternate between feminine and masculine pronouns (again, when speaking in my own voice). After much consideration, I have decided that there is no better alternative to this infelicitous practice. Because my use of gendered and non-gendered terms is not merely 'infelicitous'—not merely a matter of style—but also indicative of my stance on substantive philosophical and interpretive issues, it is advisable to give a brief explanation of my practice.

In reconstructing Rousseau's position I have adopted the no doubt risky policy of proceeding as though he recognized no important differences between men and women with respect to both how *amour-propre* manifests itself in individuals and how domestic education ought to form it.[36] I have also bracketed the noteworthy facts that, at least in *Emile*, Rousseau reserves citizenship exclusively for males and refers to the ideal associated

---

[36] My remarks here are inspired by comments made by Nannerl Keohane urging me to take more seriously the fact that, alongside his prescriptions for Emile, Rousseau devises a very different education for Sophie. I am grateful to her for this reminder, even if, as I suspect, she may not view my response to it as fully satisfying.

with moral subjectivity in general by the gender-specific term 'man' rather than 'human being'. One obvious problem of this policy is that, in the most straightforward of senses, it distorts the views Rousseau actually held. For, as both *Emile* and *Julie* make abundantly clear, Rousseau did not attribute the same nature to men and women, nor did he envisage them occupying the same or equal positions in society and state. Insofar as I abstract here from these aspects of his views, the position I end up reconstructing is not identical with the one held by Rousseau the historical figure.

My reason for adopting this policy is that, as in my paying more attention to Rousseau's philosophical descendants than to his predecessors, here, too, I am guided less by the aim of presenting a historically accurate picture of the views Rousseau actually held than by the aim of reconstructing from his texts a position that we, two-and-a-half centuries later, can recognize as the philosophically most interesting and promising core of his thought. The views Rousseau actually held concerning the different natures of women and men and their corresponding places in society—views that, admittedly, are everywhere in his texts—are no longer credible. This means that if Rousseau's views on human psychology, politics, and society are to be philosophically, and not merely historically, relevant to us, a way must be found to reformulate those views that does not take over or depend on his untenable assumptions regarding sexual difference.

A second, more serious risk that my treatment of gender faces is that it may cause important but uncomfortable truths about sexual difference to drop out of view. The truths I have in mind here have nothing to do with the important but easily established historical claim that sexist views pervade Western philosophy from its very beginnings up through (at least) the twentieth century. The more important and still unresolved issue, in my view, is the philosophical question of *how deep* the sexism of Western philosophy runs or, in other words, whether, or to what extent, its fundamental claims and strategies—the very project of Western philosophy—can survive if one gives up the assumptions about sexual inequality that are present everywhere in its representative texts. The most serious question about gender that my bracketing of the issue leaves unaddressed is whether what I treat as the salvageable philosophical core of Rousseau's thought in fact depends for its coherence or plausibility on the thesis of sexual difference. It is a weighty and not easily decided question whether it is possible to realize the *Social Contract*'s ideal of citizen or *Emile*'s ideal of man in the absence of an oppressed class of non-men and non-citizens whose domestic labor and internalized sense of themselves as 'made to please and to be subjugated' (*E* V, 358/*OC* 4, 693) serve to create the social conditions that men and citizens need in order to realize themselves as such. Is it possible to be a man and citizen while also doing one's fair share of housework, childraising, and emotional caretaking of loved ones? I proceed here on the assumption that the answer is 'yes', but I must acknowledge that this is in fact an open question deserving of further inquiry that I cannot claim to have settled or even explored in this work.

PART I

Human Nature and its Passions

1

The Nature of *Amour-propre*

In attempting to understand Rousseau's conception of *amour-propre* English speakers face two serious linguistic obstacles. First, English has no satisfactory equivalent of the French term as Rousseau uses it. Second, and obviously related to the first, until very recently English translators have consistently rendered the term in ways that suggest only the negative aspects of *amour-propre*:[1] 'vanity', 'egotism', and 'pride' all obscure the crucial point that, despite its many dangers, *amour-propre* also has a unique potential to enrich and elevate human existence. For these reasons it is important to begin this study with a detailed account of how Rousseau conceives of *amour-propre*.

Amour-propre's end

As its name indicates, *amour-propre* is a kind of self-love—a love of what is 'proper to', or belongs to, oneself. 'Self-love' in this context means self-interestedness: to love oneself is to care about one's own good (*E* IV, 213/*OC* 4, 491–2) and to be disposed to pursue whatever one takes that good to be. Yet clearly *amour-propre* is something more specific than self-interestedness in general, for Rousseau makes a point of distinguishing it from another human sentiment, or passion,[2] that could also be called self-love, *amour de soi* (or, equivalently, *amour de soi-même*). It is in distinguishing

---

[1] 'Vanity' is used by Masters (*On the Social Contract*, ed. Roger D. Masters, trans. Judith R. Masters (New York: St. Martin's Press, 1978)); 'pride' is chosen by Cranston (*A Discourse on Inequality*, ed. Maurice Cranston (New York: Penguin, 1984)); and 'egotism' is used by Cress (*Basic Political Writings*, ed. Donald A. Cress (Indianapolis: Hackett, 1987)). Allan Bloom (*E*) and Victor Gourevitch (*DI*), in contrast, leave the term untranslated.

[2] In this chapter I use 'passion' and 'sentiment' interchangeably, as Rousseau does in the following quote. In Ch. 2 I consider Rousseau's more restrictive use of the former, according to which *amour-propre*, but not *amour de soi*, counts as a passion; see Ch. 2, n. 21.

these two forms of self-love that Rousseau comes closest to defining *amour-propre*, and so it is with this contrast that I begin:

One must not confuse *amour-propre* and *amour de soi-même*, two passions very different in their nature and effects. Love of oneself is a natural sentiment that inclines every animal to attend to its own preservation and that, guided in man by reason and modified by pity, produces humanity and virtue. *Amour-propre* is only a relative sentiment, artificial and born in society, that inclines every individual to set greater store by himself than by anyone else, inspires in men all the evils they do to one another, and is the genuine source of honor. ... In the true state of nature *amour-propre* does not exist. For, since each man regards himself as the sole spectator who observes him, as the sole being in the universe who takes an interest in him, as the sole judge of his own merit, it is not possible that a sentiment that has its source in comparisons that he is not in a position to make could spring up in his soul.

(*DI*, 218/*OC* 3, 219)

The first thing to notice here is that Rousseau distinguishes the two forms of self-love in terms of the object, or good, that each inclines us to seek: *amour de soi* is directed at self-preservation,[3] whereas *amour-propre* is concerned with judgments of merit and honor, with how highly one is 'regarded'. A being that possesses *amour-propre* is moved by the desire 'to have a position, to be a part, to count for something' (*E* II, 160/*OC* 4, 421); such a being, in other words, feels a need to be esteemed, admired, or thought valuable (in some still undefined respect). Rousseau's thesis that *amour-propre* and *amour de soi* are the sources of two distinct kinds of motivation, each of which plays a central role in human life, finds another expression in his claim later in the Second Discourse that 'all our labors are directed at only two objects: the comforts of life for oneself and consideration among others' (*DI*, 219/*OC* 3, 220). Distinguishing between two sources of motivation in this way does not imply that a human action can be a manifestation of only one of these forms of self-love at a time. On the contrary, a single action can aim at satisfying both *amour de soi* and *amour-propre*, and this is the case for the great majority of

---

[3] Despite what Rousseau suggests here, the aims of *amour de soi* are not restricted to self-preservation. As N. J. H. Dent rightly points out (89–112), the good that *amour de soi* inclines humans to seek varies with their self-conceptions; to the extent that one thinks of oneself as more than a physical being, the good one seeks will extend beyond the mere necessities of life. If, for example, I take the ability to speak foreign languages as part of my good, and as good because of its inherent rewards, apart from the esteem it brings me from others, then my efforts to learn French are motivated by *amour de soi* even though they do not serve the end of preservation.

human actions. The homes we live in, the clothing we wear, even the food we eat and serve to our guests—all of these choices are typically informed not only by considerations of physical need but also by ideas about how those homes, clothing, and food express or reflect our own worth and standing, both as individuals and as members of the human species.

Although interpreters of Rousseau sometimes refer to *amour-propre* as a *belief* in one's own value that one then seeks to find confirmed in the world, it is more accurate to think of it as a *need* or *desire* to be valued, since the effects of *amour-propre* are often most visible in precisely those who are not genuinely convinced of their own worth but desperately want to be.[4] In other words, *amour-propre* is a 'passion' or 'sentiment', not (in the first instance) a belief. Nevertheless, it is an important feature of *amour-propre* that one's beliefs, or opinions—especially, beliefs about one's own merits—typically play a crucial role in determining the kind and degree of recognition one seeks, as well as in defining what will satisfy one's passionate need to 'count,' or to 'be someone'. Thus, even though *amour-propre* gives rise to a general desire for recognition that does not depend on an antecedent belief that one is worthy of recognition, beliefs about one's own worth will be hugely influential in determining both how one attempts to satisfy the promptings of *amour-propre* and the extent to which one succeeds in doing so. This feature of *amour-propre* is responsible for some of the more interesting complications that the pursuit of recognition introduces into human affairs, and I shall return to it in Chapter 2.

It is also frequently assumed, especially by moral philosophers, that what *amour-propre* directs us to seek from others is only, or primarily, recognition of our status as *morally* significant beings,[5] that is, as beings who deserve to be accorded various forms of moral respect in our interactions with others—for example, the right to have one's voice heard by others, the right to have one's needs taken into account in collective decisions, or the right not to be treated merely as a means to others' ends. But Rousseau

---

[4] This and many other features of *amour-propre* that I emphasize here can also be found in Jacques Abbadie's characterization of *amour-propre* in ch. xiv, Part Two, of *L'art de se connâitre soi-même* (Paris: Librairie Arthème Fayard, 2003), originally published in 1712.

[5] Dent uses this phrase in defining *amour-propre*'s aim (56), but he construes moral significance more broadly than the view I criticize here. Later he makes it clear that *amour-propre* also seeks recognition for 'excellent dispositions and attributes', including skills and other admirable qualities (95).

does not define the aim of *amour-propre* this narrowly. As I shall argue at length in Chapter 2, the desire for moral respect is one form *amour-propre* can take, but it is capable of assuming numerous other, less exalted forms as well. It is instructive here to recall the kind of recognition individuals seek when *amour-propre* makes its first appearance in the Second Discourse: 'Each began to look at the others and to want to be looked at himself, and public esteem came to be prized. The one who sang or danced the best, the handsomest, the strongest, the most skillful, or the most eloquent came to be the most highly regarded' (*DI*, 166/*OC* 3, 169). In this passage *amour-propre* is portrayed as leading individuals to seek not moral respect but admiration of their particular excellences, including some they acquire by birth rather than through their own efforts. The point here is that until circumstances form it in specific ways, *amour-propre* is an exceptionally plastic passion with highly indeterminate aims. This crucial point is reflected in the fact that ordinary language distinguishes a large variety of 'approbative' phenomena commonly desired by humans—for example, notice, interest, love, approval, respect, consideration, esteem, praise, admiration, applause, honor, and veneration—all of which count for Rousseau as ways in which one human being can 'count' for another.[6] In other words, *amour-propre* impels those who have it to seek some form of recognition from others, but it alone does not determine precisely how or where they will look to find it.

Relativity to others

The second principal feature of *amour-propre* alluded to in the passage cited above is its 'relative' nature, in contrast to the 'absolute' character of *amour de soi* (*E* IV, 215/*OC* 4, 494). 'Relative' here means relative *to other subjects*, and Rousseau's point is that the good sought by *amour-propre* is defined by, even partially constituted by, certain relations one has to subjects other than oneself. In fact, *amour-propre* is relative in two respects, each of which distinguishes it from *amour de soi* and helps to explain the difficulties *amour-propre* poses for beings who possess it. First, the good that *amour-propre* seeks is relative, or comparative; to desire recognition is to desire to have a certain

---

[6] This list and the term 'approbative' derive from Lovejoy, *Reflections*, 88.

standing in relation to the standing of some group of relevant others.[7] It is important to note, however, that a relative standing is not necessarily a superior or inferior one. If what one's *amour-propre* leads one to seek is simply the respect one deserves as a human being—respect one is willing to return to others in the same measure—then the standing one seeks is comparative (defined in relation to that of others) but not superior; equal standing, in other words, is still standing relative to others. This feature of *amour-propre* contrasts with the absolute (non-relative) character of *amour de soi*. If one thinks of the latter as directed at self-preservation, the point of the contrast becomes clear: the extent to which my food, my shelter, and my sleep satisfy my bodily needs is independent of how well those around me fare with respect to theirs. As long as *amour-propre* has not yet infected my pursuit of my own good, the benefit I achieve from eating my porridge is unaffected by how well your leg of lamb satisfies you.

Secondly, *amour-propre* is relative to other subjects in the further sense that, since the good it seeks is recognition *from others*, its satisfaction requires—indeed, consists in—the opinions of one's fellow beings.[8] *Amour-propre* is relative in this second sense, then, because its aim—recognition from others—is inherently social in character.[9] Here, too, *amour-propre* contrasts sharply with *amour de soi*: since the opinion of one's fellow beings is not *constitutive of* the goods sought by *amour de soi*, it does not directly and necessarily[10] tie us to other subjects, as does *amour-propre*. Of

---

[7] In distinguishing *amour-propre* from *amour de soi* Rousseau emphasizes that the former 'makes comparisons' (*E* IV, 213/*OC* 4, 493). Also: 'as soon as *amour-propre* has developed, the relative *I* is constantly in play, and the young man never observes others without returning to himself and comparing himself with them. The issue, then, is to know in what rank among his fellows he will put himself after having examined them' (*E* IV, 243/*OC* 4, 534); see also *RJJ*, 9, 112–13/*OC* 1, 669, 805–6.

[8] Rousseau uses this sense of 'relative' at *E* I, 39–40/*OC* 4, 248–9. It is also implicit at *E* IV, 213/*OC* 4, 493, in the claim that *amour-propre* demands that others confirm one's comparative judgments regarding oneself.

[9] Cooper denies this (138–41) in his otherwise excellent account of *amour-propre*. His argument that *amour-propre* need not be relative in this second sense—that it 'in certain instances … disregards others' opinions' (138)—rests on the claim that 'the Jean-Jacques of the *Dialogues* and the *Reveries* is a man largely free of *amour-propre*' (139). The argument is that if Jean-Jacques desires recognition (as he does), then the desire for recognition is separable from *amour-propre*. But, as Cooper's 'largely' shows, Jean-Jacques is *not* free of *amour-propre*, and even if he were, his seeking recognition in its absence would imply only (falsely) that the quest for recognition is possible without *amour-propre*, not that *amour-propre* can exist without the desire for others' good opinion. I see no reason to deny what Rousseau elsewhere states clearly (see previous note): that *amour-propre* is relative in that it always seeks the good opinion of other subjects.

[10] The necessity at issue here is conceptual necessity.

course, in any but the most unusual of human conditions, satisfying the needs of self-preservation will also require, as a matter of *practical* necessity, cooperation with others. Even so, the good one hopes to achieve through such cooperation—if it is truly an end of *amour de soi*—remains external and hence only contingently related to one's relations to others.

Getting clear on this feature of *amour-propre* should help us to keep in view what interpreters of Rousseau often obscure, namely, that the immediate and primary end that *amour-propre* seeks is not self-esteem[11]—nor even external *confirmation* of one's sense of self-worth—but esteem (or recognition) in the eyes of others. This is not to say that self-esteem is not an important good, nor that those who have *amour-propre* do not desire it. Rousseau's point, rather, is that beings who possess *amour-propre* care about the good opinion of others directly and for its own sake, independently of its role in producing or reinforcing self-esteem. This is certainly true of *amour-propre* as it manifests itself at the beginning of human lives: as infants we crave our parents' love not because we want them to confirm an already existent sense of self-worth, nor because we want to achieve self-esteem, but because we value their love for its own sake, as evidence that we count as beings of great value in their eyes. But this is hardly less true of *amour-propre* in its more mature manifestations, for even adults who have acquired a healthy measure of self-esteem do not therefore cease to desire, even need, the approval of others for its own sake. It is Rousseau's view that whenever human beings live together and are capable of making comparisons and judgments of value—which is to say, whenever *human* subjects exist—they are moved by the desire to be valued by others and by a concern to be seen by them as occupying a favorable position among their fellow beings.

Of course, someone who cares about her standing in the eyes of others will typically also want to share the positive valuations of herself that she desires from them (which is to say, she will desire self-esteem). Since the good that *amour-propre* seeks involves a species of *judgment*, it is hard to imagine that one could be satisfied with esteem that came only from others and not also from oneself (from one's own judgments). Although this is not the place to articulate the precise relation between self-esteem and

---

[11] *Pace* Cooper, 138, 163. That *amour-propre*, though not identical with the need for self-esteem, is intimately bound up with it is made clear at *PCC*, 154/*OC* 3, 938.

the esteem of others,[12] two preliminary remarks are in order. First, there can be no doubt that developmentally the esteem of others is a necessary condition of self-esteem, and Rousseau fully appreciates this fact. It is more controversial whether in the case of adults, being valued by others is necessary for maintaining self-esteem. Rousseau's answer, I believe, is that although it is possible, and in their best interest, for adults to develop internal sources of esteem that are not susceptible to every fluctuation in the opinions of others, maintaining self-esteem in the absence of *all* external valuation is an impossibility. More precisely, it is impossible to do so *sanely*,[13] since this would require one to occupy the mad, or madness-inducing, position of holding steadfastly to a belief that all other points of view appear to deny. Healthy self-esteem is surely not a matter of regarding oneself highly despite what everyone else thinks. In order to be healthy, self-esteem must be grounded in a realistic assessment of who one is, and it is impossible to know that one's self-assessment is well-founded if it remains wholly unconfirmed by others. Although these remarks certainly do not exhaust the topic of self-esteem, it is enough for now to have established that, apart from whatever relation it has to self-esteem, having *amour-propre* means that we value the favorable opinion of others as a non-instrumental good.

It is sometimes said that the ultimate end of *amour-propre* is not the recognition or favorable opinion of other subjects but a certain *feeling* produced by the positive judgments of others: the 'sentiment of one's own existence' (*le sentiment de sa propre existence*).[14] Although such a claim is suggested by Rousseau's own description of 'sociable man'—the man of *amour-propre*—as someone who 'draws the sentiment of his own existence' from the judgments of others (*DI*, 187/*OC* 3, 193), it is also potentially misleading. Creatures with *amour-propre* do seek a kind of feeling, but it is a sentiment with a specific intentional object—a sentiment *of* one's

---

[12] For more on this topic, see Lovejoy, *Reflections*, 100–5, 161–2.

[13] *RSW* and, especially, *RJJ* painfully exemplify, if unintentionally, how madness can result from a failure of recognition.

[14] Rousseau uses this term in many senses. The one I have in mind here finds expression at *OC* 1, 1801, where the sentiment of existence is distinguished from the desire to be happy. The former is identified with 'all that seems to extend or shore up our existence', a description that clearly fits the recognition sought by *amour-propre*. The best treatment of Rousseau's elusive concept of the sentiment of one's own existence is Cooper's, 20–30. Chitty (28) makes good use of this passage, though he mistakenly translates '*affermir*' as 'affirm' rather than 'shore up'.

existence—which is to say, an affectively tinged perception of one's own *being* as a self. In Chapter 2 I say more about what it is for Rousseau to be a self and how recognition from others plays a role in constituting a self. For now it is sufficient to note that to '*be* someone'—the ultimate aim of *amour-propre*—is, in part, to '*count as* someone' for other subjects. To find that one counts for others is, in part, to perceive that one *is* (a self), and this perception is inseparably bound up with the pleasant sense, or sentiment, of affirmation. What a being with *amour-propre* seeks, then, is not only, or primarily, a mere sentiment but a confirmation of its being as a self, which, more than just a feeling, is a public object in the sense that it is partially constituted by what others think of it.[15] Moreover, as I elaborate below, the affirmation sought by *amour-propre* is always affirmation of oneself under a certain description, or in accordance with a specific self-conception. This, too, makes its end more than just a sentiment—a merely subjective, fleeting, objectless feeling.

In articulating the second respect in which *amour-propre* is relative to others, Rousseau often draws our attention to a peculiar but important cognitive capacity that *amour-propre* both presupposes and develops: the ability to step outside one's own perspective in order to see oneself from the point of view of another. As noted, in the 'true' (but fictitious) state of nature of the Second Discourse, where enduring social relations do not exist and *amour-propre* has not yet developed, each individual 'regards himself as the sole spectator who observes him … [and] as the sole judge of his own merit' (*DI*, 218/*OC* 3, 219). For such primitive beings there exists only one perspective—one's own—from which to know and evaluate oneself and the rest of the world.[16] This original solipsism disappears, however, once *amour-propre* is awakened. According to Rousseau's hypothetical chronology, *amour-propre* entered the world at the moment when 'each began to look at the others and to want to be looked at himself, and public esteem came to be prized' (*DI*, 166/*OC* 3, 169). Because *amour-propre*

---

[15] Hegel holds a similar view about the recognition of others partially constituting who we are (our identities). See my *Foundations of Hegel's Social Theory: Actualizing Freedom* (Cambridge, Mass.: Harvard University Press, 2000), 107–9.

[16] That solipsism of this sort need not rule out all self-evaluation is suggested by Rousseau's example of the primitive human who compares himself with other species and takes pride (*orgueil*) in observing his superiority to them (*DI*, 144/*OC* 3, 166). Since the only look this man is concerned with is his own, his pride is not a form of *amour-propre* but what Dent calls 'self-estimating *amour de soi*' (98–103). See also *RSW*, 73/*OC* I, 1079.

implies a desire to be regarded in a certain way by others, beings who have this passion must take an interest in how they appear from the perspective of other subjects. Moreover, since *amour-propre* can be satisfied only when its possessor succeeds in appearing to others in ways that elicit their esteem or admiration, it provides human beings with a strong incentive to learn to view themselves as others view them (and, as we shall see in more detail later, to fashion themselves in ways that will in fact elicit the desired regard of others). In other words, *amour-propre* impels those who possess it to perfect an innate capacity[17] that would otherwise remain dormant in the human spirit—the ability to view oneself (and ultimately the world) from a perspective other than one's own particular point of view. Insofar as it implies the desire to see others regarding oneself in a certain manner, *amour-propre* is clearly a more complex form of self-love than *amour de soi*; for, among other complications, the self whose good it is concerned to achieve is not a simple, self-subsistent being but rather an 'I' that is mediated by—constructed in—the opinions of others. I return to this important point in later chapters when examining both the dangers and the promise of *amour-propre*.

Natural vs. artificial

In the passage cited above, *amour-propre* is said to be not only relative but also 'artificial' (*factice*). In this respect, too, it contrasts with *amour de soi*, a 'natural' sentiment. A careful reading of this passage shows that 'natural' here refers to three distinct qualities of *amour de soi*: it is a sentiment we share with the animals (and so is part of our biological nature); it is a benign sentiment, essential to virtue and humanity and not itself a source of human evils; and it is not 'born in society' but is (or would be) operative even in the absence of all social relations. The last point especially helps to make clear that when Rousseau calls *amour-propre* artificial, he does not mean that it is a merely accidental feature of human reality or that humans would be better off without it; he means primarily, rather, that

[17] The capacity to view the world from an external perspective is one of many cognitive capacities that are latent in the original state of nature but awakened and developed when new circumstances make them useful. Capacities that fit this description make up 'perfectibility', one of the four elements of original (non-social) human nature.

amour-propre is an inherently *social* passion, not a possible feature of human individuals 'in themselves' (apart from their relations to others). Indeed, this is *all* that Rousseau intends to claim when he denies in Part I of the Second Discourse that *amour-propre* is part of 'original human nature', for this (much misunderstood) concept refers to the basic capacities and drives that nature bestows on human beings qua *individuals*, independently of whatever social relations they may have.[18] In ascribing *amour de soi* (along with pity, perfectibility, and a primitive form of free will) to our original nature (*DI*, 139–41/*OC* 3, 140–2), Rousseau means only to claim that it, in contrast to *amour-propre*, is a passion human individuals could in principle possess on their own, even were they to exist outside all society (which, for Rousseau, no real human beings ever do). My previous discussion of the relative character of *amour-propre* makes it clear why and in what sense it is a social passion. But nothing in this account implies, even for Rousseau, that human beings can or should exist without *amour-propre*. Contrary to popular primitivist readings of the Second Discourse,[19] Rousseau does not envision human existence without *amour-propre* any more than he envisions it without love, reason, or language—all of which are just as 'artificial' as *amour-propre* and no less essential to human reality.

Granted that *human* beings never exist without it, why call *amour-propre* artificial rather than simply social? What is intended by suggesting, as the French *factice* clearly does, that *amour-propre* is something that human beings *make*? Although Rousseau does not make this explicit, the point of equating the social with the artificial (and opposing it to the natural)

---

[18] Rousseau confirms this at MCB, 302/*OC* 2, 1244–5: 'In moral inquiries…I would begin by examining the little we know about the human mind taken in itself and considered individually. I would … derive from this some … tentative bits of knowledge, but soon abandoning this dark labyrinth, I would hasten to examine man in terms of his relations, and from this I would derive a host of luminous truths that would soon dispel the uncertainty of my first arguments'.

[19] I take the term 'primitivist' from Arthur O. Lovejoy, who convincingly rebuts the common perception of Rousseau as calling for a return to (or in some other way nostalgically idealizing) the original state of nature depicted in the Second Discourse. See 'The Supposed Primitivism of Rousseau's "Second Discourse"', in his *Essays in the History of Ideas* (Baltimore: Johns Hopkins Press, 1948), 14–37. As Susan Neiman notes, however, Rousseau is sometimes guilty of encouraging the primitivist reading himself, for example in his letter to Voltaire (1756) concerning the Lisbon earthquake (in Rousseau, *The 'Discourses' and Other Early Political Writings*, ed. Victor Gourevitch (Cambridge: Cambridge University Press, 1997), 232–46). See her 'Metaphysics, Philosophy: Rousseau on the Problem of Evil', in *Reclaiming the History of Ethics*, ed. Andrews Reath, Barbara Herman, and Christine M. Korsgaard (Cambridge: Cambridge University Press, 1997), 165, n. 14.

is to emphasize that, even though humans must have social relations of one kind or another, the particular forms those relations take are highly variable and, more to the point, dependent on human will—though not, of course, on the will of any one individual. It is not, in general, up to human beings to live in society or not, but it is up to them, in some sense at least, how their social relations are configured. In other words, the social world *is* artificial in the sense that its institutions are produced by human history—by the collective actions of human beings[20]—and sustained only through the ongoing participation of their members. This crucial but unstated premise is what underlies the fundamental distinction Rousseau makes at the beginning of the Second Discourse between physical and 'moral' (or socio-political) inequality: the principal difference is that the latter 'depends on a sort of convention [in the sense of *agreement*] and is established, or at least authorized, by the consent of men' (*DI*, 131/*OC* 3, 131). In other words, the social and political inequalities that Rousseau is concerned to examine—and all truly harmful forms of inequality fall into this class—are made by human beings (rather than instituted by God or nature), not merely because the social institutions that sustain them are the creations of human history but, more importantly, because their continued existence requires the perpetual consent—the willing participation—of the individuals who live within them.[21]

But even if we grant that the social world is artificial in the sense just articulated, why should we conclude that *amour-propre*, too, is human-made? We should assent to this claim only in the same sense and for the same reasons that we admitted social relations to be artificial: although humans cannot exist as such without *amour-propre*, the particular forms it takes are highly variable and dependent on the kind of social world its possessors inhabit. If social institutions are artificial, and if concrete expressions of *amour-propre* depend on them, then there is an important sense in which *amour-propre* is artificial, too: with respect to *how* it manifests

[20] Rousseau, of course, admits that social arrangements are largely the *unintended* results of human actions, and so there is an important sense in which humans do not freely choose them. It is an open question whether Rousseau thinks it is ever possible for humans to create social institutions of their own conscious design. Settling this question would determine whether we take Rousseau's project to be of practical (e.g. revolutionary) import.

[21] Believing in the legitimacy of existing institutions is a crucial part of the consent Rousseau is talking about: we consent to inequalities that disadvantage us, in part because we believe them to be justified. Thus, Rousseau's views here constitute the beginnings of a theory of ideology.

itself in the world, *amour-propre* is just as dependent on human doings as the social institutions that shape it. The extreme malleability of *amour-propre*, as well as its susceptibility to being formed and re-formed through human interaction, are theses of crucial importance to Rousseau's thought, and they must not be lost sight of when encountering passages, such as the one cited above, that appear to ascribe a fixed, usually pernicious character to *amour-propre*. When Rousseau says that *amour-propre* 'inclines each individual to think more highly of himself than of anyone else [and] inspires in men all the evils they do to one another', 'inclines' and 'inspires' must be read as 'disposes' or 'makes possible', not as 'compels' or 'necessitates'. As I emphasized earlier, Rousseau does think that *amour-propre* is the principal source of the evils that beset human beings, but he does not believe that it leads to evils necessarily, in all its possible forms. Thinking more highly of oneself than of others is certainly one common way that *amour-propre* manifests itself, but because of *amour-propre*'s artificial character—because the forms it takes are always the effects of contingent circumstances that depend on human will—it is by no means necessary that it do so. As we shall see in more detail in the following chapters, the effect of Rousseau's claim that *amour-propre* is artificial is to direct philosophy's attention away from the project of describing and accommodating the deficiencies of a fixed human nature to the task of investigating, and criticizing where appropriate, the social relations that shape *amour-propre* and give human motivation its concrete form.

With these points about the artificial character of *amour-propre* in mind, it is possible to understand more precisely the source of its great plasticity. In short, *amour-propre* is capable of assuming highly variable forms because of the extent to which an individual's 'opinions'—more precisely, his conception of himself—mediate his pursuit of social recognition.[22] We noted earlier that beliefs about oneself help to determine the kind and degree of recognition one seeks from one's fellow beings,[23] as well as what counts as satisfying one's *amour-propre*. The self-conceptions at issue here

---

[22] Cohen emphasizes this feature of *amour-propre* (109–11, 121), and Dent (25, 30) acknowledges it as well.

[23] According to *Emile*, the most important factor in determining whether a person's *amour-propre* assumes inflamed or benign forms—whether 'his character will be humane and gentle or cruel and malignant'—is his self-conception ('what position he [feels] he has among men') (*E* IV, 235/*OC* 4, 523).

consist not only in beliefs about the extent of one's own merit or worth but also in the ideals one measures oneself by and aspires to achieve. Because these self-conceptions are themselves highly malleable, *amour-propre*, too, is capable of assuming an impressive variety of concrete forms.

Two features of these self-conceptions are relevant to understanding the plasticity of *amour-propre*. First, self-conceptions are shaped by historical and social circumstances that, far from being dictated by nature, are themselves highly variable. Processes of socialization give particular shape to the desires and ideals that motivate individuals, and real social institutions inevitably encourage certain ways of finding recognition while ruling out others. Capitalism, for example, affords its participants different forms of social recognition from those that were available under medieval feudalism or Eastern-bloc socialism; similarly, states that safeguard individual rights accord their members a kind of recognition that cannot be had in a despotic regime. Secondly, even though Rousseau regards these social and historical constraints as powerful forces beyond the control and choice of the individuals whose self-conceptions they shape, he does not believe that such forces completely determine how human beings define themselves. In other words, humans by nature have free will (*DI*, 140–1/*OC* 3, 141–2) and, through this, the ability to reflect on and transform their ideals and self-assessments. Rousseau believes (similarly to Sartre after him) that freedom is at work—in the form of voluntary acceptance or assent—even when humans simply take over the roles and ideals handed to them by their social world. This is the thought behind Rousseau's claim, cited above, that moral inequality 'depends on ... convention' and is perpetuated 'by the consent of men'. Living by self-conceptions that are socially prescribed—simply accepting, for example, that wealth denotes personal merit, or that the poor deserve their lot—still requires our participation and 'consent'. This feature of Rousseau's view is extremely important to the strategy he settles on for solving the seemingly intractable problems posed by human *amour-propre*. For if the particular forms our *amour-propre* takes are shaped by our self-conceptions, and if the latter depend, at least to some extent, on our own wills, then it is conceivable that certain kinds of human intervention—most obviously, education but also institutional reform—might be capable of transforming human individuals such that they are able to satisfy their need for recognition from others in ways consistent with the happiness and freedom of all.

Even granting these points, one might ask whether *amour-propre*'s artificiality really distinguishes it from *amour de soi*. For if the good that the latter sentiment inclines humans to seek also varies with their self-conceptions,[24] is it not just as vulnerable to the influences of history and society as *amour-propre*? Although it is important to see that in humans *amour de soi* is far from being a given sentiment with a fixed, biologically determined object, there is still some sense to Rousseau's distinguishing it from *amour-propre* in terms of the contrast between the natural and the artificial. First, as is the case with all animals, the biological nature of human beings provides *amour de soi*'s aim with a certain core content that is presocially determined and invariable across societies. In the case of *amour-propre*, in contrast, virtually everything in the content of its ends is subject to determination by society, history, and human freedom. In other words, even though a significant degree of plasticity characterizes both forms of self-love, nature places far fewer constraints on what will satisfy the need to count as somebody for others than it does on the human being's non-relative good, an essential part of which is defined by the requirements of physical survival.

Secondly, Rousseau's distinction between the natural and the artificial is meant to draw our attention to the fact that *amour-propre*—like free will and the latent cognitive faculties that constitute perfectibility, but unlike *amour de soi*—differentiates the human from the merely animal and so removes human beings from the realm of the purely natural. Implicit in this view is the idea, central to Rousseau's thought, that it is primarily *amour-propre*, in its many possible and actual vicissitudes, that is responsible for the numerous and significant differences we take to separate the human race from other animal species. This relative, artificial passion, in other words, is what makes possible the by far greatest part of those phenomena and circumstances that we regard as making up the distinctively human condition. Finally, calling *amour-propre* artificial is also Rousseau's way of signaling that it, in contrast to *amour de soi*, has the capacity to lead us away from our true good—from nature in the normative sense—in ways that our concern for our non-relative good cannot. Explaining precisely why *amour-propre* has this capacity is a major goal of Rousseau's thought and the main task of the following chapter.

[24] See n. 3 above.

Amour-propre and *amour de soi*

There is a good deal of uncertainty in the secondary literature, some of it due to Rousseau himself, concerning the precise relation between *amour-propre* and *amour de soi*.[25] Some interpreters deny that this distinction can be drawn as sharply as Rousseau does in the passage that I have explicated here and that I regard as the canonical statement of *amour-propre*'s nature.[26] (Recall its claim that 'one must not confuse *amour-propre* and *amour de soi-même*, two passions very different in their nature and effects.') Much of this uncertainty stems from Rousseau's apparent retraction of this strict demarcation of the two when he asserts in *Emile* that *amour de soi* is the 'source', 'the origin and principle', of all other passions, including *amour-propre*, and that 'all other passions are in a sense only modifications' of the more original *amour de soi* (*E* IV, 212–13/*OC* 4, 491). Resolving this uncertainty depends on holding apart two different questions: whether the two passions are distinct with respect to their *nature* (because they have, say, different structures or effects or aims); and whether they are *genetically* distinct (because both are equally primordial and neither develops out of the other). The passage from the Second Discourse on which I have relied so heavily asserts that the passions have different natures—different structures, effects, and aims—whereas the passage from *Emile* denies that they are genetically distinct.[27] Even when claiming, in the latter, that *amour de soi* is the source or origin of *amour-propre*, Rousseau continues to distinguish the passions with respect to their nature (or structure) in ways that are consistent with the distinction he draws in the Second Discourse.[28] Immediately after claiming in *Emile* that *amour-propre* is 'in a sense' a modification of *amour de soi*, he reiterates one of the distinctions highlighted in the Second Discourse (relativity in the

---

[25] Chitty offers a more comprehensive account of the relation between *amour-propre* and *amour de soi* (27–50). Though I disagree with certain details of his account, it is the best in the literature. No doubt some of what I say here comes from him.

[26] Dent, for example, asserts that *amour-propre* is a subspecies, or 'extension' of *amour de soi* (118). Although this view finds some support in the passage from *Emile* cited here, it is incompatible with others, for example, the statement that '*amour de soi-même* is always good and always in conformity with order' (*E* IV, 213/*OC* 4, 491), whereas *amour-propre* is not.

[27] It is the genesis of *amour-propre* rather than its nature that is at issue when, in describing Emile's adolescence, Rousseau refers to 'the point where *amour de soi* turns into *amour-propre*' (*E* IV, 235/*OC* 4, 523). I discuss the sense in which *amour-propre* is an outgrowth or modification of *amour de soi* below and in Ch. 4 (in the text surrounding note 24).

[28] That Rousseau never stops distinguishing the two passions according to whether they are absolute or relative is confirmed by *E* IV, 215/*OC* 4, 494.

first sense discussed above): *amour de soi* 'regards only ourselves', whereas *amour-propre* 'makes comparisons' (*E* IV, 213/*OC* 4, 493).[29] Relativity in the second sense also continues to figure prominently in *Emile* as a feature that distinguishes *amour-propre* from its counterpart.[30] On the basis of these textual considerations, but also for philosophical reasons, it is important to hold to the distinction between the two forms of self-love as I have articulated it here: *amour-propre* and *amour de soi* are 'very different' passions with respect to their structures, effects, and aims; a desire or need counts as a manifestation of the former, and hence not of the latter, if, and only if, it is relative to other subjects in the two senses I have outlined above. Below I discuss a further respect in which the two passions are fundamentally distinct: they represent independent sources of value for human beings; the ends of *amour-propre* are sought for their own sake, not merely because they are a means to achieving *amour de soi*'s ends, and vice versa.

This is not to say, of course, that the two passions have no common features. Both are passions (though, as I discuss in Chapter 2, Rousseau denies even this in those instances when he distinguishes passions from sentiments), and, more important, both are species of self-love in the broadest sense. What makes each a species of self-love is that both passions motivate individuals to pursue their own good (as conceived under a certain description). And to repeat: self-love counts as *amour-propre* whenever, and only when, the good sought is relative in the two senses highlighted in both the Second Discourse and *Emile*. This point holds the key to understanding Rousseau's claim that, despite these differences in nature, *amour de soi* is the origin, or source, of *amour-propre*. For the latter is nothing but a particular form that a more primordial non-relative self-love tends to assume when certain developmental and historical conditions obtain, namely: when, first, the cognitive capacities on which comparison and reflection depend have been awakened and strengthened through struggles for survival motivated solely by *amour de soi*; and, secondly, humans have begun to lead a sufficiently settled existence that regular intercourse among individuals and primitive social bonds can arise.[31] These conditions make

---

[29] See also his remark that renouncing comparisons and being content with being good in one's own eyes transforms *amour-propre* into *amour de soi* (*RSW*, 73/*OC* I, 1079).

[30] e.g. at *E* I, 39–40/*OC* 4, 248–9, and *E* IV, 213/*OC* 4, 493.

[31] Chitty thinks that material dependence is also a precondition of *amour-propre* (52–3, 62–3). But this contradicts Rousseau's own genealogy, in which the first instance of wanting to be regarded by

it possible for humans to conceive of their own good in radically novel ways, and the basic impulse of self-love in general—to seek one's own good—acquires a shape so different in structure, effect, and aim that it makes sense to speak of two fundamentally distinct forms of the human concern for one's own good.

In sum, then, *amour-propre* is a form of self-love that is the source of the enduring, though malleable, need human beings have in society to count as someone of value, both in the eyes of others and relative to the value of others. Formulated in this way, Rousseau's doctrine of *amour-propre* forms part of his psychological theory of the fundamental motivators of human action. Its task as a psychological theory is to delineate the kinds of ends that humans *in fact* tend to seek, and it does so by appealing to a prior understanding of the basic sentiments, or passions, common to all (socialized) human beings. Viewed from this perspective, Rousseau's account of *amour-propre* claims that in one form or another the recognition of others is a universally desired end; that the drive for recognition cannot be extinguished in human beings;[32] and that (therefore) social, moral, and political philosophy must take very seriously the implications of this fundamental human need. Further, the dual relativity of *amour-propre* implies that the urge to compare one's own standing or merit with others'—and even, as I argue in Chapter 3, some form of the desire to be *better* than others—as well as the need to have one's comparative standing or merit confirmed by the judgments of others, are basic, permanent features of the human condition.[33] Even in the best of societies, according to Rousseau, individuals will be driven to compare their standing or merit to others', and self-esteem will never obviate the need for social recognition.

The theoretical and normative status of *amour-propre*

Rousseau thinks of his basic theses about human nature, including his account of *amour-propre*, as having roughly the same theoretical status as

others precedes the division of labor and material dependence more generally (*DI*, 166–7/*OC* 3, 169–71).

[32] Rousseau need not deny that some individuals might come not to care about or seek recognition from others, but he is committed to viewing such cases as both rare and pathological. For social and political philosophy, then, such cases are negligible.

[33] *RSW*, 73–6/*OC* 1, 1079–82; *E* IV, 235, 245, 339/*OC* 4, 523, 536, 670; *E* V, 436/*OC* 4, 806; *DI*, 183/*OC* 3, 189.

the first principles of Newton's physics.[34] Though not exactly empirical generalizations, they derive their support from the success with which, on the assumption of a very small number of basic principles regarding 'the first and simplest operations of the human soul' (*DI*, 127/*OC* 3, 125), they make sense of the vastly diverse forms of human behavior we know from our own experience, as well as through the testimony of history and of what we would now call anthropology.[35] Although Rousseau's claims regarding *amour-propre* have considerable force from this point of view alone, they are meant to be supported by considerations of a less empirical nature as well.[36] Rousseau never articulates these more philosophical arguments for the fundamental status that *amour-propre* (and its twofold relativity) has in his account of human nature, but their underlying ideas are suggested in his texts, and so it is appropriate to indicate here, though only briefly, where they are to be found.

The first of these ideas concerns the fundamental role that comparison plays for Rousseau not just in the strivings of *amour-propre* but in distinctively human activities of all sorts, especially in phenomena as central to human life as language and reason.[37] (Nietzsche expresses essentially the same view when he locates the origin of civilization in those relations in which one person 'measures himself against another' and when he argues that activities such as establishing equivalences through comparison 'constitute thinking *as such*'.[38]) When, for example, Rousseau reconstructs the process through which human language could have originated, comparison of particulars plays a central role in explaining the capacity for concept formation (*DI*, 147–8/*OC* 3, 149–50; *OL*, 254/*OC* 5, 381). In the narrative of the Second Discourse, the newly acquired ability to make simple comparisons

---

[34] This is no doubt one meaning of Kant's characterization of Rousseau as the Newton of the moral world. Rousseau himself suggests this analogy when he compares his 'hypothetical and conditional reasonings' in the Second Discourse with the method of physics (*DI*, 132/*OC* 3, 133).

[35] See n. 18 above.

[36] In this regard Rousseau's theory can be compared with Sartre's more ambitious (and also more obscure) attempt to deduce the realm of being-for-others from some more basic feature of subjectivity—some 'lack' intrinsic to the nature of consciousness itself—that explains why, necessarily, conscious subjects seek a recognized presence for others (Jean-Paul Sartre, *Being and Nothingness*, trans. Hazel E. Barnes (New York: Washington Square Press, 1956), 135–46, 376).

[37] 'Reflection is born of the comparison of ideas' (*OL*, 268/*OC* 5, 396).

[38] Friedrich Nietzsche, *On the Genealogy of Morals*, trans. Walter Kaufmann and R. J. Hollingdale (New York: Random House, 1967), II.9.

is followed immediately by 'the first movement of pride (*orgueil*)'[39]—a consciousness of one's own superiority that, though at first only a pride in one's species, soon turns into *amour-propre*'s concern for one's 'rank as an individual' (*DI*, 162/*OC* 3, 166). In the context of these developments all that is needed for *amour-propre* to be born is for humans to develop a more settled existence in which they come into repeated contact with the same individuals. In such circumstances they naturally—without thinking about it—apply their capacity for making comparisons to the qualities of individuals, which gives rise to the first 'sentiments of preference' and, immediately thereafter, to the desire to be preferred—and hence compared and evaluated—by others (*DI*, 165–6/*OC* 3, 169). The clear implication is that the human tendency to compare the relative merits of individuals, though artificial in Rousseau's technical sense, is no less basic to human life than the foundations of reason and language.

The second claim regarding *amour-propre*'s relativity to other subjects—that it includes the desire to have one's standing confirmed by others—is also bound up with non-empirical, philosophical considerations, in this case concerning the intersubjective nature of judgment in general. I have already hinted at this point in suggesting that since the good sought by *amour-propre* consists in a *judgment* of one's relative standing, satisfying this passion requires that others confirm the standing one claims for oneself. The alternative to finding this confirmation would be the madly narcissistic, or irrational, position of stubbornly holding on to a belief (in this case, about oneself) that everyone else denies. A healthy, or rational, striving for recognized standing seeks an objectively valid assessment of one's merit, but it is impossible to know that a given view of oneself is warranted if it remains unconfirmed by others. (I say more about the intersubjective conditions of objectivity in Chapter 6 when articulating the conditions under which political laws are objectively binding on, or obligate, individuals.) The claim here is not that the aspiration to objectivity in our judgments is inborn or otherwise operative from the beginning of life. What is developmentally primitive in *amour-propre* is the desire for others' recognition, broadly understood, without regard, at first, to

[39] This is pride, not yet *amour-propre*, because (i) it is a looking at oneself that does not require or seek the opinion of others; and (ii) the comparative standing of individuals is not at issue. In other words, the two species of relativity that define *amour-propre* are lacking.

whether that recognition is objectively warranted. The desire to count in relation to others survives childhood and adolescence, but once constituted as rational subjects, adults cannot be genuinely satisfied in this desire unless the standing they seek to achieve appears to them, to some extent at least, objectively valid, which is to say: recognized by others. This is why, apart from all merely psychological theses, even adults who have a substantial and non-pathological reserve of self-esteem can never be completely free of the need for recognition from others.

It is important to note that Rousseau's psychological claims, which ascribe a central role to *amour-propre* in the explanation of human motivation, do not by themselves establish the normative status of *amour-propre* in his social and political theory. Recognition from others may be universally desired, but is it also a *desirable* end, one *worthy* of being desired by human beings? In other words, does Rousseau also regard the end that *amour-propre* leads us to seek as part of our *good*, as an end that it is rational for us to pursue, and important for social theory to take account of, given the kind of beings we are and ought to be? And, if recognition from others is a good in this sense, what makes it one?

One implication of Rousseau's view that *amour-propre* and *amour de soi* are distinct passions, each playing a fundamental role in human motivation, is that the value recognition has for those who seek it is not to be explained by appealing to some further good that recognition promotes. Instead, his psychological theory takes the passion to secure the good opinion of others as a kind of brute fact of human nature:[40] once humans have attained a minimal level of cognitive and social development, they naturally care about their standing in others' eyes, and they value that standing for its own sake rather than merely instrumentally, as a means to some other good. In other words, Rousseau's account of human psychology does not derive the value of *amour-propre*'s ends for those who have it from the value that the ends of *amour de soi* have for them. This is what it means to say that the two are distinct passions, 'very different' in their aims. Even if *amour de soi* were understood in the widest possible sense as self-love in general—as a concern for one's well-being, regardless of how that well-being is conceived—then *amour-propre* could be said to be one manifestation of *amour de soi* (a concern

[40] This is not the *original* human nature of Part I of the Second Discourse (what human creatures are like independently of social relations) but of *human* nature (what humans are like once their social attachments are factored into their original nature).

for one's well-being, construed as a valued presence for others), but this would not amount to deriving the need for recognition from some more original need, such as biological survival.[41]

Rousseau's psychological theory establishes that human beings desire recognition and regard it as valuable for its own sake, but it does not tell us whether normative social and political theory ought to regard recognition, or social esteem, as a central human good, or indeed, as any kind of good at all. If a desire to inflict cruelty on others, or to take walks in the rain, were shown to be intrinsic to human nature, philosophy would still need to ask: but are these *good* ends for humans to pursue? This question is bound up with fundamental issues about the normative structure of Rousseau's philosophy that, unfortunately, Rousseau himself does not explicitly address. Thus, if an answer to this question is to be found, it must be reconstructed from what is implicit in Rousseau's attempts to define the outlines of a good social order (via his version of the social contract) and, in conjunction with that, to determine, in *Emile* and other texts, what kind of life it is best for human individuals to lead.

It can appear that Rousseau assumes a direct relation between the psychological fact that humans naturally desire a particular end and the normative claim that achieving that end is good. Such a view might be thought to be implicit in Rousseau's description of the original state of nature in the Second Discourse, and it is at least suggested by the quasi-theological pronouncement with which *Emile* begins: 'Everything is good as it leaves the hands of the Author of things; everything degenerates in the hands of man' (*E* I, 37/ *OC* 4, 245). The implication of this maxim can easily appear to be that, because it comes directly from the hands of God, nature itself, including all that belongs to (original) human nature, must be good. This in turn would imply that if human beings in fact desire a certain end because of their nature, it is *ipso facto* good for them to pursue it.

There are two problems, however, with this way of establishing the normative status of the ends arising from *amour-propre*. First, the special status of *amour-propre* as a passion that is universal (shared by all actual human beings) but not, strictly speaking, natural (in the special sense articulated

---

[41] When *amour-propre* first appears in the Second Discourse, the desire to be looked at by others is not explained as arising out of previous self-preservative impulses but is presented instead as a new kind of desire that comes on the scene once humans have achieved a certain level of social and cognitive development (*DI*, 166/ *OC* 3, 169).

above) makes it unclear whether the principle 'everything natural is good' applies in this case.[42] Second, and more important, Rousseau in fact never relies on this principle to *establish* the goodness of human nature or of the ends humans naturally pursue. 'Everything natural is good' is not an unquestioned starting point of Rousseau's thought but a controversial thesis that he recognizes must be argued for. It is no exaggeration to claim that Rousseau's three major philosophical works constitute a single extended argument for the goodness of nature (especially, human nature).[43] It is not my aim to reproduce Rousseau's complex argument for this thesis here, nor does my treatment of *amour-propre* depend on its being true. Nevertheless, understanding the type of argument Rousseau employs to prove the goodness of original human nature—the union of *amour de soi*, pity, perfectibility, and free will—is relevant to determining whether and, if so, on what basis Rousseau takes the recognition of others that all humans seek to constitute a genuine good.

The central theoretical device of Rousseau's moral and political thought—a social contract that results in a civil association governed by a general will—implicitly sets up two broad conditions that universally shared ends must satisfy in order to be regarded as human goods, and so as goods that a rational society must aim to make available to all. These conditions are *universal satisfiability* and *compatibility with the human essence* (freedom).[44] The implicit principle underlying Rousseau's position is that

---

[42] It might at first seem obvious that Rousseau's principle does not apply here, given his insistence that *amour-propre* comes not from nature but from society. But if, as I have argued, Rousseau believes both that *amour-propre* arises whenever humans live together in society and that humans are by nature dependent and so in need of social intercourse, then excluding *amour-propre* from 'human nature' appears highly arbitrary and considerably weakens his thesis that human nature is good. In fact, since *amour-propre* is capable of assuming forms that do not lead to human evils, Rousseau is committed to regarding it, too, as good in the sense at work in his claim that the rest of human nature is good. (See the following note.) Cohen (103) implicitly endorses this point by including 'a sense of self-worth' in his description of 'the complex natural endowment' of humans.

[43] Roughly, the Second Discourse shows that (original) human nature itself is not the source of evil, misery, and servitude, while the *Social Contract* and *Emile* demonstrate that the ineradicable dependence of humans and their consequent need to live in society can in principle be reconciled with their essential aspiration to be free, happy, and unalienated. Together these three works show that the misery and evil that pervade human history are not inevitable consequences of either the (original) nature of human individuals or of their need for society, or of the combination of the two. My views on this topic have been influenced by Cohen.

[44] The view that freedom constitutes the essential nature of humanity (its highest and only unconditional ideal) is expressed in Rousseau's claim that 'to renounce one's freedom is to renounce one's status as a man' (*SC* 1.4.6). For an account of how Rousseau understands freedom in this context, see Neuhouser, *Foundations* ch. 2.

THE NATURE OF *AMOUR-PROPRE* 51

a human end is good only if its achievement is systematically compatible with a social order that is able to satisfy the fundamental human interests of all (relevantly associated) individuals. In other words, what our natural desires lead us to seek is good for Rousseau only to the extent that their satisfaction can coexist with the basic requirements of the *happiness* (or well-being) and *freedom* of all our fellow beings.[45]

The two conditions named above give content to Rousseau's principle as follows. The first, universal satisfiability, requires of an end that it be satisfiable in principle for all members of a society at once. If this were not the case, the basic happiness of some would necessarily be purchased at the expense of others', and this Rousseau thinks is impermissible. According to this criterion, personal security counts as a morally unobjectionable end because it can be realized simultaneously for all individuals: the protection of my body and personal belongings poses no necessary obstacles to the protection of others'. To want to be the sole determiner of laws, in contrast, would not be recognized as a legitimate aspiration even if it were natural to humans, since it obviously cannot be universally fulfilled: if I were to succeed in my quest, all others would necessarily fail in theirs. The second condition, compatibility with the human essence, requires of an end that its realization be compatible with the basic requirements of each person's ability to be free or, equivalently, to avoid 'being subject to someone else's will' (*LWM*, 260/*OC* 3, 841). If the ends of some could be achieved only at the expense of others' freedom, and so only on the condition that others fail to realize their essential nature, those ends would be morally impermissible and so not part of a person's genuine good. If, for example, being a domestic servant were incompatible with remaining the master of one's own will, then the desire to surround oneself with servants would be morally objectionable, no matter how widespread or 'natural' it was.

How, then, do these considerations bear on the normative status of *amour-propre*? The position they imply is that the recognition of others, regardless of how urgent a need it represents or how deeply ingrained it is in human nature, will not count for Rousseau as a genuine human good unless it can be shown to satisfy the two conditions just discussed. As I said above, Rousseau does not simply assume that so deep-seated a need as

---

[45] For more on the structure of Rousseau's social contract and on how he understands these two fundamental interests, see ibid. 184–94.

recognition from others *must* be reconcilable with the basic requirements of human freedom and happiness. His guiding intuition, however, is that the obstacles *amour-propre* poses for the realization of those ideals are not inherent in the basic features of the human condition but rather the product of poorly ordered social institutions and of improper education. The task that Rousseau undertakes on the basis of his intuition is to show, contrary to Hobbes, that the universal quest for the recognition of others is both satisfiable for all and compatible with universal freedom. If he is able to establish this, Rousseau will have made significant progress towards his goal of 'justifying' human nature by showing that the recognition of others that all humans desire is, in appropriate forms, a worthy end for them to pursue. In addition, he will have discovered an important part of the solution to the problem of how a genuinely human social existence is possible.

The most important element of Rousseau's strategy rests on his insight that *amour-propre* is a highly malleable passion that can seek satisfaction in a nearly infinite variety of concrete forms. One of Hobbes's mistakes, according to this view, is to have characterized the ends of human pride too narrowly—as desires for *advantage* over others (*L*, xvii.8)—and so to have guaranteed from the start that no systematic and harmonious satisfaction of this passion would be possible. Rousseau's approach, in contrast, is to distinguish between the highly general need to be recognized by others (which all humans have) and the specific forms this generic need assumes in concrete social circumstances (which are historically contingent and subject to modification).[46] This approach enables him to separate the pernicious, or inflamed, forms of *amour-propre* with which we are so familiar from the wealth of potentially benign forms this passion is in principle capable of assuming, given the appropriate circumstances. Rousseau's strategy, then, is first to survey the depressingly familiar instances of *amour-propre* in order to discover how and why the need for others' recognition so often goes awry. (This is the topic of Chapter 2.) Once he has located the sources of *amour-propre*'s dangers, he proceeds to ask whether it is feasible, given the constraints of human nature, for the need to be recognized by others to take forms that bypass these pitfalls, making universal satisfaction that is consistent with the freedom of all a realistic possibility. (This is the task of Chapter 5.)

---

[46] Cohen nicely articulates this crucial distinction (108–11).

Before proceeding to these parts of Rousseau's theory, it is important to note that the argument just outlined, according to which the human drive for recognition can in principle meet the moral criteria of universal satisfiability and compatibility with the freedom of all, does not exhaust Rousseau's claim that recognition is a significant human good. This argument, if successful, shows that a certain universally shared desire is able to survive a kind of moral reflection, fundamental to Rousseau's practical philosophy, that in effect establishes the permissibility of acting on that desire. Yet Rousseau's view of the goodness of *amour-propre* goes beyond what is established by this forerunner of Kant's categorical imperative test. In addition, Rousseau believes, apart from all psychological theories about the desires we in fact have, that it is in general *good* that humans possess *amour-propre*, for we would lack something of great importance if we did not. In brief, *amour-propre* is good not only because its end is in fact highly valued by human beings and because it can be achieved in morally permissible ways but also because: 1) the human need for recognition is at the very heart of a number of goods that are both valuable in themselves and responsible for much of what gives human lives meaning, including love, friendship, and all types of affirmation by others; and 2) in seeking to satisfy the longings of *amour-propre*, human individuals are unwittingly led to develop a variety of cognitive and conative capacities without which such 'spiritual' goods as rationality, morality, and self-determination would not be possible. These claims will be examined in Chapter 7; now it is time to turn our attention to Rousseau's account of the many dangers of *amour-propre* and why those dangers derive from its very nature.

PART II
Diagnosis

2

The Dangers of *Amour-propre*

Now that we have examined the basic character of *amour-propre*, it is time to reconstruct Rousseau's account of why it is the principal source of the enslavement, conflict, vice, misery, and self-estrangement that pervade human reality. The first question to be addressed—and the central topic of this chapter—is how *amour-propre* helps make possible the evils mentioned above. My concern here is not to explain why those evils are so widespread—why *amour-propre* so frequently gives rise to them—but merely to understand how the features of *amour-propre* outlined in the previous chapter *make them possible*. Implicit in this undertaking is the view that in the absence of *amour-propre*, these human evils would be non-existent or, at worst, extremely rare. In other words, Rousseau's account of *amour-propre* is predicated on the view that the elements of original human nature—the pity, *amour de soi*, perfectibility, and free will that human individuals possess 'in themselves', independently of social relations—cannot by themselves explain the apparent human tendency to fall into conditions of enslavement, conflict, vice, misery, and self-estrangement.

This view rests on two crucial claims: first, that humans naturally possess a sensitivity to the pains of other sentient creatures—pity—that tends to moderate their pursuit of their own well-being; and, second, that *amour de soi* by itself (without *amour-propre*) cannot explain the evils Rousseau thinks it necessary to account for. To the latter claim it might be objected that, given basic conditions of scarcity, *amour de soi* is sufficient to engender enduring conflict, as well as certain forms of vice, misery, and enslavement. Rousseau's response, however, is that, in the absence of *amour-propre*, scarcity would be only a contingent and exceptional feature of human existence, since circumstances are rare in which the earth's fruits are too meager to meet only the non-relative needs of *amour de soi*. Rousseau's view is that society, not nature, is by far the principal source of scarcity and that scarcity seems to us so pervasive a character of the world only because the world we imagine is always one in which *amour-propre* is already at work—that is, a world in which, for reasons to be explored in this chapter, the needs of humans are multiplied and complicated far beyond those that 'nature' alone imposes on them.

To understand how *amour-propre* makes it possible for the evils of human existence to arise is at the same time to grasp the various ways in which *amour-propre* can go awry. Thus, by the end of this chapter, we will have before us the basic ideas needed to undertake the task of Chapter 3: constructing a more comprehensive account of 'inflamed', or pernicious, *amour-propre* than can be found in the current literature. (Inflamed *amour-propre* is simply any form of *amour-propre* that tends to produce one or more of the evils mentioned above.[1]) As we shall begin to see by the end of the present chapter, *amour-propre* can be inflamed in a number of ways that must be distinguished. Doing so (in Chapter 3) will enable us not only to grasp the complexities of *amour-propre* and its dangers but also to discover (in Chapter 4) possible solutions to the problems it creates.

The present chapter takes the following course: In the first half I consider the most common way of characterizing inflamed *amour-propre* (as a yearning to be recognized as *better than* others) and suggest some reasons for doubting the adequacy of this account. In the second half I examine five fundamental features of *amour-propre* in general (in any of its forms) and show in detail how each is responsible for one or more of the dangers Rousseau attributes to *amour-propre*. By taking note of the diversity of ways in which *amour-propre* is capable of producing human evil, we shall see that seeking to be recognized as superior to others is only one of the ways in which that passion can go awry, thus laying the groundwork for a richer, more adequate account of the varieties of inflamed *amour-propre* in Chapter 3.

[1] Rousseau uses 'inflamed' and its variations only once to modify *amour-propre* (*E* IV, 247/*OC* 4, 540), but it has become standard practice to use the term, as I do here, to refer to *amour-propre* in any of its pernicious manifestations. This practice is due largely to Dent, who uses the term frequently and tends to equate 'inflamed' with both 'excessive' and 'perverse' (52, 256). Arthur M. Melzer also uses the term in *The Natural Goodness of Man* (Chicago: University of Chicago Press, 1990), 93.

Inflamed *amour-propre*: The prevailing view[2] and its problems

Inegalitarian amour-propre

It can be tempting to think that Rousseau offers a relatively simple account of what causes the human quest for recognition to go awry and of how *amour-propre* must be configured if the problems associated with it are to be resolved. Most commentators who address these issues focus on a single aspect of Rousseau's account that they take to hold the key to diagnosing and solving the ills of inflamed *amour-propre*. According to this interpretation, what makes *amour-propre* inflamed is simply the desire to be recognized as superior to one's fellow beings—inflamed self-love is just *inflated* self-love—and what makes *amour-propre* benign is merely the pursuit of equal standing with others. On this account, the single source of *amour-propre*'s tendency to produce enslavement, conflict, vice, misery, and self-estrangement is the perverted desire to achieve superior status relative to others, and, by implication, the necessary and sufficient condition for rendering *amour-propre* harmless is the cultivation of what could be called egalitarian *amour-propre*.[3] Joshua Cohen provides an especially clear formulation of this view:

Amour-propre comes in two forms, corresponding to two ways I might value myself. On the one hand, I might regard my worth as equal to that of others. If I do, then I will think that others ought to take my well-being equally into account, to treat my concerns and theirs as on a par. ... The second, inegalitarian form of self-regard is to think oneself more worthy of regard than others, and find it insulting if they reject this elevated conception. ... [Human vices] reflect a conception of one's relative worth that issues in a desire—indeed a demand, a sense of entitlement—to live a better life than others. And this sets the central

---

[2] To be precise: that there exist both malign (inflamed) and beneficial forms of *amour-propre* is far from being the prevailing view among commentators. Among those who recognize this, however, the prevailing view is that inflamed *amour-propre* is nothing more than inegalitarian *amour-propre*. (One exception is Timothy O'Hagan, *Rousseau* (London: Routledge, 1999), 173–5.) Also, those who do not recognize this distinction typically treat the danger of *amour-propre* as due exclusively to its inegalitarian tendencies.

[3] Dent uses the term 'equable *amour-propre*' (60). Although his excellent account of *amour-propre* is considerably richer than the simple model I am sketching here, he does sometimes appear to endorse it. He defines inflamed *amour-propre*, for example, as the '*strident* demand for superior position and title' (58). Moreover, he tends to locate the solution to its ills exclusively in the fostering of egalitarian self-conceptions (60–1, 70).

question for an explanation of vice: *How does a generic, not-intrinsically-inegalitarian concern to be treated with respect come to be particularized as a desire and demand to be treated as a better?* If Rousseau can answer this question[,] ... he will have accounted for the origin of vice without supposing it to be an original disposition, whether express or latent.[4]

Cohen's view is attractive not only for its simplicity but also because it highlights what is undeniably a central theme in Rousseau's philosophical texts: the profound importance of human equality. It is indisputable that the Second Discourse assigns great weight to socio-political inequalities in explaining human ills; the *Social Contract* continues in this vein by making political and economic equality central to its solution to the fundamental conflict between dependence and freedom;[5] and in *Emile* Rousseau locates 'the error most to be feared' in a child's upbringing in the presumption that one is 'of a more excellent nature' than others (*E* IV, 245/*OC* 4, 537).[6] More important, the suggestion that egalitarian *amour-propre* is the key to solving the problems Rousseau is concerned with has substantial philosophical plausibility. Both Cohen and Dent give compelling accounts of how the drive to achieve superior status necessarily produces conflict and unhappiness once it infects some number of individuals. The basic ideas are these: first, since inflamed *amour-propre* requires others to put themselves in the undesirable position of valuing others more than themselves, satisfying inflamed desires for recognition will be difficult and perhaps impossible; secondly, if individuals conceive of the standing they seek as requiring recognition of their superiority, then recognition becomes an inherently scarce good and so an enduring object of competition, conflict, and unmet desires; finally, by inspiring in individuals the constant desire to fare better than their peers, inflamed *amour-propre* saddles those who have it with an insatiable need to improve their own lot in the face of their competitors' advances, resulting in endless frustration and misery for all concerned. (I elaborate on these ideas below.)

---

[4] This quote is cobbled together from three paragraphs in Cohen, 109–11.

[5] I articulate this interpretation of Rousseau's political theory in Neuhouser, *Foundations of Hegel's Social Theory: Actualizing Freedom* (Cambridge, Mass.: Harvard University Press, 2000), ch. 2.

[6] In fact, Rousseau identifies 'the error most to be feared' as believing oneself worthier of happiness than others. But two paragraphs later he equates the latter with believing oneself 'to be of a more excellent nature and more happily born than other men'.

Respect vs. esteem

Interpretations that trace the dangers of *amour-propre* back to inegalitarian self-conceptions clearly get something right about Rousseau's position. I aim to show, however, that this monistic understanding of inflamed *amour-propre* leaves out a good deal of the complexity and richness of Rousseau's view of the dangers inherent in the human need to win the recognition of others. The tendency to focus exclusively on inegalitarian self-conceptions derives, I suspect, from how Kant appropriated the doctrine of *amour-propre* for the (narrower) purposes of his moral philosophy. (For Kant, the pernicious form of self-love can be defined as taking one's own happiness—rather than the moral law, which also takes the happiness of others into account—as the supreme criterion for action (*KPV*, 5: 73–4); since this is in effect to regard oneself as worthier of happiness than others, it can plausibly be viewed as embodying an inflated sense of self-worth.) Merely getting persons to think of themselves as equal to their fellow beings looks most plausible as a remedy for inflamed *amour-propre* when attending exclusively to the question of what *moral* status it is appropriate for individuals to assign to themselves and to others. It is no accident that when Cohen, for example, characterizes the self-conceptions that determine which of its two forms *amour-propre* will assume, he focuses exclusively on the degree of moral respect one claims for oneself and grants to others. For Cohen, to suffer from inflamed *amour-propre* is to regard oneself as inherently superior to one's fellow beings, and this attitude finds expression in the beliefs that one is by nature entitled to a better life than others and that one's own well-being deserves more consideration than others' in determining the obligations of all. Non-inflamed *amour-propre*, in contrast, is defined by the belief that all persons have the same 'natural worth'—are equally deserving of moral consideration—in virtue of their 'common human nature'.[7]

This understanding of the danger of *amour-propre* conceals the complexity of Rousseau's position in a number of ways, but the easiest to see is in its implicit assumption that moral respect alone is, or could be, sufficient to satisfy the needs of *amour-propre*. More precisely, this interpretation overlooks the distinction sometimes made between respect and esteem[8]

---

[7] Cohen, 109, 110.

[8] This point is inspired by the distinction between self-respect and self-esteem articulated by David Sachs in 'How to Distinguish Self-Respect from Self-Esteem', *Philosophy & Public Affairs* 10 (1981),

and tacitly assumes that the longings associated with *amour-propre* can be satisfied simply by achieving the former. For philosophers who make this distinction, respect is an intrinsically moral form of valuing persons. It is the attitude to persons that Kant, for example, places at the center of his moral theory, and it consists, roughly, in according equal moral status to the interests or ends of all individuals. To respect a person in this sense is to regard him as possessing a set of rights that all persons possess simply in virtue of being human (or, as Kant understands it, in virtue of being a free, rational agent). Respecting others, then, involves recognizing their fundamental dignity as human beings—as beings whose interests and desires place moral constraints on others' actions. Manipulation, degradation, exploitation, disregarding the wishes of others without reason[9]—in short, all forms of dehumanization—are ways of violating others' status as moral beings and so of failing to display the respect due to them as persons.

As Kant himself recognizes, the (moral) respect of persons (*Achtung*) can be distinguished from forms of esteem (*Verehrung*) that are directed at individuals' particular attributes and achievements.[10] As I construe this distinction here, to esteem someone is to regard him as worthy of praise, admiration, or emulation for some specific quality or achievement. Unlike respect, esteem is not a *recognition of rights* that individuals enjoy in virtue of possessing a certain status (as beings of a certain sort) but a valuing of persons that involves a *positive appraisal* of the esteemed person's particular qualities or achievements.[11] This difference manifests itself in the fact that respect is an inherently practical attitude—one must 'display' one's respect

346–60. See also the papers contained in *Dignity, Character, and Self-Respect*, ed. Robin S. Dillon (New York: Routledge, 1995). The distinction I draw here between respect and esteem does not correspond in any rigorous way to common usage, which often treats the two as identical. Rousseau, too, generally treats *estimer* and *respecter* as interchangeable. Yet making the distinction is philosophically necessary, insofar as it helps to clarify and make sense of Rousseau's project. Axel Honneth also highlights a similar distinction in *The Struggle for Recognition*, trans. Joel Anderson (Cambridge: Polity Press, 1995), 111–24.

[9] These examples come from Sachs, 348.

[10] Immanuel Kant, *The Metaphysics of Morals*, ed. Mary Gregor (Cambridge: Cambridge University Press, 1996), 6:467–8.

[11] This way of differentiating respect and esteem is inspired by Stephen Darwall's distinction between recognition respect and appraisal respect in 'Two Kinds of Respect', in Dillon (ed.), *Dignity, Character, and Self-Respect*, 181–97. Darwall's main concern is not to distinguish respect from esteem (184), and the distinction he makes does not completely overlap with the one I make here. The most important difference is that Darwall (correctly) allows for forms of recognition respect beyond the moral respect for persons as such (183–5)—for example, recognition of the consideration a person deserves by virtue of occupying a particular role, such as that of parent, client, elder, etc.

for others by regulating one's conduct in accordance with norms that define how persons as such deserve to be treated—whereas esteem is less a matter of acting in certain ways than of holding certain approving opinions concerning the merits of the esteemed.

Beyond this, esteem differs from respect in that it is not something to which all persons are entitled simply in virtue of their common nature; it is accorded to persons not on the basis of properties that all humans share as such but rather for particular qualities, capacities, and achievements that vary widely from individual to individual. More precisely, esteem is typically accorded to a person for his *excellences*, for the ways in which he 'stands out' from his fellow beings and elicits their praise or admiration.[12] Excellences constitute a very large class of nearly limitless variety, which includes particular achievements (having scaled Mt. Everest), natural abilities (bodily grace), cultivated talents (fluency in a foreign language), and even purely innate characteristics (having lovely eyes). It is, of course, possible to be esteemed for distinctively moral attributes—living a morally exemplary life is a kind of excellence—but here, too, esteem is accorded on the basis of particular achievements and is distinct from the respect (the respectful treatment) due not just to the virtuous but to all persons. The distinctness of these two modes of valuing persons is made evident by the fact that it is possible—and, in civilized intercourse, frequently necessary—to display respect for individuals whom one in no way esteems.

Rousseau on respect and esteem

Although Rousseau does not explicitly distinguish between respect and esteem, his depictions of the manifestations of *amour-propre* abound with examples of both. This is most evident in the passage of the Second Discourse, cited in Chapter 1, in which *amour-propre* makes its first appearance in the human world.[13] According to this passage, immediately after individuals have begun to desire to be esteemed by others as 'the handsomest, the strongest, the most adroit, or the most eloquent', they also begin to

---

[12] Although individuals are typically esteemed for qualities that differentiate them from others, it will be left open for now whether *in principle* only qualities that not everyone possesses can be the object of esteem. (It might be thought, for example, that the ability to speak a foreign language might continue to elicit esteem even in a world where everyone in fact had learned to do so.) The more basic point is that esteem, unlike respect, is directed at qualities of individuals beyond those they possess simply in virtue of the kind of being they are.

[13] I am indebted to Terence Irwin for pointing this out to me.

demand a kind of recognition that is clearly a form of respect rather than esteem:

As soon as men had begun to appreciate one another and the idea of consideration had taken shape in their mind, each one claimed a right to it, and one could no longer deprive anyone of it with impunity. From here arose the first duties of civility, even among savages, and from it any intentional wrong became an affront, because along with the harm that resulted from the injury, the offended man saw in it contempt for his person that was often more unbearable than the harm itself.

(*DI*, 166/*OC* 3, 169–70)

There can be no doubt that the duties of civility referred to here provide individuals with a kind of recognition that is importantly different from the valuation they seek in wanting to be acknowledged as the handsomest or the strongest: in the former case their desire is to be treated by others in accordance with standards of human dignity that apply to all persons as such, whereas in the latter they seek to be valued for some specific excellence that (in the examples Rousseau gives) marks them as different from their peers.

Several issues are raised by Rousseau's juxtaposition of these two different ways in which primitive individuals seek to be recognized. The most urgent is a conceptual issue that bears on how precisely the quest for esteem is to be understood. This question arises because, rather than defining this crucial phenomenon, Rousseau merely presents us with examples of it: individuals, assembled for the first time in a public arena, are moved by the desire to be recognized by others as 'the one who sang or danced the best, the handsomest, the strongest, the most skillful, or the most eloquent' (*DI*, 166/*OC* 3, 169). What all these examples of the search for esteem have in common is the desire to be regarded by others as the *best* in some specific respect, and this naturally conveys the impression that a wish to be recognized as best (in some respect) is intrinsic to—a necessary part of—any desire for esteem. This impression, however, is false, and recognizing that will be of significance later when it is time to consider how the human need for esteem might be widely satisfied without engendering the panoply of evils that are the 'natural' consequences of inflamed *amour-propre*. At this point it is sufficient to note that, as Rousseau himself realizes, there is no necessary link between the quest for esteem and wanting to be recognized as the best. Emile, for example, finds honor in being recognized as 'a man of good sense' (*E* IV, 339/*OC* 4, 670) and as a skilled carpenter (*E* V, 437–8/*OC* 4, 807–9) without needing or wanting to be regarded as the best carpenter or the most sensible man. In cases such as these, esteem is accorded to someone not for being best but for realizing an ideal defined by the intrinsic merit of a thing (one's work or character of mind) rather than by how it compares with the qualities or achievements of others.[14] I shall postpone for now the more difficult question of whether esteem might nevertheless contain an ineliminable element of comparison with others—and so implicitly involve being recognized as better than others in some way, even if not necessarily as the best. It might be, for instance, that what counts as being good at carpentry depends on what the average carpenter is able to do, or that being good at something elicits esteem only when it is not a common occurrence. In any case, as we shall see, Rousseau's solution to the problems that arise from the desire for esteem does not depend on supposing that esteem can be rid of all elements of comparison with others or of all desires to be better than others in some specific respect.

If Rousseau is aware, however, that being recognized as the best is not intrinsic to winning esteem, why do all the examples he provides here involve striving for precisely that? If we rule out coincidence or sloppiness as the explanation—contrary to appearances, there is little of either in Rousseau's texts—one interesting possibility remains: these most primitive attempts to win esteem are instances of wanting to be seen as the best because for humans this is the 'natural' form the quest for esteem takes. Or, formulated more precisely: given the constraints of human nature (the nature of *amour de soi* is especially relevant), in the absence of the complex social and educational institutions that can mitigate *amour-propre*'s dangers, *seeking to be recognized as the best is the natural (most likely) form for the desire for esteem to assume.* This is primarily because normal human development is such that yearning to be 'in the first place' is *amour-propre*'s 'default' configuration. My concern here is not to argue for this claim—I do that in the next chapter—but merely to forestall at this early stage of my inquiry a possible confusion about the nature of esteem that is encouraged by how Rousseau depicts its first appearance in the Second Discourse: although

[14] I am indebted to David Estlund and Bernard Reginster for making me aware of this possibility and its importance.

(for reasons not yet articulated) wanting to be recognized as the best is a common and 'natural' way for humans to seek esteem, the former is not necessary to the latter.

Finally, one further point about how the practices of respect and esteem are introduced into the Second Discourse merits our attention: Rousseau presents these two forms of wanting to be recognized by others as successive developmental stages in *amour-propre*'s 'history': the demand for respect appears to develop *out of* the earlier and (presumably) more primitive desire to be thought best in some specific respect. Nevertheless, there is no account given here—and none, I think, to be constructed—that explains why the earlier stage must, or even is likely to, give rise to the later. Despite this lacuna in Rousseau's account—it is not the only such gap in the Second Discourse[15]—two points can be inferred from this sequence of stages. First, the desire to be valued for one's particular excellences is a more primitive manifestation of *amour-propre* than the demand for respect. 'More primitive' here does not imply 'inferior' but refers instead to the cognitive complexity of the phenomenon at issue. The point, then, is that the duties of civility require more sophisticated concepts and self-understandings than the practices associated with the simple desire to stand out as the strongest or most beautiful. For, as they are described here, the practices of respect presuppose not only the moral idea of what a person is *entitled* to demand from others but also the ability to conceive of oneself abstractly, as a 'person' who shares a fundamental nature and identical rights with all other individuals despite the many particular qualities that differentiate them.

The more important point implicit in Rousseau's depiction of the demand for respect as arising out of earlier desires for esteem is that, though distinct, the two phenomena are enough alike to count as manifestations of a single passion (*amour-propre*). The point here is not simply that esteem and respect are both avenues by which individuals can achieve recognized standing for others but also that there exists an economy of *amour-propre*

---

[15] I do not mean to imply that such lacunae represent defects in his account. Rousseau's aim in the Second Discourse is not to prove that events must have happened as they did or even that they are likely outcomes of his hypothetical starting point. His aim, rather, is to 'venture some conjectures' (*DI*, 125/*OC* 3, 123) as to how human society might have evolved in order to show that its present condition could have developed out of more innocent beginnings and that therefore present evils need not be imputed to a fixed human nature. In the passage at issue here Rousseau's aim is not to explain the origin of the duties of civility but to point out the kinship between desires for (what I call) respect and esteem.

such that finding one species of recognition can lessen the urgency of one's pursuit of the other. In other words, being respected as a person helps to satisfy the general and protean human need to count as someone for others, and this can alleviate the need to achieve standing in others' eyes on the basis of one's particular qualities and accomplishments.

Critique of the prevailing view

Interpretations that regard egalitarian *amour-propre* as the key to solving the evils depicted in the Second Discourse are forced to place great significance on this 'economic' feature of *amour-propre*, for they are committed to the view that, given the right social and psychological conditions, respect by itself can satisfy the human longing to have a recognized worth. These interpretations, I have suggested, get something right about Rousseau's view, but they err insofar as they suppose that the demand to be respected as an abstract person, equal to all others, can or should completely replace the desire to be esteemed for one's particular excellences. Acquiring an egalitarian conception of one's inherent worth is an important part of the solution Rousseau envisages, but—to his credit as a theorist of human affairs—he never falls prey to the illusion that respect alone could satiate the need of humans to 'count for something' in the eyes of their fellow beings. Even though Rousseau portrays the demand for equal respect as developing out of the more primitive desire to be admired for one's particular qualities, he nowhere suggests that the former can completely replace the latter. In the Second Discourse, individuals' desires to be valued as handsome or strong do not disappear once the practices of civility are established; on the contrary, they flourish, increasing in both intensity and variety. And in case one is tempted to view the survival of the desire for esteem as merely a feature of the corrupt society portrayed in the Second Discourse, it is worth remembering that even the well-educated Emile does not cease to care about his excellence as others perceive it simply because he has learned to regard himself as the moral equal of all human beings (*E* IV, 339/*OC* 4, 670–1).[16] Even in the First Discourse—which seems to take a dimmer

---

[16] Further evidence is that even after his *amour-propre* has been properly formed, Emile badly wants to win the race he has entered, and to do so with Sophie watching him (*E* V, 436/*OC* 4, 806). Sophie, too, has 'a strong love of praise', even though her desire for esteem, like Emile's, is subject to certain conditions, for example, 'that she can believe that the good that is said of her is actually thought' (*E* V, 399/*OC* 4, 754).

view of *amour-propre* than the writings that follow it—Rousseau recognizes that public esteem can be an important force in motivating humans to develop and employ their talents, thereby contributing to the well-being of all.[17]

But, textual evidence aside, why ought we to be suspicious of the suggestion that simply ensuring respect for everyone could suffice to solve the wide array of problems Rousseau attributes to *amour-propre*? One answer is suggested by imagining oneself in the position of those primitive creatures described in the Second Discourse who, assembled in front of their huts, strive to win recognition from their fellow beings as a gifted singer or dancer, as worthy of admiration for specific qualities or achievements that distinguish them from others. What reaction would they be likely to have if, in place of esteem for their excellences, they were to receive assurance that henceforth their status as moral persons was to be respected by all, that they would never again be treated as merely a means to others' ends or have their wants and interests disregarded by others without reason? Without underestimating the importance of moral respect to individuals' sense of their worth, it is safe to assume that such an assurance would not satisfy the specific longing that motivated their efforts to be esteemed, admired, or deemed worthy of emulation on the basis of their particular qualities. A plausible explanation for this can be found by considering the aspect of oneself that is affirmed by others in the practice of respect. Persons are accorded moral respect on the basis of some quality they share with all other humans, which, depending on the moral theory one espouses, might be freedom, rationality, or the ability to anticipate pain. But human individuals are, and take themselves to be, more than just the universal quality that makes them persons and hence worthy of respect. In addition to recognition of their dignity as a human being, they also long for evidence of their worth as the particular beings they are; they desire to be valued, admired, and loved for their distinctive accomplishments and even for their natural (and sometimes trivial) endowments and properties.

[17] For example: i) Rousseau expresses his admiration for individuals like Bacon, Descartes, and Newton, whose achievements are 'monuments to the glory of the human mind' (*DSA*, 27/*OC* 3, 29); ii) he endorses 'respect for the truly learned' (*DSA*, 5/*OC* 3, 5); iii) he admits that 'the wise man ... is not insensitive to glory' and that emulation can animate virtue to the advantage of society (*DSA*, 23/*OC* 3, 26); and iv) he praises the strategies of literary academies, which attempt to use the motive of honor to inspire individuals to 'make themselves worthy by means of useful works and irreproachable morals' (*DSA*, 24/*OC* 3, 26).

Given what humans are like, finding respect without esteem is unlikely to be psychologically satisfying, and in cases where it is—where one's sense of worth is exhausted by one's abstract human dignity—it seems appropriate to speak of a kind of self-estrangement, that is, an alienation from the part of oneself that makes one a specific individual.

There is a further reason to doubt that respect alone could satisfy *amour-propre*. This consideration has to do not with which aspects of the self are affirmed by respect or esteem but with *how* the self is affirmed in each. The inadequacy of respect alone stems not only from its inability to confirm a person's worth as a particular individual but also from the kind of recognition it provides. This point is bound up with a difference between respect and esteem mentioned earlier, namely, that respect is conferred primarily through behavior, whereas esteem consists in the holding of certain opinions (about the esteemed person). Again, without underestimating the importance of this essentially external form of recognition, it is natural for individuals to desire, in addition, affirmation from others that springs from a more internal source, one located in the 'inner' depths of consciousness. Being thought of highly by others can, of course, have implications for how one expects to be treated by them; still, when one desires others' esteem, it is their ('true') opinions one cares about and not, in the first instance, their external actions. What the person who seeks esteem wishes to evoke from others is unfeigned expression of their approval, admiration, amazement, or delight, not a demonstration of their practical commitment to treat all persons as moral equals. It is significant that Rousseau frequently highlights this feature of the quest for esteem when characterizing *amour-propre*; it is precisely what he means to capture, for example, in claiming that *amour-propre* is relative in the second sense distinguished in Chapter 1: what *amour-propre* seeks is signs of one's worth *in the eyes of others*, a mode of affirmation that *consists in* the favorable opinions of other evaluating beings.

Rousseau's extensive treatment of *amour-propre* is inspired, in part, by the view that because the need for esteem is so deeply rooted in (socialized) human beings—because respect on its own cannot entirely satisfy our longing to count as someone for others—a social theory that aspires to do justice to the difficulties *amour-propre* introduces into human affairs must take full account of the need for esteem and of the messiness and complexity that attend it. Doing so requires investigating not only the specific dangers this need poses but also how social institutions can be arranged so as to avert those dangers while still affording individuals ample opportunities to satisfy this crucial aspect of their need to achieve standing in the eyes of others. One thing, however, is clear even before this task is begun: once esteem from others is acknowledged as an enduring and significant human need—a need that social theorists ought not to count on banishing from human existence (*E* IV, 212/*OC* 4, 491)—it becomes much less plausible that simply making *amour-propre* egalitarian could cure the evils depicted in the Second Discourse.[18] One reason is that the desire for esteem stands in some tension with the belief in the equal worth of all persons that is constitutive of egalitarian *amour-propre*. If esteem is directed primarily at individuals' excellences—at ways in which they stand out from their fellow beings—then seeking esteem can easily seem to require that one try to raise oneself above the crowd rather than rest content with equal recognition. Moreover, the fact that excellences come in varying degrees means that esteem, too, is likely to be meted out unequally. These considerations alone cast doubt on interpretations that focus exclusively on egalitarian *amour-propre* as the remedy for human evils. Yet, as we shall see, even they do not exhaust the ways in which such interpretations fail to do justice to the full richness and complexity of Rousseau's account of the dangers of *amour-propre*.

Explaining *amour-propre*'s dangers

It is time to begin a more systematic reconstruction of Rousseau's view of the dangers that *amour-propre* introduces into the human world. As I suggested above, the Second Discourse concerns itself with five distinct evils, all of which it regards as effects (or partial effects) of generalized *amour-propre*: enslavement, conflict, vice, misery, and self-estrangement (or alienation).[19] Our immediate task is to understand how the characteristics of *amour-propre* outlined in Chapter 1 explain its tendency to produce each of these evils. This will provide us with the resources we need to inquire,

[18] This was seen most clearly by Hegel, whose social theory makes individuals' need for esteem for their particular qualities a central concern; see Neuhouser, *Foundations*, 14, 92, 98–9, 108–10, 143–4, 156.
[19] Melzer suggests a sixth: the disunity of the soul (63–8).

in Chapter 5, whether it is possible to direct the expression of *amour-propre* in such a way that these evils are avoided, making the quest to count as someone for others compatible with freedom, peace, virtue, happiness, and unalienated selfhood. In reconstructing Rousseau's view I divide the sources of *amour-propre*'s dangers into five categories, corresponding to the five basic features of *amour-propre* set out in Chapter 1.

a) *The satisfaction* amour-propre *strives for gives being to the self*

One important characteristic of *amour-propre* that contributes to its capacity to wreak havoc in human society is the ferocity and power with which it grabs hold of individuals and moves them to act. None of the other problematic features of *amour-propre* would ultimately be of much consequence to human affairs, if *amour-propre*, like natural pity, were a sentiment that spoke only 'under certain circumstances' and with 'a gentle voice' (*DI*, 152, 154/*OC* 3, 154, 156). Rousseau draws our attention to the ferocity of *amour-propre* when he notes in the Second Discourse that once civility had become an established social practice, 'any intentional wrong became an affront, because along with the harm that resulted from the injury, the offended man saw in it contempt for his person that was often more unbearable than the harm itself. It was thus that... vengeances became terrible, and men bloodthirsty and cruel' (*DI*, 166/*OC* 3, 170).[20] Similarly, in *Emile* Rousseau associates the awakening of *amour-propre* with the birth of the passions, which, in distinction to the gentler sentiments,[21] introduce feverishness and agitation into Emile's demeanor and signal a 'stormy revolution' in his emotional makeup (*E* IV, 211/*OC* 4, 489–90). And in a later text, Rousseau describes the violent physical and 'involuntary' effects of his own wounded *amour-propre*, when 'anger and indignation take possession of my senses': 'flashing eyes, an inflamed face, trembling limbs, a throbbing heart—... and reasoning can do nothing about it' (*RSW*, 76/*OC* 1, 1083).

In emphasizing its passionate nature, Rousseau draws our attention to three separate features of *amour-propre* that distinguish it from a gentler

---

[20] See also note xvi, *DI*, 218/*OC* 3, 219–20.

[21] Rousseau does not always give 'passion' the narrow meaning it has here. Sometimes the term is used very broadly to include gentle sentiments, such as pity, but in the passages cited here 'passion' is used in a more restrictive sense that implies the potential for stormy, feverish emotion. See the editor's note to this passage, *OC* 4, 1454–5.

sentiment, such as pity. The first is simply its capacity, when unsatisfied, to inspire acts of violence and cruelty—acts that otherwise, on Rousseau's view, have no basis in human nature. The second is *amour-propre*'s ability to 'consume' (*DI*, 184/*OC* 3, 189) those it affects, leading them to forsake other, less urgently felt pursuits and to focus single-mindedly on winning the esteem they feel deprived of, often at the expense of their other, 'non-relative' interests. The third feature that makes *amour-propre* such a potent and unruly force is hinted at in the suggestion that Emile's acquisition of a single new passion effects a 'revolution' in his character, as well as in his claim that *amour-propre* 'excites and multiplies passions' (*DI*, 184/*OC* 3, 189). What Rousseau appears to have in mind in these remarks is *amour-propre*'s virus-like capacity to infect virtually all of life's activities, investing them with its own significance and commandeering them in service of its own, foreign ends. Like flames that rush in to fill an oxygen-rich room, *amour-propre* threatens to engulf every human enterprise it touches. It is true that when Emile's *amour-propre* is awakened, he acquires a set of motivations he previously lacked. But it would be wrong to suppose that these new motivations simply take their place alongside those he had before. Rather, each of Emile's previous projects is transformed (or has the potential to be transformed) by his newly acquired desires. His interest in woodworking, for example, is no longer exhausted by the satisfaction to be had from imposing a form on inanimate nature and creating objects of beauty and utility. For now, in addition, his work can serve to display to others a quality of himself that enhances his standing in their eyes. This feature of *amour-propre* is extremely important to Rousseau's project in the Second Discourse, since it is crucial to his account of how private property originates and multiplies inequalities, thereby helping to generate the evils the Discourse is concerned to explain: once it is common practice to see one's worth reflected in things, even the commodities of life cease to be valued primarily as means to comfort or survival, becoming instead objects to be owned, accumulated, and paraded before others. With this development, the passion to acquire standing in the eyes of others enters a vast, new arena, one that will afford it ample opportunities to assume novel and unexpected forms in response to its own evolving demands.

Each of the features that give *amour-propre* its passionate character is explained by the fact that something of great importance is at stake in its activity. Its ferocity, its power to consume those who have it, its ability to infect every human enterprise with its own meaning—all are signs of the overriding significance with which the aims of *amour-propre* are invested. In this regard it is no accident that Rousseau's account of the bases of human motivation gives *amour-propre* roughly the same fundamental status it accords to the self-preservative drives of *amour de soi*. This equality of status is a reflection of the fact that in both forms of self-love what is at stake is, in some sense, the very being of the self. This is obvious in the case of *amour de soi*, for which physical survival is the first and overriding concern, but it is no less true for *amour-propre*, which aims at what might be called the self's moral, or spiritual, survival. This is the idea Rousseau means to communicate when he says repeatedly that in being recognized by others, an individual acquires a 'sentiment of his own *existence*' (*DI*, 187/*OC* 3, 193; my emphasis).[22] The failure to find recognition from one's fellow beings does not, of course, pose a threat to one's existence as a physical entity, and yet, as ordinary language acknowledges, a person who lacks standing in the eyes of others is, in some meaningful sense, a 'nobody'. The kind of existence at issue here is akin to what Sartre, under the influence of Rousseau and Hegel, has called 'being-for-others',[23] and the sign of such being is not physical presence in space and time but rather 'moral presence',[24] as manifested in the various kinds of impact one can have (as a valued subject) on the behavior of others. Dent nicely captures Rousseau's idea of moral presence and its relation to *amour-propre* in the following passage:

[Being recognized by others] is testimony to personal power and force in encounter and contention with other persons. The display of personal power is a proof to oneself of one's possession of real, effective existence as having living presence … in … the world, particularly the world of other humans. We crave, as the condition of having any sense of ourselves as living, vital, existences at all, proofs of our reality; this we secure only by enforcing ourselves upon our surroundings such that we experience a world showing the effects of our presence.[25]

If, generally speaking, the capacity to produce effects in the world is the sign of a being's existence, or reality, then being valued by others, insofar

---

[22] See also *E* I, 42, 61/*OC* 4, 253, 279–80; and *E* IV, 270/*OC* 4, 570–1.   [23] Sartre, Part III.

[24] The term comes from Dent, who gives an excellent account of what such presence consists in (21–6, 49–50, 56–8). 'Moral' here contrasts with 'physical' and so has a wider sense than 'ethical' or 'duty-related'.

[25] Dent, 49.

as it is exhibited in their speech and action, can be taken to confer on the self a being, or reality, of a certain, distinctively human kind: to achieve recognition is to acquire a confirmed existence for others as a 'real', effect-producing subject.[26]

Understanding the passionate character of *amour-propre* is important to Rousseau because it plays a crucial role in explaining why, as Hobbes is famous for noting, conflict is so pervasive a feature of human intercourse. It is not, for Rousseau, the urgency of self-preservation but rather the 'desire for reputation, honors, and preferences' that 'makes all men competitors, rivals, or... enemies' (*DI*, 184/*OC* 3, 189). Rousseau's suggestion is that if ordinary conflicts of interest were unaffected by the needs of *amour-propre*—if such conflicts were not regularly transmuted into contests over the worth and dignity of the opponents—struggles among humans would be rare, short-lived, and mostly without enduring significance. When another individual steals the fruit I have gathered for my next meal, what prompts me to seek revenge—what prompts me to expend more energy in retrieving it than finding another would require—is less that I am hungry than that, in addition, my *amour-propre* has been wounded. For Rousseau, then, it is not material scarcity but unfulfilled *amour-propre* that is most responsible for the warlike relations among individuals that can easily appear to constitute the enduring, 'natural' condition of humankind.

b) Amour-propre *seeks relative (comparative) standing*

A second source of *amour-propre*'s dangers is its relative character in the first of the two senses distinguished in Chapter 1. The point here, it will be recalled, is that the standing sought by *amour-propre* is always defined relative to that of other individuals. In other words, the recognition *amour-propre* strives for is a positional good, which implies that doing well for oneself (finding recognition) consists in doing well in relation to others. This means that the extent to which I find my need for recognition satisfied depends on how well—or how badly—those around me fare with respect to theirs. This feature of *amour-propre* is fraught with danger precisely because it is so easy for humans to take 'doing well' (in relation to others) to imply 'doing better', in which case the quest for recognition becomes a quest to be more highly valued than others. (It is a question of deep importance whether the

---

[26] Dent, 50.

drive for superior status is unavoidable in human beings or merely the result of contingent though widely obtaining social and psychological conditions. This question will be addressed later, when considering whether it is possible to find a solution to the manifold problems to which *amour-propre* gives rise. For now it is sufficient to note that superior status is in fact a widely pursued human end and, more important, to understand how this fact helps to account for many of the evils Rousseau wants to explain.)

It is easy to see how *amour-propre* becomes the source of serious problems once individuals take the view that having their worth affirmed requires being recognized not merely as good but as superior to others (the hallmark of what I called above inegalitarian *amour-propre*). Even though this aspect of Rousseau's analysis has been clearly articulated by other interpreters and summarized briefly above, it will be useful to note again four basic problems that tend to arise when even a small number of individuals seek to satisfy their *amour-propre* by being recognized as worthier than others. First, one individual's desire to be recognized as superior by a second encounters an initial obstacle in that it appears to demand of the second that she (at least in some respect) value the first more than herself. Rousseau expresses this point, somewhat imprecisely, in his claim that '*amour-propre*, which makes comparisons, is never content and never could be, because this sentiment, in preferring ourselves to others, also demands that others prefer us to themselves, which is impossible' (*E* IV, 213–14/*OC* 4, 493).[27] Regardless of whether we agree that it is psychologically impossible for humans to regard others as worthier than themselves, Rousseau's remark points to a genuine and systematic problem the quest for superior status faces when pursued by a sufficient number of one's fellow beings: my desire to be recognized as superior to you stands, prima facie at least, in conflict with your similar desire with regard to me.

The second difficulty implicit in the widely shared desire for superior status is that, when success is defined only in terms of achieving more than others, the systematic satisfaction of *amour-propre* becomes impossible. This is because when *amour-propre* assumes an inegalitarian form, social esteem necessarily becomes a scarce good; or, as Rousseau puts the point: 'all could not want preference without there being many malcontents' (*E* IV, 215/*OC* 4, 494). The claim here is not, as in the previous paragraph,

---

[27] One source of imprecision here is that Rousseau fails to restrict his claim to inflamed *amour-propre*.

that it will be psychologically difficult for individuals who themselves desire superiority to acknowledge the worth of others. Rather, Rousseau is making the conceptual point that the very nature of such an end precludes collective satisfaction and guarantees systematic conflict for those who pursue it. If some are to achieve superiority, others must end up in an inferior position, and so, rather than being accessible to all, recognition must become the object of endless competition, conflict, and frustrated desires.

The third problem that results from the desire for superior standing is the 'rat race' phenomenon, or the struggle to 'keep up with the Jones's'. This problem stems from the fact that superiority, even if attained, is insecure and short-lived as long as it is achieved in relation to others who desire the same. In order to outdo the competitor who has just overtaken me or to maintain the position of pre-eminence I now occupy, I must constantly be engaged in enhancing my own current standing. In such a situation, individuals are burdened with a nearly limitless need to better their own positions in response to or in anticipation of their rivals' advances, resulting in a restless and unceasing game of one-upmanship. The problem here is not merely that the only satisfaction *amour-propre* can find will be fleeting and insecure but also that needs and desires become boundless in a way that is inimical to human happiness. Whereas '*amour de soi* ... is content when our true needs are satisfied' (*E* IV, 213/*OC* 4, 493), *amour-propre*, in its inegalitarian form, quickly multiplies our desires and perceived needs beyond any plausible conception of what our 'true' needs might be.[28] Such ever-expanding desires impose on those who have them the need to expend vast amounts of labor and energy in pursuit of the goods and honors they hope will satisfy their drive for superiority. But no matter how elaborate and exhausting, such schemes are doomed to fail, first because the labor they require typically outweighs the satisfaction they bring and, secondly, because once individuals' motivations have been permeated by inflamed *amour-propre* to this degree, they lose the capacity to enjoy their

---

[28] See also *RJJ*, 144/*OC* 1, 846. Rousseau's talk of 'true needs' ought not to be construed as referring to a historically fixed or biologically determined set of 'true' human needs. Rather, his view is best understood as grounded in a moral criterion for what constitutes false human needs, according to which, a need is false if the attempt to satisfy it stands in conflict either with one's own happiness or freedom, or with the systematic satisfaction of the fundamental interests of all. In other words, false needs are (perceived) needs we would be better off without, because they either enslave us or result in our frustration and misery.

possessions and achievements for the intrinsic (non-relative) pleasures they afford. This condition represents a genuine perversion of human desire, for such beings 'value the things they enjoy only to the extent that others are deprived of them and, without any change in their own state, ... would cease to be happy if [others] ceased to be miserable' (*DI*, 184/*OC* 3, 189).

The three points just discussed demonstrate how the quest for superior standing tends to engender both conflict and unhappiness (frustrated desire) among those who pursue it. There is, however, a further problem with inegalitarian *amour-propre*, namely, its tendency to produce vice, or immorality. In this context, vice is usually understood as a callous disregard for the sufferings of others or, in its more pernicious forms, an inclination to harm others or to take delight in their misfortunes.[29] For Rousseau an important part of this inclination to harm others—and a ubiquitous feature of 'civilized' society—is the disposition to inflict not physical but moral suffering through scorn, contempt, derision, and a host of similar attitudes that aim at humiliating—lowering the standing of—those one seeks to be better than. For if a self has both a physical and a moral existence, it stands to reason that an inflamed *amour-propre* bent on lowering others in order to raise itself will not hesitate to attack the selves with which it is in competition at both sites of their being.

Defined in this way, vice requires a suppression of our natural pity (our sensitivity to others' pains), and so the propensity to vice that is so widespread among civilized beings is not simply a consequence of human nature but demands some further explanation. Rousseau finds this explanation in the essentially comparative nature of the desire for superior status: if doing well for oneself is conceived in terms of doing better than others, then it is possible to further one's own well-being by doing harm to those with whom one compares oneself. Once I measure my own standing in relation to others', I can further my standing either by improving my own lot or, what is sometimes easier to do, by worsening yours. Thus, inegalitarian *amour-propre* provides humans with an incentive they would otherwise lack to rejoice at, or even to seek, the adversity of others. This is precisely the point Rousseau invokes when explaining the origin of vice in the Second Discourse: 'the fervor to raise one's relative fortune, less out

---

[29] Vice also includes dishonesty, hypocrisy, deceit, and dissimulation. That Rousseau believes them, too, to be engendered by inegalitarian *amour-propre* is evident at *DI*, 171/*OC* 3, 175.

of true need than in order to place oneself above others, inspires in all men a base inclination to harm one another' (*DI*, 171/*OC* 3, 175).

There is a second sort of vice that *amour-propre* is capable of engendering: the will to dominate others. Rather than regard the will to dominate as a basic urge of human nature, Rousseau explains it as a deformation of *amour-propre* that is a possible (and common) but by no means necessary characteristic of human beings. Taking this view enables Rousseau to understand domination as an end humans seek for its own sake rather than merely for its instrumental value (where commanding the powers of others is sought only insofar as it helps to satisfy self-preservative or other non-relative needs). This is because he regards the 'spirit of domination' or 'the desire to command' (*E* I, 67–8/*OC* 4, 289–90) as, at root, the desire for recognition from others of a type of superior standing: making oneself into the master of others' wills is one way of finding confirmation of one's favored status not only in the behavior of those who obey but also in the eyes of those who witness that obedience and regard it as natural or legitimate. (In Chapter 4 I expand on the connection between *amour-propre* and the will to dominate, as well as on the social and psychological conditions that foster it.)

c) Amour-propre *seeks standing in the eyes of others*

As I have argued, *amour-propre* is relative to others in a second sense as well, and it, too, is a source of human ills. Because the good sought by *amour-propre* is to be regarded in a certain way by others—because it involves a concern for how one appears *to other subjects*—beings who have this passion are directly dependent on others for the satisfaction of one of their most keenly felt needs. For such beings, relations to others are necessary not only as a means to satisfying non-relative needs but also because the favorable opinion of others is an essential part of the good they seek. Some of the danger that springs from this aspect of *amour-propre* can be understood in light of Rousseau's larger view concerning the dangers of dependence in general.[30] (Dependence in this context is opposed to self-sufficiency: an individual is dependent when he has to rely on the cooperation of others in order to satisfy his needs.) Rousseau's social and political thought is founded on the idea that any form of dependence carries with it the danger that

---

[30] For more on the threat that dependence poses to freedom, see Neuhouser, *Foundations*, 64–73.

individuals will have to compromise their freedom in order to satisfy the needs that impel them to seek the cooperation of others. If freedom consists in 'not being subject to someone else's will' (*LWM*, 260/*OC* 3, 841)—or, equivalently, in obeying only one's own will[31]—then dependence poses a standing threat to being free, since it opens up the possibility that in order to get what I need I may have no choice but to tailor my actions to conform to the (often arbitrary) wills of those on whose cooperation I rely. When constantly faced with a choice between getting what one needs or following one's own will, it will be no surprise if satisfaction frequently wins out over freedom.

Applying this principle to *amour-propre*, Rousseau warns that depending on others for esteem often results in the loss of freedom:

> Even domination is servile when it is connected with opinion, for you depend on the prejudices of those you govern by prejudices. To conduct them as you please, you must conduct yourself as they please. They have only to change their way of thinking, and you must perforce change your way of acting.
>
> (*E* II, 83/*OC* 4, 308)

Rousseau's thought is that someone who needs recognition will regularly be subject to the temptation to let her actions be dictated by the values and preferences of others and, so, to determine her will in accordance with their wishes or values rather than her own. But this is precisely how Rousseau defines enslavement, or loss of freedom, and it is for this reason that he views *amour-propre* as a serious threat to our capacity to be free. Moreover, it should be noted, this threat to freedom follows solely from the dependence-producing character of *amour-propre* in general and, so, is not contingent on whether *amour-propre* assumes an illegitimately inegalitarian form or is in some other respect inflamed.

If we think more carefully about what the loss of freedom consists in when it is a result of dependence stemming from *amour-propre*, we see that it is difficult to distinguish it from a loss of *integrity*.[32] The defining feature of

---

[31] This formulation is implicit in Rousseau's statement of the fundamental problem of political philosophy, which glosses freedom as 'obeying only oneself' (*SC*, I.6.iv). See also *RSW*, 56/*OC* 1, 1059, where freedom is said to consist in 'never doing what [one] does not want to do'.

[32] The loss of integrity might be regarded as more a kind of alienation than a loss of freedom. But loss of integrity is distinct from what Rousseau calls existing (exclusively) outside oneself, which I take to be the essential feature of alienation (or self-estrangement). As my discussion below makes clear, the latter consists in having too little capacity for self-affirmation. Thus, although the two may occur

enslavement is that one obeys—acts in accordance with—the will (ends, preferences, or values) of another. This definition implies that the unfree person has an identifiable will of his own but, for whatever reason, is unable to act in accordance with it. What does this failure to follow one's own will look like, though, when it is due to the sort of dependence that *amour-propre* creates—that is, when a person obeys the will of another in order to satisfy his need for recognition? Evidently this: such a person does whatever he can to shape himself—his visible actions and traits—in ways that will elicit the approval and esteem of his fellow beings; in other words, he makes his own activity and ends conform to what others value for the purpose of raising himself in their estimation. The reason it might be more accurate to describe this as a loss of integrity than as a loss of freedom is that it is unclear whether a person who lives his life in accordance with other people's values merely in order to win their recognition can be said to *have* any values—and, so, any will—of his own at all (beyond, of course, the overriding desire to be recognized). It is not so much, then, that a person of this sort fails to follow his own will as that he fails to have one in the first place.

However we name this phenomenon, it is clear that Rousseau regards it as one of the most pernicious of *amour-propre*'s potential effects. It is precisely the evil he means to bring to our attention in passages such as the following:

> Emile ... values nothing according to the price opinion confers on it. ... He will concern himself with [others'] opinion only insofar as it relates immediately to his person, and he will not worry about arbitrary evaluations whose only law is fashion or prejudice. ... He will hardly seek advantages that are not clear in themselves and that need others' judgments in order to be established; ... still less will he seek those that are not at all connected with his person, such as being of nobler birth, being esteemed richer, more influential, or more highly considered, or making an impression by great pomp. ... He will not precisely say to himself, 'I rejoice because they approve of me' but rather 'I rejoice because they approve of what I have done that is good. I rejoice that the people who honor me do themselves honor. So long as they judge so soundly, it will be a fine thing to obtain their esteem.'
>
> (*E* IV, 338–9/*OC* 4, 669–71)

One way of formulating Rousseau's point would be to say that Emile does not pander to others' expectations of him: he does not adopt others'

---

together, alienation is distinct from what I am calling the loss of integrity: adopting the values of others blindly, without concern for their validity.

standards without first considering whether they reflect what, in his own judgment, is truly of value. This implies that integrity should be thought of as a solidity of character—a moral backbone—that refuses to accord value to something merely because others think it good. In place of blindly pursuing whatever the crowd prizes in order to win its esteem—in place of taking 'fashion and prejudice' as his 'only law'—the person of integrity insists on being able to see for himself why a thing is good before he makes it his own end. This converges with my earlier suggestion that to lack integrity is to have no values of one's own—or, more precisely, to have insufficient independence of judgment regarding the good to be able to resist the temptation to adopt others' valuations merely for the sake of winning their favor. The same point could also be formulated in this way: the person who lacks integrity fails to constrain her pursuit of recognition by any criteria of her own for what makes someone *worthy* of others' esteem; such a person, in effect, mistakenly treats the favorable opinion of others as an unqualified good, one whose value is unconditioned by the *worthiness* to be well thought of.[33]

What makes the lack of integrity an evil in Rousseau's eyes is that, like enslavement (and like the alienation discussed below), it amounts to a failure to realize an essential characteristic of genuine selfhood, or subjectivity. To the extent that an individual values only in imitation of others, he surrenders his status as an independent, value-conferring subject. By letting others' opinions count as the sole criterion of the good, he repudiates the authority he possesses as a rational being to determine what is good on the basis of his own judgment and insight.

The passage just cited might be read as implying that there are in fact two forms the loss of integrity can take. In addition to valuing something merely because others do, Rousseau seems to point to a second form as well, namely, espousing (for whatever reason) the *wrong* values, such as nobility of birth, wealth, social influence, and pomp, rather than those that relate directly to one's 'person' (or character). This condition might, too, be considered a loss of integrity since adopting false or arbitrary values is evidence of a corrupted capacity to follow one's reason and discern clearly what things are good 'in themselves' (that is: good in truth, because of the nature of things). Despite appearances, though, the

---

[33] My discussion of integrity has been shaped by helpful interchanges with Bernard Reginster.

lack of integrity is best construed as a single phenomenon, the essential character of which is most clearly exhibited by the first of these cases. This is because, as Rousseau presents it here, the second case (subscribing to the wrong values) is to be explained as a consequence of the first (having no independent standards of worth to impose on one's search for recognition). If someone pursues the showy and superficial in lieu of the truly valuable—if she turns her back on what in the absence of distorting influences reveals itself rather clearly as the good—what can explain her error other than that her vision of the good has been blinded by an inflamed desire to win esteem from others at whatever cost? Rousseau's claim that valuing the wrong things is always—or nearly always, since the bad values need to find a beginning somewhere—the consequence of an unrestrained desire to be well thought of by others[34] is predicated on the controversial assumptions that under 'natural' conditions the good is easily discernible and that very little can derail this process beyond the lure of public esteem. But while Rousseau's claim may be exaggerated, it does draw our attention to how another widely observed human failing—the inability to keep sight of the things that matter most—has one of its sources in the temptation to seek the good opinion of others without regard for the true value of what they prize. Rousseau's view, then, is that it is this temptation, intrinsic to *amour-propre*, that accounts for a large part of the tendency of humans both to lose their integrity (as independent, value-determining subjects) and, under the sway of the crowd, to embrace corrupt values.

There is a further, closely related danger that follows from the fact that *amour-propre* seeks a good that consists (in part) in the judgments of others. This danger is best conceived of as *alienation*, even though Rousseau himself does not use the term in this context. 'Alienation' here denotes the self-estrangement Rousseau has in mind when he criticizes the civilized individual for existing 'outside himself', as in the following passage:[35]

---

[34] On this point Rousseau may have been influenced by Augustine's *Confessions*, which appears to trace the impulse to sin to temptations that arise only in the company of others. This is especially evident in its telling of the theft of the pears, a deed that is made sense of only by invoking the young Augustine's desire not to feel shame in front of his peers (*Confessions*, trans. R. S. Pine-Coffin (New York: Penguin, 1961), II: 8–9).

[35] The best recent philosophical exploration of alienation is Rahel Jaeggi, *Entfremdung* (Frankfurt am Main: Campus Verlag, 2005). Her account is inspired more by Hegel than Rousseau, but she agrees that the concept of alienation is implicit in and central to Rousseau's thought (24–5).

There is a kind of men who set some store by how they are looked upon by the rest of the universe, who know how to be happy and content with themselves on the testimony of others rather than on their own. This is, in fact, the true cause of all these differences: the savage lives within himself; sociable man, always outside himself, knows how to live only in the opinion of others; and it is, so to speak, from their judgment alone that he draws the sentiment of his own existence.

(*DI*, 187/*OC* 3, 193)

Rousseau uses similar language elsewhere in the Second Discourse in referring to 'this ardor to be talked about, this furor to distinguish oneself, which nearly always keeps us outside ourselves' (*DI*, 184/*OC* 3, 189), and in *Emile* he describes the same phenomenon in terms of 'basing [one's] own existence only on the judgments of others' (*E* IV, 215/*OC* 4, 494).[36]

Existing outside oneself certainly sounds like a species of alienation, or self-estrangement, but in what precisely does it consist, and how does it differ from the loss of freedom described above? According to the passages just cited, existing outside oneself involves gaining the sentiment of one's own existence from the judgments of others. As we saw above, having a sentiment of one's own existence is central to what it is for Rousseau to be a self in a moral, or non-physical, sense. It involves a sentiment (or sense)—and, so, a more than purely cognitive affirmation—that one is 'somebody,' that one has a non-instrumental worth or dignity superior to the value accorded to mere things. Because the valued self that is the object of this sentiment depends for its being on the confirmatory attitudes and behavior of other subjects, there is a genuine sense in which the self of a creature who possesses *amour-propre* exists externally. This implies that the source of my own existence (as a self) lies not only in me but also in others and, so, that my very being depends in some respect on the uncertain, possibly arbitrary opinions of my fellow beings. The point here is not, as it was above, that *amour-propre* can lead to a loss of freedom (to a state of affairs in which I may have to act in accordance with others' wills instead of my own). Rather, what is at stake in Rousseau's talk of the self's existence is a person's stable, enduring sense of her own worth; it is affirmation of self, not practical self-determination, that gives substance, and thus being, to the self.

---

[36] '*ne fonder leur propre existence que sur les jugements d'autrui*'. Bloom's normally reliable translation omits the crucial 'only' in this sentence, the importance of which will become apparent below.

It would be a grave error, however, to conclude from this that existing outside oneself is equivalent to self-estrangement. On the contrary, external existence must be carefully distinguished from alienation if Rousseau is to have a coherent response to the problems of *amour-propre*. (It is no accident that one needs the same distinction to make sense of Hegel and Marx, for whom externalization (or objectification), a necessary stage in the constitution of subjectivity, must be held distinct from alienation, a condition in which this process has in some respect gone awry.[37]) Given his view of the self as completed only through the recognition of others, Rousseau is committed to holding that the human subject must always exist to some extent outside itself. In other words, for Rousseau, too, external existence (in the judgments of others) is necessary for selfhood in any of its forms and does not by itself constitute self-estrangement. Where, then, does the difference lie? A careful reading of the passages cited above suggests that what makes the self's external existence an instance of alienation is that one exists *always* outside oneself, that one lives *only* in the opinion of others, that one can be happy with oneself on the basis of their judgment *alone*. An alienated self, then, is not one that merely needs the recognition of others but one that at the same time has no, or only very meager, internal resources for self-affirmation; an alienated self contains within itself none, or too little, of the sources of its own being. Understood in this way, alienation is made possible by the self's external character, but it is by no means a necessary consequence of selfhood.

Perhaps the best way to clarify what it means to lack sufficient internal resources for self-affirmation is to examine why having too few is a bad thing—why, in other words, alienation is an evil. The first reason is that, without such resources, our enjoyment of the specific good to which *amour-propre* directs us is bound to be contingent, inconstant, and perpetually insecure. Even in the best of worlds, other subjects are imperfect sources of esteem, capable both of withholding recognition altogether and of providing it at the wrong times, in the wrong amounts, and for the wrong reasons. Thus, in the absence of any resources for affirming myself from within, my very being (as a valued self) is vulnerable to a host of vicissitudes outside my control; my existence is insubstantial—unsteadfast—in the way

[37] Georg Lukács makes this point in his 1967 Preface to *History and Class Consciousness* (Cambridge, Mass.: MIT Press, 1971), xxiii–xxv, when he insists on the distinction between objectification (*Vergegenständlichung*) and alienation (*Entfremdung*).

that a log's ashen remains are subject to being reduced to a pile of dust by a single tap from without. The second reason alienation is bad is that being overly dependent on the recognition of others can interfere with one's achieving not only the good of affirmation but other essential goods as well. Too great a need for the affirmation of others—craving it at every moment, in exaggerated amounts, or for every imagined merit—makes one easy prey to the temptation to sacrifice other essential goods (health, peace of mind, security, freedom) in pursuit of the recognition one desperately longs for.

Alienation, then, is the state of existing outside oneself (depending on others' opinions for the affirmation of self) to a degree that is detrimental to one's overall well-being. Understood in this way, alienation represents a danger of *amour-propre* that cannot be traced back simply to its tendency to assume an inegalitarian form (as the desire for superior status). The problem that gives rise to alienation is not that one conceives of one's own worth so as to require the inferiority of others. The problem, rather, is that one relies too much on what others think to confirm whatever conception of one's worth one has. Even someone who wants only to be recognized as as good as everyone else can be plagued by too intense a need to have this status confirmed by those around him. This means—as we shall see again below—that inflamed, or pernicious, *amour-propre* cannot simply be equated with seeking superior status. It means, too, that there will not be a single remedy to the ills to which *amour-propre* gives rise. As this part of my analysis has shown, the task faced in finding a remedy for these ills is to discover not only how individuals can be brought to have sufficiently egalitarian conceptions of their worth but also how they can learn to find within themselves a substantial part of the affirmation they need in order to enjoy a stable and satisfying sentiment of their own existence.

Given the dangers inherent in the self's urge to exist outside itself, it can easily seem that the best response to *amour-propre* might be simply to strive, as far as is humanly possible, to rid oneself of the desire for external affirmation. At the end of his life, when he had become the object of his contemporaries' ridicule and scorn as well as the victim of his own paranoia, Rousseau embraced such a strategy as the only way to cope with a relentlessly hostile world: 'By retreating into my soul and severing the external relations that make it demanding, by renouncing comparisons and preferences, [my *amour-propre*] was satisfied with my being good in my own eyes. ... Pressed from all sides, I remain in equilibrium because, no longer attached to anything else, I depend only on myself.'[38] While such an attempt to escape 'the yoke of public opinion' might be the only strategy available to those who inhabit a corrupt and malevolent world, even in his most zealous moments of self-detachment Rousseau recognized the extreme costs as well as the ultimate impossibility of attempting to live without the recognition of others. Having tried as hard as possible to pay no heed to his revilers' attacks, he admits in the end that he is unable to do so:

> in the midst of men ... *amour-propre* then plays its game. The hatred and animosity I see in their hearts ... tear my own heart apart with pain. ... [This is] the result of a foolish *amour-propre* whose complete folly I sense, but which I cannot overcome. The efforts I have made to become inured to these insulting and mocking looks are unbelievable. ... Not only have I not been able to succeed, I have not made any progress; and all my painful but vain efforts have left me just as easy to disturb, to grieve, and to render indignant as before.

> (*RSW*, 75/*OC* 1, 1081–2)

But even if Rousseau had possessed the psychological strength to silence his longing for esteem under these extreme conditions, his personal victory would not have constituted a philosophical solution to the problems of *amour-propre*. For the project I am reconstructing here is concerned not with how a given individual might best respond to his particular circumstances but with whether, in principle, the human need to count as someone for others can be systematically satisfied, given the constraints of human nature and the world we inhabit. As I have emphasized throughout, the suppression of *amour-propre* is not an acceptable solution to this problem, and not merely because, as Rousseau's example confirms, it is a practical impossibility for most of us. It will become clearer in Chapter 7, when we consider the positive potential of *amour-propre*, why Rousseau cannot regard the self-sufficiency he strove for towards the end of his life as a general solution to the problem of *amour-propre*: the radical narcissism that consists in being wholly self-contained—in having no external existence in others—precludes the development of human beings' highest potential; that is, reason, virtue, and self-determination depend for their

---

[38] The two parts of this quote come from different paragraphs, the first at *RSW*, 73/*OC* 1, 1079; the second, at *RSW*, 71/*OC* 1, 1077.

very existence on the human urge to count as someone in the eyes of others.

d) Opinion (or judgment) is constitutive of the good sought by amour-propre

A fourth source of the evils that *amour-propre* introduces into human affairs comes from the fact that *opinions*, especially opinions of others, constitute an essential part of the good that *amour-propre* seeks. This claim is closely related to the one just discussed in that both appeal to the importance *amour-propre* leads us to place on the judgments of others. But whereas the previous point emphasized the dependence-producing implications of this fact—that *amour-propre* seeks something that by its very nature can only be had from others—the present point focuses on the fact that esteem is based on *opinions* others have of oneself rather than on the realities those opinions are supposed to reflect. The principal danger posed by this feature of *amour-propre* is the possibility that individuals will come to care more about perception than reality. If it is opinions of one's merits that matter in the end, then appearing to be excellent will seem just as desirable as actually being so. And, since getting others to perceive one as excellent is frequently easier than being so, giving the appearance of excellence will often be a natural strategy to pursue in the quest for social esteem. In certain of its non-ideal forms, then, *amour-propre* can be accused of fostering a 'metaphysical' perversion of sorts—an inclination to invert the proper relation between appearance and reality.

We encountered above one form this inversion of appearance and reality could be said to take in discussing the tendency of inflamed *amour-propre* to be guided by 'apparent' values (birth, wealth, social influence) at the expense of 'real' ones (freedom, happiness, well-founded esteem). A second form this inversion takes, however, is a disposition to appear (to others) to be other than one is, and this, for Rousseau, accounts for the widely observed duplicity, pretense, and hypocrisy of human beings, and so, for much of the vice that infects their interactions: 'To be and to appear to be became two entirely different things, and from this distinction arose ostentatious display, deceitful cunning, and all the vices that follow in their wake' (*DI*, 170/*OC* 3, 174; LCB, 52/*OC* 4, 966–7). Elsewhere Rousseau suggests that it is not only vice that results from the wish to appear other than one is but also self-estrangement, though in a different sense from the one discussed above (existing only outside oneself, in the opinion of others). When the self that I am and strive to be for others is based on how I appear rather than on how I am, there is an important and straightforward sense in which the self I labor to maintain is illusory and thus alien to who I really am: 'as for my Emile, if... he just once prefers to be someone other than himself, ... everything has failed. He who begins to become alien to himself does not take long to forget himself entirely' (E IV, 243/OC 4, 535). To distinguish here between a real and an illusory self is not to fall into a specious essentialism that elevates some of a person's traits into her 'true' self and regards others as merely accidental to her 'real' identity. The point, rather, is that a self becomes false and alien to itself—'forgets itself entirely'—when it attempts to establish its existence as a recognized self by means of properties it affects but does not in truth possess.

e) Amour-propre's strivings are mediated by a self-conception (a conception of one's own merit)

Finally, *amour-propre* is dangerous because, in all but its most primitive forms, satisfaction is mediated by one's self-conception, including a conception of how much and what kind of recognition one deserves from others. The kind and degree of recognition that will satisfy my yearning to be someone is not objectively fixed—for example, by physiological need—nor can actual satisfaction be guaranteed by the fact that those around me are unstinting and reasonable in their assessment of my merits. What satisfaction requires, rather, is that the recognition I receive be commensurate with the recognition I take myself to deserve. This adds to the problematic character of *amour-propre*, insofar as it opens up a new way in which the quest for recognition can go awry: even if I am fortunate enough to find other subjects who assess my merits impartially and grant me the recognition I deserve, there is always the possibility that this will fall short of my own perception of my due and so fail to satisfy my *amour-propre*. Moreover, my inflated self-conception poses obstacles to satisfaction not only directly (for me) but indirectly as well—that is, for all who share the social world with me. This is because taking myself to be consistently slighted by others makes me, in turn, less inclined to recognize them;[39] perceiving my world as stingy and withholding elicits the same quality in myself, which then

---

[39] This is reminiscent of Rousseau's characterization of vanity (*vanité*) as 'demanding everything and granting nothing' (E V, 430/OC 4, 798).

elicits it further in others, resulting in an overall scarcity of recognition that nourishes all the evils whose existence Rousseau wants to explain.

Obviously, this problem will be greatly exacerbated if humans have the tendency, whether by nature or the force of circumstances, to exaggerate their own merits and thus demand more recognition from others than they have reason to expect. Rousseau believes that even minimal powers of observation suffice to reveal that self-overestimation, with all its expected consequences, is a widespread phenomenon. He also believes, of course, that the principal source of this phenomenon is not human nature itself but social arrangements that can in principle be other than they are. When I later consider the possible solutions to the problems posed by *amour-propre*, it will be necessary to say more about where the tendency to exaggerate one's own merits comes from and why it occurs so frequently. For now it is enough to get a sense of the numerous complications this tendency can bring about by noting that, like inflamed *amour-propre* generally, self-overestimation takes a variety of problematic forms. One form consists in deluding oneself about the actual magnitude of one's excellences or achievements, especially relative to others'. My rendition of Hamlet's soliloquy may be elegant and precise, but it is probably not, as I am tempted to think, flawless or unsurpassable. Alternatively, one can accurately perceive what one is or has done but exaggerate its significance. I may in fact be the first to distinguish the thirty-eight senses in which Rousseau speaks of 'nature', but this does not (by itself) make me the most important philosopher of my generation. Finally, it is possible to regard one's qualities or deeds as warranting praise or admiration when in fact they do not. To believe my light skin color to be an excellence or my intimidating demeanor a sign of strength is to overestimate my merits by taking pride in—and expecting others to admire—features of myself that no one has good reason to value. Unfortunately, any of these ways of exaggerating one's merits poses substantial obstacles to the general satisfaction of *amour-propre*, making it even more unlikely than it otherwise is that individuals will succeed in finding the standing for others they so forcefully desire.

3

The Varieties of Inflamed
Amour-propre

In the previous chapter I examined the various ways in which *amour-propre* poses dangers for human well-being. My task here is to use the results of that inquiry to construct a more precise and comprehensive account of what inflamed *amour-propre* consists in than previous interpreters have provided. (Recall that 'inflamed' designates any form of *amour-propre* that tends to produce one or more of the human evils thematized in the Second Discourse.) By surveying the various ways the passion for recognition can go awry, I offer in this chapter a greatly expanded characterization of inflamed *amour-propre*, one that goes far beyond what I have called the prevailing view, which simply equates inflamed with inegalitarian *amour-propre* (the drive for some form of superior standing in the eyes of others). This expanded account of inflamed *amour-propre* will allow me to examine, in Chapter 4, how both *amour-propre* and the social world must be configured if the dangers posed by the drive for recognition are to be averted, or at least minimized.

I begin with a summary of the different ways in which *amour-propre* can qualify as inflamed that is guided by the analysis of the preceding chapter. Each of the five dangers explored there can be taken to point to a distinct variety of inflamed *amour-propre*.

a) *Amour-propre* is inflamed when it gives rise to desires for recognition that are 'feverish' in at least one of three senses: (i) one's passion is overheated and so prone to inspiring acts of violence or cruelty; (ii) one's passion is all-consuming, leading one to seek recognition from others at the expense of one's other vital interests; (iii) one's passion is restlessly imperialistic, turning nearly all of life's activities into a quest for prestige, thereby multiplying one's desires boundlessly, far beyond what one's non-relative needs require (so that, for example, the simple need for clothing is magnified into a craving for the latest and most expensive fashions). In each of these cases inflamed *amour-propre* can be seen as a natural (understandable) response to being deprived of an extremely important human good, having a confirmed existence as a self for others.

b) *Amour-propre* is inflamed when it leads humans to seek forms of superiority to others that (i) necessarily create a scarcity of recognition, thereby ensuring widespread frustration of the universal desire for recognition; (ii) inevitably produce greed and frustration by generating perverse and boundless desires for things or qualities that are taken to bestow prestige on their possessors; (iii) foster vice either by giving individuals reason to rejoice at, or even to cause, others' misfortunes or by leading individuals to satisfy their need for recognized standing through relations of domination. (Because the issues associated with the desire for superior status are extremely complex, I will say a good deal more below about when and in what forms this desire is to be considered inflamed.)

c) *Amour-propre* is inflamed when an individual needs the good opinion of others so intensely that he is inclined to sacrifice his freedom (to act in accordance with others' wishes and values rather than his own) in order to obtain their recognition, or when the sources of his sentiment of existence are so preponderantly external to himself (so heavily dependent on others' assessments) that his sense of self is unstable and inordinately vulnerable to the changing, sometimes arbitrary opinions of others.

d) *Amour-propre* is inflamed when its possessor cares so much about how others think of her that she takes appearing to be excellent to be just as desirable as actually being so, with the result that duplicity, pretense, and hypocrisy recommend themselves as effective strategies for acquiring recognition.

e) *Amour-propre* is inflamed when a person has an exaggerated sense of the value of his own qualities and achievements and demands that the recognition he receives from others reflect his own inflated self-assessment, thereby ensuring not only his own dissatisfaction but also that of others (since he is then disposed to be as stingy in

his recognition of others as he perceives them to be with respect
to him).

It should be obvious by now that this systematic analysis of *amour-propre*'s
dangers yields a much more complex understanding of inflamed *amour-
propre* than the prevailing view. For in addition to a pathological striving
for superior status, *amour-propre* can be inflamed in a number of other ways
as well: when one craves recognition too fiercely or lets the pursuit of it
take up too large a part of one's life (a); when social esteem is accorded as
much importance as (or more than) freedom or independent selfhood (c);
when one attempts to appear other than one is in order to win esteem for
illusory qualities and achievements (d); when one overestimates one's own
merits and demands that others concur in one's inflated judgments (e).

The problem with the view that equates inflamed with inegalitarian
amour-propre, however, is not merely that it recognizes only one species of
inflamed *amour-propre* but also that its central concept—inegalitarian *amour-
propre*—is too coarsely defined to distinguish between pernicious forms
of the desire for preeminence and those that are benign, perhaps even
necessary and beneficial. In other words, this view requires us to dismiss all
forms of the desire for preeminence as inflamed *amour-propre*. This certainly
simplifies Rousseau's theory, but it also diminishes its richness, part of
which resides in the many resources it offers for providing a more fine-
grained analysis of the desire for superior status—and thus a more nuanced
account of the roles it can play in healthy human interactions—than a
simpler conception of inflamed *amour-propre* allows for. In the remainder of
this chapter I explore the many ways in which Rousseau's position on the
desire for superior status is both more complex and more interesting than
the view that all forms of that desire are destructive of human well-being
and, so, inflamed.

When is the quest for superiority inflamed?

In the previous chapter I presented a number of textual and philosophical
reasons for rejecting the view that solving the problems posed by *amour-
propre* requires nothing more than fostering the egalitarian form of that
passion—that is, educating individuals to conceive of themselves as equal
in (moral) standing to all other human beings. My objections there centered

around the claim that respect and esteem are importantly different forms of recognition and that, although both address the longing to count as someone in the eyes of others, finding the former does not obviate the need for the latter. In articulating these points the question arose whether—and, if so, to what extent—some form of the wish to be recognized as superior to others might be intrinsic to the desire for esteem and hence ineliminable in a world where the needs for both respect and esteem were present. If esteem is typically accorded to persons for their excellences—for the ways they 'stand out' from their fellow beings—might not superiority to others, in some form, be a necessary aim of one who seeks esteem? And, if so, how are we to distinguish acceptable, perhaps even healthy, versions of the desire for superior standing from pernicious ones? It is time now to address these important issues in some detail. In doing so my aim is to arrive at a more adequate understanding of the conditions under which the desire for preeminence is to be considered inflamed[1]—one that is not only more precise than the prevailing view but also more faithful to the twisted complexity of human reality once individuals are affected by the urge to acquire standing for others.

Let us begin by reviewing the progress we have made thus far in clarifying the connection between esteem and the quest for superior standing. First, in introducing the distinction between respect and esteem, I argued that, Rousseau's earliest examples notwithstanding, the wish to be the *best*—even best merely in some specific respect—is not intrinsic to the desire for esteem. (Though, as I argue in the following chapter, the desire to be best is also no merely contingent feature of human psychology; on the contrary, it is the form *amour-propre* tends to assume first in the normal course of human development.) Secondly, I suggested some reasons for thinking that even if esteem does not require being recognized as the best, it might nevertheless require being recognized as *better* than others, at least in some specific respect. The most important of these reasons is that, in distinction to respect, esteem is typically accorded to individuals for particular excellences,[2] and—as the etymology of that

---

[1] An interesting contemporary version of this project is begun by Thomas E. Hill, Jr., in 'Social Snobbery and Human Dignity', in his *Autonomy and Self-Respect* (Cambridge: Cambridge University Press, 1991), 155–72.

[2] There is an important species of esteem that seems not to have this relation to excellences, namely, the love sought from parents or lovers. (For evidence that Rousseau counts love as a form

word suggests—excellence involves standing out in some way from one's fellow beings.[3] Given this, it is hard to see how the quest to win esteem could avoid some attempt to raise oneself above others in particular ways that will attract attention and admiration. The fact that one can strive to realize ideals defined by the intrinsic merit of the goal itself rather than by comparison with others—one can strive to be a man of good sense rather than a man of better sense than most—does not undermine this point. For it is unlikely that being good in some respect will succeed at eliciting esteem from others unless being so is an uncommon achievement. But if this is so, then being good will involve being better. Or, more precisely: *to the extent that it satisfies the need for esteem from others*, being good requires some element of being better, and this means that the desire for superior standing cannot be entirely excised from the basic longing for esteem.

It might be thought that this conclusion can be avoided by distinguishing more carefully between external conditions the world imposes on the success of a particular project and what one essentially desires or aims at in undertaking that project. Emile, it will be remembered, desires to be, and to be esteemed by others as, a man of good sense and a skillful carpenter. If it so happens that winning this esteem requires being better than others in those respects, then Emile might be thought to welcome, even to delight in, his superiority without it being the case that superiority itself was what he desired or aimed at. That Emile is pleased by a consequence

of esteem, see *E* IV, 214/*OC* 4, 494; see also Honneth, 95–6.) Indeed, one who desires this kind of love will likely feel resentment and outrage if made to believe that his being loved is conditional on qualities and achievements that mark him as better than others. Here, it might be thought, is a form of esteem that eschews comparisons and seeks recognition on the basis of one's particularity and distinctness, not because of one's superior qualities. But while this example shows that not all esteem is tied to excellence, it does not undermine the claim that the longing for esteem includes a desire for preeminence. For even if I do not want to be loved by my parents or lover because of my excellent qualities, it is essential to what I want that they love me best (or, in the case of parents, better, at least, than all non-family members). Oedipal jealousy and a lover's revenge bear witness to the fact that both familial and romantic love contain a forceful demand for superior standing in the eyes of another. Rousseau explicitly notes this fact: 'To be loved ... one has to make oneself more lovable than another, more lovable than every other, at least in the eyes of the beloved object' (*E* IV, 214/*OC* 4, 494).

[3] Hume, at least, thought so. He writes that qualities that elicit pride (and esteem) must be 'peculiar to ourselves, or at least common to us, with a few persons' since 'every thing which is often presented, and to which we have long been accustom'd, loses its value in our eyes; ... goods, which are common to all mankind, and have become familiar to us by custom, give us little satisfaction.' He supports this claim by noting that health, for example, 'is seldom regarded as a subject of vanity, because 'tis shar'd with such vast numbers' (David Hume, *A Treatise of Human Nature* (Oxford: Clarendon Press, 1967), 291–2). For more on the moral importance of pride for Hume, see Donald C. Ainslee, 'Skepticism About Persons in Book II of Hume's *Treatise*', *Journal of the History of Philosophy* 37 (1999), 469–92.

of his actions—even a necessary and foreseeable one—does not imply that he desired or intended that effect. But this objection rests on an error. Although it is sometimes useful to distinguish what an action aims at from its unintended effects (even when those effects are foreseen and perhaps also welcomed), this distinction is not relevant here. It is important to remember that Emile desires not only to *be* good (as a carpenter and man of sense) but also to be *esteemed* as good by others; the recognition of his peers is part—though only part—of what motivates him to endure the discipline and hard work that being a good carpenter or a man of good sense requires. Rousseau's thesis that *amour-propre* is an ineradicable feature of human reality implies—correctly, in my judgment—not only that in general humans cannot help but be pleased when they encounter esteem from others but also that they cannot help but be motivated to pursue that end. For Rousseau it is a basic psychological fact about humans that, even where excellence has it own intrinsic rewards, it is seldom pursued for those reasons alone. Humans are creatures who *seek* social esteem, and given the close and transparent connection between the basis of that esteem (excellence) and superiority to others, they can be said to seek that superiority as well. To deny this would be akin to saying that a candidate for the U. S. Presidency has the desire to be President but not the desire to receive more votes than her opponent. While it may be true that a candidate wants to receive the most votes only because that is what it takes to become President, this is not a reason to deny that she also desires an electoral majority. Yet, as this analogy makes clear, to say that certain forms of the desire for preeminence characterize even non-inflamed *amour-propre* is not to imply that preeminence is desired in those cases as an end in itself or for its pernicious effects. Just as candidates for office need not desire to win the most votes for its own sake or in order to humiliate their opponents, so it is possible to seek superior standing for reasons other than its potential to make one's rivals envious, resentful, or unhappy with their lot.

That Rousseau agrees that even healthy (non-inflamed) *amour-propre* will incorporate some form of the desire for preeminence is expressly confirmed by his description of Emile as he emerges from his exemplary education: 'He will have the pride (*l'orgueil*) to want to do everything he does well, *even to do it better than another.* He will want to be the swiftest at running, the strongest at wrestling, the most competent at working, the most adroit at games of skill' (*E* IV, 339/*OC* 4, 670; emphasis added).[4] Rousseau's position on the ineradicability of the desire for preeminence echoes the common perception that the spirit of competition is an inescapable feature of human reality and that it is possible to distinguish a benign, even useful form of this competitiveness—a healthy desire to do better than others—from a malicious and destructive drive for superiority. My task here, then, is to determine what Rousseau has to say concerning how that distinction is to be drawn. My aim, in other words, is to refine our understanding of inflamed *amour-propre* by articulating more precisely when the desire for superiority is likely to result in the scarcity, vice, and unlimited wants that were picked out above as the principal dangers of that desire.

My discussion above of the connections among the ends of *esteem, excellence,* and *preeminence* (or superiority) suggests a partial answer to this question: if a quest for superior standing is to avoid being inflamed, superiority may be sought neither for its own sake nor as a means to harming one's competitors but only because achieving preeminence (in some specific respect) is necessary to being esteemed by others as excellent (in some specific respect). In addition, the kind of preeminence one seeks must be taken, by the person himself, both to constitute a genuine excellence and to be worth pursuing, at least in part, for that reason. In other words, preeminence must be desired not only because achieving it will be rewarded with esteem from others but also in part because one judges the quality with respect to which one strives to 'stand out' to be genuinely good and, so, worthy of pursuit independently of its power to confer esteem on someone who achieves it. Hence Emile, insofar as he strives to be a better carpenter than most, does so only because it is important to him to be esteemed by others as an excellent craftsman. And though he regards this esteem as valuable for its own sake, his pursuit of esteem is at the same time informed by his commitment to an independent ideal—being a skillful carpenter—that places substantial constraints on what will count for him as acceptable, or satisfying, recognition.

In sum: it is permissible to seek esteem for its own sake—we would hardly be human if we did not—and because of this it is permissible as well to seek certain kinds of preeminence (though not preeminence for its own

---

[4] Once again, I would insist that there is no reason Emile must desire to be the *best* at any of these pursuits.

sake or for the sake of harming others). Yet even though there is nothing wrong in seeking esteem for its own sake, pursuing it *unconditionally* is a sign of inflamed *amour-propre*. Moreover, one of the conditions constraining the healthy pursuit of social esteem is that the preeminence sought be pursued, in part, because one judges it to constitute a genuine excellence. In effect, the latter condition dictates merely that *amour-propre* be constrained by the virtue of integrity as defined in the previous chapter. A person who fails to constrain his pursuit of esteem by his own criteria for what makes someone worthy of esteem makes the approval of others into an unqualified good, and this—inflating the value of social recognition at the expense of being an independent, value-establishing subject—is clearly an instance of inflamed *amour-propre*.

There is a further, less subjective condition that Rousseau places on the non-inflamed pursuit of preeminence. It is not enough that one merely *take* a certain form of preeminence to be good independently of its esteem-conferring power; one's judgment that it is so must also meet certain criteria of objectivity or well-foundedness. This part of Rousseau's view is expressed in a series of remarks towards the end of *Emile* that describe the results of the educator's successful efforts to prevent inflamed *amour-propre* from establishing itself in his charge's character. Though I have already examined these passages in discussing integrity, their importance for clarifying the nature of inflamed *amour-propre* makes it worth citing them again. The well-educated Emile, it will be remembered, 'values nothing according to the price opinion confers on it' (*E* IV, 338/*OC* 4, 669). Instead,

> he will concern himself with [others'] opinion only insofar as it relates immediately to his person, and he will not worry about arbitrary evaluations whose only law is fashion or prejudice. ... He will hardly seek advantages that are not clear in themselves and that need others' judgments in order to be established. ... [Emile] will not precisely say to himself, 'I rejoice because they approve of me,' but rather, 'I rejoice because they approve of what I have done that is good. ... So long as they judge so soundly, it will be a fine thing to obtain their esteem.'
>
> (*E* IV, 339/*OC* 4, 670–1)

As these passages show, Rousseau focuses not so much on the objective correctness of Emile's judgments about which forms of preeminence are worth pursuing as on the fact that in making those judgments he relies on his

own, non-arbitrary standards of the good, that is, standards Emile subscribes
to independently of prejudice and fashion. This is not because Rousseau is
unconcerned with the correctness of Emile's judgments but rather because,
as explained in Chapter 2, he believes that once one appreciates the merely
conditioned value of social esteem—once one attributes value to esteem
only when it accords with genuine worthiness—the main obstacles to a
clear perception of the good have already been removed. On this view,
to have independence of moral judgment—fostering Emile's confidence
in his own judgment is a main concern of Books I–III—is already to
possess more or less everything one needs to be a sound judge of what it is
worthwhile for humans to pursue.

It is worth pausing to note an intriguing implication of Rousseau's view
that a person with non-inflamed *amour-propre* seeks esteem only to the
extent that it reflects his own independent judgment of the good. Although
Rousseau makes less of this consequence than he might have—it is left
to Hegel, especially in his analysis of master and slave, to exploit it as
the key to solving the problem of intersubjective recognition—the crucial
idea is presented clearly enough in the final lines of the passage just cited:
in the case of non-inflamed *amour-propre*, a person finds the esteem of
others satisfying only when it is accompanied by his own judgment that
the person esteeming him is a 'sound judge' of the good. This means that
when the desire for esteem takes the form it should, there is *internal to
that desire itself* an implicit demand on the seeker of esteem to esteem,
in turn, the person from whom the first esteem is sought. Or, more
precisely: a necessary implication of my non-inflamed *amour-propre* is that
I can find your recognition of my excellence satisfying only if I also
recognize you as a worthy judge of me. In effect, then, healthy satisfaction
of *amour-propre* is impossible unless recognition of some sort proceeds
in both directions. To say, however, that satisfying recognition must go
both ways is not to say that recognition must be precisely symmetrical.
If I am to find healthy satisfaction in your recognition of me as a fine
interpreter of Hamlet, then you are recognizing me for that excellence and
I am recognizing you as a competent judge of theatrical talent. In other
words, the type of reciprocity that this example shows to be built into
the idea of satisfying esteem, important as it is, does not by itself warrant
the strong conclusion that most interpreters of Hegel—perhaps even
Hegel himself—proclaim too hastily, namely, that *equality* of recognition

among subjects is implicit in the ideal of *amour-propre*'s satisfaction. This consideration shows that some kind of reciprocity of recognition is required for the healthy satisfaction of *amour-propre*, but it leaves room for a nearly endless variety of human relations characterized by reciprocal but not strictly symmetrical recognition.

Formulating the principle of non-inflamed pursuits of superiority

The upshot of the preceding section might be loosely formulated as the claim that if *amour-propre* is to count as non-inflamed, preeminence and esteem must be valued in the right measure and for the right reasons. Not surprisingly, though, these are not the only constraints on the non-inflamed quest for preeminence that follow from Rousseau's account of the dangers of *amour-propre*. For one thing, the constraints just discussed do not respond to the problems that arise due to the inherently comparative quality of the good that *amour-propre* desires: even if humans seek preeminence only as a means for achieving esteem that is commensurate with genuine excellence, what is to be said about the host of problems—conflict, dissatisfaction, and the will to harm others—that follow from the inherent scarcity of positional goods like superior standing? Here I shall argue that it is possible to introduce more systematicity into Rousseau's position than his texts suggest. I shall claim that a general principle underlies Rousseau's apparently haphazard treatment of these issues and that it is best captured by the following elaboration of b) above:

(b*) *Amour-propre* is inflamed when it urges one to seek a kind of preeminence in relation to others that would make it impossible for them to have similar aspirations and at the same time find a rationally acceptable level of satisfaction in their quest for recognition.

In other words, Rousseau's position is best understood as taking desires for preeminence to be manifestations of inflamed *amour-propre* only when they fail to meet some (rather complex) criterion of universalizability. A particular desire for preeminence can be tested by this criterion by imagining a world in which that kind of desire were generalized—possessed by all, or by many—and then asking whether in such a world the needs of *amour-propre* (when configured as hypothesized) could in principle be adequately satisfied for all.

This criterion clearly rules out the form of desire for preeminence that commentators have most often identified with inflamed *amour-propre*, namely, the demand to be accorded greater moral respect than others (the demand that one's own well-being and concerns count more than those of one's fellow beings). For, clearly, not everyone can regularly have his interests figure more prominently than others' in collective decisions. At the same time, this criterion explains why it is acceptable to want to be the most highly regarded—to be loved[5] above everyone else—by some other particular individual (such as one's lover), as well as, of course, why the demand to be such for everyone is inflamed: the former—to count as best in the eyes of one other person—is in principle achievable by all, whereas the latter—to be the best for everyone—is not.

Things become more complex when we consider the desire to be recognized as superior to others with regard to some particular talent or accomplishment. The universalizability criterion I have attributed to Rousseau does not rule out all such desires, because a desire to do better than others in some particular respect is compatible with others satisfying similar desires of their own. (Wanting to do better in *all* respects, however, is not compatible with others wanting the same.) There are two reasons the desire to excel in some particular way satisfies Rousseau's criterion. First, human excellence takes numerous forms, and so it is possible for many—in principle, for everyone—to excel in at least some significant respect. Second, one person's excellence in a given area does not preclude others from excelling in the same field. Even though excelling entails being better than most, being among the best in a field is compatible with a number of others belonging to that group as well. In other words, wanting to excel need not be a manifestation of inflamed *amour-propre* since—to borrow a phrase from Locke's justification of a different sort of inequality[6]—in winning the esteem one seeks, one does not rob others of the chance to find esteem that is 'enough and as good as' what one has found for oneself.

---

[5] See n. 2 above for evidence that Rousseau counts love as a form of esteem.

[6] John Locke, *Second Treatise of Government*, in Peter Laslett, ed., *Two Treatises of Government* (New York: Cambridge University Press, 1963), §27.

But beyond this, Rousseau's criterion ought not to be construed as ruling out even the desire, not just to excel, but to be the best in some particular area of endeavor. This is an issue of some importance, first because the desire to be best—to be a 'star' of some kind—appears to be sufficiently common among civilized human beings that a social theory that required its eradication could reasonably be dismissed as utopian. Despite his great (and justified) fear of precisely this desire, Rousseau nevertheless seems to recognize the pervasive tendency of human beings to be motivated by it. (Recall that even the educated Emile 'will want to be the swiftest at running, the strongest at wrestling, the most competent at working, the most adroit at games of skill' (*E* IV, 339/*OC* 4, 670).[7]) A second reason for hesitating to condemn all forms of wanting to be the best (in some specific respect) is that there is good reason to think that humanity in general would be poorer without it. The argument for this that Rousseau would be most likely to accept is that the desire to be a star can serve as a powerful motivator for individuals to put themselves through the excruciating labor of perfecting their natural talents, the results of which—the brilliant lecture, the exquisite poem, the perfectly executed jump—enrich the lives of everyone.[8]

Nevertheless, it seems obvious that such a desire—to be recognized, for example, as this generation's best soprano—would fail the test of universalizability since realizing this desire would make it impossible for others to do the same. Even if we universalize not this particular desire (to be the best soprano) but the more general desire to be best in some respect, it seems unlikely that all, or even most, could satisfy this demand of *amour-propre*. For despite the multiplicity of forms of human excellence, there are not so many of genuine significance that everyone could in principle be the best in one of them.

---

[7] Further evidence of Rousseau's belief in the pervasiveness of the desire to be the best is his claim that the first sentiment aroused in Emile once his *amour-propre* has been awakened is 'to desire the first position' (*E* IV, 235/*OC* 4, 523).

[8] Despite Rousseau's ambivalence about the desire to be a star, this argument is suggested by the First Discourse's claims that human knowledge is born of ambition and the 'furor to distinguish oneself' (*DSA*, 16, 18/*OC* 3, 17, 19), and that academies foster excellence by honoring the most accomplished men of letters (*DSA*, 24/*OC* 3, 26). In the Second Discourse Rousseau says that the 'universal desire for reputation … trains … talents and powers' and that 'to this furor to distinguish oneself … we owe what is best … among men,' including virtue and science (*DI*, 184/*OC* 3, 189). Other such examples abound in his writings.

How, then, could such a desire to be the best not be ruled out by Rousseau's criterion? Only if it is possible for all to aspire to be the best (in some non-trivial respect) and at the same time satisfy their *amour-propre* to a rationally acceptable degree. This is indeed possible if certain conditions obtain. First, it must be the case that those who are disappointed in their wish to be best have enough other sources of recognition available to them that they can satisfy their basic need to be someone for others (and so find an acceptable degree of recognition). This condition will be met when a variety of other avenues to finding esteem are open to them and, more important, when they inhabit a social world that accords a substantial level of equal moral respect to all (by guaranteeing, for example, equality before the law, individual civil rights, rights of political participation, due consideration of one's interests in collective decisions, etc.). Secondly, those who fail to realize their desire to be best must not be so attached to their aim that they regard it as the *sine qua non* of a satisfying life; their desire must not be so strong, in other words, that reconciliation to disappointment is psychologically impossible. This is a less stringent condition than might be initially thought. One should not underestimate the human capacity to dream ambitiously, to let such dreams animate one's life, and then in the end to reconcile oneself without resentment to their failure to come true. Finally, the system of rewards that frustrates the desire to be best for some must be rationally acceptable to all. This, too, will be the case if esteem is commensurate with genuine merit (rather than awarded on the basis of birth, money, or personal connections), and if everyone benefits appreciably from such a system in the end. Happily, the latter condition is likely to be met if only the former obtains. This is because those who succeed at establishing themselves as the best win recognition on the basis of genuine excellences that they in fact possess and because, in general, the cultivation of excellences tends to benefit many individuals beyond those who possess them.[9] Thus, even though many people will necessarily be disappointed if all aspire to be best in some respect, the system of rewards that requires this outcome is nevertheless one that all can rationally endorse, since all benefit from it and since it deprives no one of the chance to find a satisfying measure of recognition of other types.

---

[9] This is very close to the thought that motivates Rawls to propose the difference principle as one of the conditions under which material inequalities, even rather large ones, are rationally acceptable.

Further refinements

As the preceding sections suggest, it is no simple matter to specify all the conditions that a desire for preeminence must meet to qualify as non-inflamed. Although it is probably useless to attempt a comprehensive survey of such conditions, it may be helpful to supplement the points already made by examining some important remarks in *Emile* concerning how an adolescent's *amour-propre* must be formed if he is to be able to be pleased with 'what rank among his fellows' he ascribes to himself after 'comparing himself with them' (*E* IV, 243/*OC* 4, 534), while at the same time avoiding the many pitfalls associated with thinking oneself better than others. (Meanwhile, it is worth noting Rousseau's admission in this passage that Emile's concern about his rank in relation to others, including his desire to fare favorably in this comparison, is an unavoidable consequence of *amour-propre*'s relative nature.[10]) It is in these remarks that Rousseau singles out believing that one is 'of a more excellent nature' than others as 'the error most to be feared' in a young man's education (*E* IV, 245/*OC* 4, 537).[11] One clear implication of these remarks is that under some conditions it is permissible for Emile to take delight in, and even to seek, superiority to others. Moreover, the condition Rousseau regards as the most important of these is that Emile not fall prey to the illusion that his superiority is due to his being 'of a more excellent nature'.

What exactly is it, though, to believe oneself 'of a more excellent nature'? Commentators who overemphasize the importance of egalitarian *amour-propre* will take Rousseau to be insisting here on the necessity of always bearing in mind the equality of worth all individuals possess in virtue of their common human nature. Equality of worth in this sense is expressed in the belief that all individuals deserve to be treated with equal moral respect because of some fundamental quality (free will, reason, or the capacity for pain) they share with all other humans. (Recall that moral respect, in contrast to esteem, has to do with regarding persons as equal, rights-bearing individuals whose interests and desires place moral constraints on others' actions.) Rousseau certainly believes in the equality

[10] See also *E* IV, 245/*OC* 4, 536.

[11] Rousseau makes a similar point when he says that instilling in Emile a sense 'of the true relations of man'—a sense of the fundamental equality of all humans—should be his tutor's foremost aim if the evils of inflamed *amour-propre* are to be avoided (*E* IV, 219/*OC* 4, 501).

of all humans in this sense—as well as in the importance of forming Emile's *amour-propre* so as to accommodate it—but it is plainly not what he has in mind in the paragraphs referred to here. In order to see this, and to grasp the complexities of the point he is making,[12] it is necessary to reproduce a good deal of the lengthy passage at issue:

in considering his rank in the human species and seeing himself so happily placed there, Emile will be tempted to honor his reason for the work of yours [the tutor's] and to attribute his happiness to his own merit. He will say to himself, 'I am wise, and men are foolish.' In accusing them, he will despise them; in congratulating himself, he will esteem himself more, and in feeling himself to be happier than they, he will believe himself worthier to be so. This is the error most to be feared, because it is the most difficult to destroy. If he were to remain in this condition, he would have gained little from all our care; and if it were necessary to choose, I do not know whether I would not prefer the illusion of prejudices to that of pride [*l'orgueil*].

Great men are not deceived about their superiority; they see it, feel it, and are no less modest because of it. ... They are less vain about being raised above us than they are humbled by the sentiment of what they lack, and with the exclusive goods they possess they are too sensible to be vain about a gift they did not give themselves. The good man can be proud [*fier*] of his virtue because it is his; but of what is the man of genius [*l'homme d'esprit*] proud? What did Racine do not to be Pradon? What did Boileau do in order not to be Cotin?

... if as a consequence of my care Emile prefers his way of being, of seeing, and of feeling to that of other men, Emile is right. But if he therefore believes himself to be of a more excellent nature and more happily born than they, Emile is wrong. He is deceived. One must undeceive him or, better, anticipate the error for fear that afterward it will be too late to destroy it.

(*E* IV, 245/*OC* 4, 536–7)

The details contained in these three paragraphs are remarkably complex—and perhaps not entirely consistent—but their most striking feature is that the 'error' Rousseau describes at the beginning and emphasizes throughout does not appear to have much to do with believing oneself to be of a more excellent *nature* than others. Rather, his central concern appears to be Emile's temptation to believe, falsely, that he is *worthier of happiness* than his fellow beings, though not in the sense emphasized by the

---

[12] Darwall makes many interesting points relevant to the topic of the rest of this chapter: for what characteristics and under what conditions it is appropriate to expect esteem from others (184, 186–90).

exponents of egalitarian *amour-propre*—thinking one's own interests ought to carry more weight than others' in the making of law—but in the sense of taking oneself to *deserve* the superior happiness one in fact enjoys. Emile's (hypothesized) belief that he is worthier of happiness than others could, of course, be grounded in a belief about his nature—if, for example, he regarded his superior happiness as a birthright, or as something he deserves on the basis of some special natural endowment. But this is not what, at first glance, Rousseau appears to be most concerned with. Instead, the error at issue seems to be the tendency to take credit for some excellence (Emile's superior rank among men) that is in fact the work of someone else (his tutor)—for something, in other words, that is the result of fortuitous circumstances or luck rather than Emile's own efforts or constitution. Rousseau's point, presumably, is that Emile would be deceived if he were to believe himself responsible for his happy condition, since its true cause is his tutor's pedagogical wisdom (in conjunction with a variety of external circumstances), not any quality of Emile's. This account of Emile's error, however, omits all mention of his taking himself to be 'of a more excellent nature' and 'more happily born' than others. The most plausible way of accommodating these apparently crucial elements of Rousseau's text is to suppose that Emile, as imagined here, attributes his advantaged position not to his own hard work and effort but to some superior quality—his wisdom, or reason—that he takes himself to possess by nature (innately). In other words, what Rousseau describes as 'the error most to be feared' must be Emile's belief that he deserves the advantaged position he enjoys because it is a consequence of his own superior natural endowment.

This way of construing the error of which Emile is to be steered clear poses an important interpretive dilemma, for it attributes two quite different errors to Emile—both recognizable as pride or vanity—and so is ambiguous with respect to which Rousseau sees as the error 'most to be feared'. Is Emile's principal mistake that he takes his happy position to be due to some special quality or achievement of his own (either innate or acquired), when in fact it is due to his good fortune in having received an exemplary education? Or, is it rather his belief that being well born (in whatever respect) gives him a reason to esteem himself for—take pride in—his natural excellence and to think himself deserving of the benefits it enables him to enjoy? In other words, is Emile deceived because he misdiagnoses the source of his superior position, attributing it to some

quality of his rather than to fortuitous circumstances and the efforts of
others, or because he assumes that his natural advantage is a legitimate
source of pride or merit? (Note that Rousseau is clear about one thing:
Emile does not err in believing, and in delighting in the fact, that his way
of being—his character, values, and tastes—*is* superior to others'.)

The best response to this dilemma is to conclude that there are two
grievous errors to which Emile is susceptible and that Rousseau has not
sufficiently distinguished them to have a clear view as to which poses the
real (or greater) danger. More precisely: it is possible to pick out a single
error that is 'most to be feared'—taking oneself to *deserve* the superior
happiness one enjoys (which is one way of believing oneself worthier of
happiness than others)—but there are two ways of succumbing to this
error that Rousseau fails to distinguish. That there are two wrong paths to
be distinguished here is supported by the fact that, in neighboring passages
of *Emile* and elsewhere, Rousseau goes on at some length about the issues
at stake in both of the errors I have distinguished here. The first type
of error—ascribing responsibility for one's advantaged position to oneself
rather than to good fortune and the efforts of others—is one of Rousseau's
main topics in the thirty or so pages preceding the long passage cited
above (*E* IV, 219–45/*OC* 4, 500–36). Throughout these pages Rousseau
emphasizes the importance of instilling in Emile 'a sense of [his] true
relations...to the species' (*E* IV, 219/*OC* 4, 501), and by this he clearly
means Emile's essential equality with other men in the sense that all share
the same basic 'human' condition.[13] A central part of Emile's education,
then, is directed at bringing him to appreciate the pain, weakness, mortality,
and—especially—the vulnerability to misfortune common to all human
beings: 'Men are not naturally kings, or lords, or courtiers, or rich men. All
are born naked and poor; all are subject to the miseries of life, to sorrows,
ills, needs, and pains of every kind. Finally, all are condemned to death.
This is what truly belongs to man. This is what no mortal is exempt from'
(*E* IV, 222/*OC* 4, 504).

In this first case, then, pride or vanity—a form of inflamed *amour-
propre*—consists in both an overestimation of the extent to which one
is responsible for the advantages one enjoys and, based on this, a smug

---

[13] Note again, this is not the moral equality vaunted by those who see egalitarian *amour-propre* as a
sufficient solution to the problem of inflamed *amour-propre*.

blindness to the fortuitousness and fragility of one's fortunate condition. Pride in this sense is directly related to having an inflated sense of what one deserves, or merits, and thus can easily be connected to the thought, emphasized in the passage above, that one is worthier of happiness than others. To rid a person of this type of pride would be to remove an important source of her sense of deserving, or being entitled to, the happy position she occupies. For the upshot of this aspect of education is the realization that, even if the advantages one enjoys are due in part to one's own efforts or qualities, these are insufficient by themselves—in the absence of good fortune and others' assistance—to produce the advantages one is tempted to regard as one's own achievement. In fact, the sense that one deserves what one enjoys is lessened by this realization in two ways. First, recognizing the significant role played by chance in determining life's outcomes poses a direct challenge to the idea that the person herself—or anyone at all—is responsible for how her life has turned out. Second—and especially important for considerations of distributive justice—recognizing the extent to which one's own efforts and endowments require the help of others if they are to be translated into real advantages undermines the belief that the rewards of those efforts and endowments belong exclusively, or even mostly, to oneself. If such rewards are always the product of an undisentangleable web of cooperative ventures, then there is an important sense in which they belong first to us and only secondarily to me.[14]

The second error—believing that purely natural qualities are a legitimate source of pride or merit—presents more complications than the first. Some version of this error undoubtedly plays a role in the passage I am attempting to understand, since it is clearly what is at issue in the claims that great men 'are too sensible to be vain about a gift they did not give themselves' and that it is right to be proud of one's virtue but not of one's natural genius. Moreover, it is almost certainly what Rousseau has in mind when he refers to Emile's being deceived in believing himself 'of a more excellent nature and more happily born' than others.[15] Even if one might want to dispute

---

[14] This point, I take it, is also behind Rawls's conviction that the benefits of social cooperation must accrue to us all. It is also one of the principles underlying Rousseau's famous claim that 'the right each ... individual has to his own resources is always subordinate to the right the community has to all' (*SC*, I.9.vii).

[15] This opinion is shared by the editors of *OC* 4, who equate 'more happily born' with 'more happily endowed' (1488 n. 3).

Rousseau's claim, his basic thought seems clear enough: it is irrational to honor oneself for qualities bestowed on one without one's participation. Doing so is a vain overestimation of self because it involves taking credit for something that is not the product of one's own efforts; it moves beyond a simple delight at one's natural advantages to presume, mistakenly, that one is worthy of—that one merits—the happiness they result in.

Yet despite its initial plausibility, this part of Rousseau's view is confused. The most pressing problem lies not in his general principle—that it is wrong to pride oneself on qualities that one in no way helps to bring about (though this, too, will need to be refined later)—but in the way he applies this principle in the passage cited above. In specifying the attitudes to one's own excellences that are consistent with non-inflamed *amour-propre*, it makes sense to distinguish between those of one's qualities for which one is to some degree responsible and those (purely natural qualities) for which one is not. The problem with Rousseau's account is that the examples he gives—virtue and intelligence (or genius)—undermine the point he wants to make since neither fits comfortably into either of the two categories he means to distinguish. This is because, on the one hand, virtue is not primarily a self-given quality. If it were, the entire project of *Emile* would be incoherent, since its premise is that a virtuous character can be acquired only through a process of education that is imposed on one from without. Even if the exercise of virtue also requires effort on the part of the person educated, the fact remains that a large part of one's virtue is due to the work of others rather than to one's own. If we take Rousseau's pedagogical thesis seriously, it will be hard to maintain that a person's virtue is any more substantively his (the result of his own doing) than other qualities he happens to have acquired from the fortuitous circumstances of his life.

On the other hand, genius—or, more precisely, the observable expressions of genius that actually elicit our admiration or pride—is itself far from being a purely natural endowment, and this makes it much closer to the case of virtue than Rousseau allows.[16] This point is vividly made, in spite of Rousseau's intentions, by the rhetorical questions he poses in defending his claim that the virtuous man, but not the man of genius, can be proud of his

---

[16] The two cases are not completely alike, however, since great cultural achievements presuppose extraordinary natural endowments, whereas virtue does not. Yet, as explained above, this does not imply that one's virtue comes more from one's own efforts than intellectual greatness does, since the former requires the educator's work and other fortuitous circumstances.

excellence: 'What did Racine do not to be Pradon? What did Boileau do in order not to be Cotin?' Rousseau's suggestion—that we esteem Racine and Boileau for natural qualities they played no role in bringing about—is patently false. For we esteem great authors not primarily for their natural talents but for the use they have made of those talents in their literary work. This means that the excellences for which *l'homme d'esprit* is admired require his own participation, just as those of the virtuous man require his.[17] If 'the good man can be proud of his virtue because it is his' (his own doing), then the man of genius ought to be permitted to take pride in his achievements to the extent that the same is true of them.[18]

But if it is wrong for Emile to believe that he has earned the fruits of his excellences, what attitude to them ought he to take? It might be thought that Rousseau's answer follows straightforwardly from the distinction he seems to appeal to between merely celebrating or delighting in one's excellences, on the one hand, and taking credit for them, on the other: even if Emile's excellences depend on good luck and the efforts of others, and even if he deserves no credit for the special gifts he was born with, it is nevertheless both natural and unobjectionable that he take delight in his excellences and in the happy place in the world they secure for him. In other words, it is appropriate for Emile to take satisfaction in, and perhaps even to strive for, superior position, but he commits a grievous mistake the moment he starts to believe that he deserves (for either of the reasons distinguished here) the happy position he enjoys.

Rousseau expresses this point by saying that although it is fine for Emile to 'congratulate himself' (*se féliciter*) on his superior position, he ought not to 'esteem himself more' (*s'estimer d'avantage*) because of it. Rousseau's use of *s'estimer* seems to imply that the attitude Emile should take to his

---

[17] There is, of course, a distinction between the two cases that Rousseau might have meant to signal: Racine and Boileau could not have done what they did without exceptional natural talents, whereas virtue, according to Rousseau's central thesis, is open to all, including those without special natural gifts. (As Rousseau never tires of pointing out, neither Emile nor Sophie possesses exceptional natural qualities.) Still, it is hard to see how this distinction is relevant to Rousseau's point that it is irrational to pride oneself on qualities or achievements one played no role in bringing about, since both kinds of excellence require effort and since, as explained above, virtue depends on many factors other than one's own effort, such as the educator's work and other fortuitous circumstances.

[18] Unless, of course, it is permissible to take pride only in accomplishments that have *moral* worth. Rousseau does say that Emile 'will concern himself with [others'] opinion only insofar as it relates immediately to his person' (*E* IV, 339/*OC* 4, 670), but this is not a reason to saddle Rousseau with the moralistic view that only moral excellences are legitimate sources of esteem. Presumably 'person' in this passage means something like 'character' in a broad sense of that term.

excellences is that, however delightful and gratifying, since they do not ultimately come from him (from either his natural talents or his own efforts), they ought not to be a source of pride he takes in himself or of esteem he receives from others. Emile, according to this reading, should take satisfaction in his excellences but not want to be esteemed because of them. This conclusion, though, is at odds with what Rousseau says about the attitude individuals of extraordinary talent ought to take to their excellences (as well as with what healthy common sense and custom say about the matter). While Rousseau's emphasis here is on the humility of great individuals, he also clearly implies that they properly take a certain limited pride in their natural gifts: they are 'no less modest' for being clear-sighted about the source of their excellence, and their humility makes them merely *less* prideful ('less vain') than they might otherwise be.

The only way to reconcile this claim with the fact that the excellences at issue here are not deserved advantages (since they are natural gifts and, so, not due to the efforts of those who possess them) is to assume that the domain of what it is natural and fitting to take pride in and to receive esteem for does not completely overlap with the domain of the deserved. In other words, even excellences one is in no way responsible for are appropriate objects of a certain positive attitude that Rousseau refers to here as congratulation (from oneself or from others) and pride (in one's own favored attributes). Since this attitude consists in affirmation, approval, or admiration of the person who possesses the favored quality, it is a species of esteem in the general sense in which I have been using the term here. Forms of appreciation such as these, when directed at one person by another, are properly regarded as instances of recognition since they are ways in which one person expresses to another that she takes him to possess a certain value or worth. In admiring even the natural qualities of others, we bear witness to the value we accord to those qualities and, by extension, to the persons who possess them.[19] (Rousseau does not imagine that human beings naturally are, or ever ought to be, capable

---

[19] The idea that to affirm a person's purely natural qualities is to accord a certain value *to her* is supported by the fact, well known to psychologists if not to philosophers, that the development of a healthy sense of self-worth in children requires being affirmed by others for their natural qualities—their smile, the sheen of their hair, the rich color of their skin. This, of course, can lead to serious problems if such purely contingent excellences come to be the only or primary source of a person's sense of self-worth; still, it is normal and fitting, for both adults and children, that part of one's 'sentiment of self' have a source of this sort.

of distinguishing themselves so starkly from their properties—even their 'given' properties—that they might fail to experience another's affirmation of their charming smile, say, as an affirmation of them.) When in the passage cited above Rousseau contrasts the attitude of congratulation with that of esteem, he must be read as using *estimer*—a word with many shades of meaning in ordinary discourse—in a special, restrictive sense that implies that the esteemed person merits or deserves the favored condition she is being esteemed for; as Rousseau makes explicit in the very same sentence, esteeming someone in this narrow sense includes regarding her as worthy of (*digne de*), or as deserving, her happy state.

The upshot of these considerations is that not all forms of esteem in the broadest sense—not all forms of recognizing the value of others on the basis of their particular qualities—presuppose a judgment that the esteemed persons are responsible for their excellent qualities and, so, merit or deserve them and their benefits. Rousseau believes that we deserve our excellences and the happiness they bring only to the extent that they are the products of our own efforts, and, presumably, it is only insofar as this condition is met that we are correct in believing that we deserve the happiness we enjoy. (Moreover, *pace* Rousseau, it is rarely, if ever, the case that an excellence is due entirely to a person's own efforts.) Yet the fact that a person does not deserve the excellences he enjoys does not imply that they are not appropriate objects of certain forms of esteem that express affirmation, approval, or admiration of the one who possesses such favored qualities without assuming that he is responsible for them. In other words, to take pride in one's undeserved excellences and to want to be appreciated by others because of them does not yet constitute inflamed *amour-propre*. As my reconstruction of Rousseau's position here implies, *taking pride in one's undeserved excellences remains unobjectionable as long as it is tempered by an appreciation of the role that luck and the work of others have played in bringing them about.* Such pride is consistent with—indeed, demands—the realization that one does not deserve all the advantages one enjoys and, consequently, that one is not worthier of happiness than those who enjoy less.

Finally, in the passage I have been examining here Rousseau seems to equate being 'worthier of happiness' with having 'a more excellent nature' and being 'more happily born'. This means that the error 'most to be feared' in a child's education—taking oneself to deserve one's superior happiness—could also be characterized as believing oneself to be of a more excellent nature than others. In the paragraphs above I have tended to construe the idea of being better than others by nature as the thought that one's natural endowment—one's innate talents and qualities—is superior to others' (and, by implication, a sufficient explanation of one's more fortunate position in the world). But this is not the only sense 'a more excellent nature' can have. As Kantian interpreters of Rousseau make clear, there is a second way of understanding this idea as well, namely, as the demand that one's own happiness carry greater weight than others' in determining what all are permitted and obligated to do. Some version of this idea—concerning the amount of respect one merits in relation to others—clearly plays a role in Rousseau's account of the kind and extent of esteem it is appropriate for individuals to seek for their excellences. For, as I noted above, much of his discussion immediately preceding the cited paragraphs is devoted to the importance of instilling in Emile a feeling for his essential equality with other human beings. The sentiment that Rousseau means for Emile to absorb and to live by is that, despite their many differences, all humans share a single condition—all are subject to suffering, mortality, and the vicissitudes of fortune—and because of this, especially because all are alike in the capacity to feel pain, no one's happiness deserves to be treated as less important than another's. Regardless of whether one agrees that equal susceptibility to pain is the best foundation for the right to equal moral respect, Rousseau's commitment to the importance of such respect is clear enough. What is less clear is how his discussion of this topic contributes to the project of clarifying the conditions under which pride in one's unearned excellences remains benign.

Here is my suggestion: in addition to requiring that pride in one's excellences be accompanied by a recognition of the extent to which they depend on luck and the work of others (and of the extent to which the advantages they confer are therefore undeserved), Rousseau means to impose a further condition on pride of this sort as well: although it is appropriate for an individual to take a certain pride in her excellences (and, so, in the particular ways she surpasses others), these are not to be taken as indicators of some more substantial superiority of soul or nature—a superiority such as we allude to in ordinary discourse when we accuse an arrogant person of thinking she is 'better than' other people (or, perhaps, 'a better *person*' than others). It is tempting to say that someone who thinks herself better than others because of her superior qualities or achievements commits the simple error of taking her excellences to be markers of self-worth when in truth they are not.[20] But this explanation is not precisely right. If the position I have been reconstructing in this chapter is correct, then it *is* legitimate to derive a sense of self-worth of a certain sort from the ways in which one excels. This implies that there will even be a sense in which the person with certain superior qualities or achievements is justified in believing herself better than others. ('Great men', remember, 'are not deceived about their superiority; they see it, feel it, and are no less modest because of it' (*E* IV, 245/*OC* 4, 537).) Of course, Emile might justifiably take himself to be better than others merely along some specific dimension—as a carpenter or a man of good sense—but in the passage cited above he is portrayed as believing even that, overall, he is a superior specimen of human excellence compared with his fellow men. As we have seen, part of what allows Emile to enjoy this high opinion of himself and to take it as a basis for self-esteem without succumbing to the temptation to think himself 'better than' others is his recognition that without good luck and the wisdom of his tutor, he could not have attained the favored position he enjoys. Moreover, Emile feels, and expresses in his actions, the natural concomitants of this attitude: an absence of contempt for those less favored than he and a sense of humility for all that he knows himself still to lack. But a further reason Emile avoids falling into inflamed *amour-propre* is surely that he refuses to exaggerate the significance of his excellence by taking it as indicative of a more substantial superiority (of soul or nature) than the fact of his excellence warrants. For all the pride he takes in his superior qualities and position, Emile, we might say, does not think himself a better *person* than others.

Although 'person' is not a technical, or even univocal, term for Rousseau, he does employ it in precisely the sense at issue here in that crucial passage of the Second Discourse where the distinction between respect and esteem is implicitly introduced. Immediately after they first experience the wish to be regarded by others as the handsomest or strongest or most graceful, those primitive individuals who gather in front of their huts begin to conceive of themselves as what we, with Rousseau, would call 'persons': 'As soon as ... the idea of consideration had taken shape in their mind, *each one* claimed a *right* to it, and one could no longer deprive anyone

---

[20] I am indebted to Jason Hill for discussion of these issues.

of it with impunity. From here arose the first *duties of civility*, and ... any intentional wrong became an affront because ... the offended man saw in it contempt for his *person* that was often more unbearable than the harm itself' (*DI*, 166/*OC* 3, 170; emphases added). A passage such as this, together with the urgency Rousseau accords to Emile's acquiring a sense of his essential equality with all humans once his *amour-propre* has awakened, strongly suggests that, despite the pride he takes in his superior position, Emile escapes thinking himself 'better than' others because at the same time he attributes equal *personal* worth to all. And, as this passage implies, to attribute equal personal worth to all is to respect the right of each person to be treated in accordance with a conception of personal dignity that applies to everyone; it is, in short, to recognize the personhood of all individuals by according them a basic moral respect simply because they are human beings.[21] As we saw above, the central feature of this personal dignity is the right to have one's happiness or interests carry the same weight as all others' in constituting the laws or principles that dictate what each is permitted and obligated to do. In other words, Emile takes pride in his superior qualities and position but does not regard them as entitling him to a higher moral status than those less favored than he, and, in conformity with this, he lets his treatment of others be guided by the basic principle of human morality that declares the essential humanity of all individuals inviolable. My reconstruction of Rousseau's position makes clear why there need be no conflict between the pride Emile takes in being an excellent specimen of humanity and his unbending commitment to the equal dignity of persons. First, since respect is primarily a practical attitude one takes to others—an action-guiding, normative commitment to treat everyone in accordance with the ideal of the equal worth of persons—it does not directly contradict the (more theoretical, or constative[22]) judgments on the basis of which esteem is accorded differentially to individuals for their particular qualities or achievements. In other words, it is possible to value (esteem) certain individuals more than others because of the particular

---

[21] This point plays a prominent role in Rousseau's summary account of the mature Emile's attitude to others: 'No one will be more exact than Emile in observing all the signs of respect that are founded on the order of nature' (*E* IV, 337/*OC* 4, 668).

[22] This is not to suggest that these judgments are value-free but only that, unlike the basis for according respect, they i) depend on ascertaining some particular fact about the object of esteem; and ii) do not necessarily have implications for how the esteemer acts towards the esteemed.

merits one discerns in them and, at the same time, to commit oneself to treating all individuals in accordance with the idea that, as persons, they have equal worth. Secondly, whatever tension might remain for Emile between the equal respect he must show to all persons, on the one hand, and the unequal esteem he will accord to individuals for their particular excellences, on the other, will be mitigated by his recognition that those excellences depend on a convergence of good luck, hard work, and help from other people. With the awareness of this fact firmly ingrained in him, Emile avoids the temptation of believing that differences in the extent to which individuals flourish are somehow reflective of differences in intrinsic merit and, so, indicators of a superior right to partake of the diverse goods that human life offers.

Before we conclude this chapter, one final question deserves our attention: how does my reconstruction of Rousseau's account of inflamed *amour-propre* differ in the end from the much simpler, Kantian suggestion with which the chapter began, namely, that what makes *amour-propre* inflamed is simply the desire to be recognized as superior to others and that cultivating egalitarian *amour-propre* is all that need be done to render that passion benign? As the attentive reader will have noticed, my discussion in the final sections of this chapter of the conditions under which the desire for preeminence counts as benign gives some reason to doubt that the difference between the two interpretations of Rousseau's position is as great as it initially seemed. This is because there are important respects in which non-inflamed *amour-propre*, as I have characterized it, implicitly incorporates a commitment to some version of the very principle that Kantian interpretations emphasize, the *moral* equality of all persons. In imposing conditions of universalizability on permissible desires for preeminence, for example, Rousseau's position evaluates *amour-propre* by considering the effects such desires would have on others' ability to attain the fundamental goods that define human well-being. In this instance at least, the standpoint from which desires for preeminence are criticized as inflamed is one that recognizes the right of all individuals to be able to satisfy the fundamental human need for recognition. In a second instance, too, the idea of universal moral equality plays a substantial role in defining constraints on permissible desires for preeminence: a person's pursuit of and delight in the advantages she enjoys counts as non-inflamed only if it is accompanied by an attitude of humility informed by a kind of moral egalitarianism, namely, the recognition that all humans share a single basic predicament and nature; that excellence is not an indication of desert in any robust sense; and that having achieved superiority to others (in specific respects) never entitles one to greater moral respect than the less advantaged.

These considerations should suffice to show that, for Rousseau himself, the presence or absence of egalitarian *amour-propre*, in precisely the Kantian sense, plays a major role in distinguishing inflamed from non-inflamed forms of the passion for social esteem. And, accordingly, instilling in individuals a commitment to the equal moral worth of all persons will be a central goal of Rousseau's program for eradicating the evils that unreformed *amour-propre* tends to produce. At the same time, focusing solely on the need for a sense of the moral equality of all human beings—in effect, *equating* inflamed *amour-propre* with the desire for superior standing—causes important elements of Rousseau's position to be lost sight of: first, that not every desire for preeminence—not even every desire to be recognized as superior (in some specific respect)—is inflamed; second, that *amour-propre* poses many dangers to human existence beyond those bound up with the quest for superior standing;[23] and, finally, that since respect alone can never wholly satisfy the human need for recognition, a complete solution to the problem of *amour-propre* will require a set of social—not merely political—institutions that, beyond insuring equal respect for all citizens, creates a space within which individuals can pursue their many and diverse needs for esteem without producing a world of enslavement, conflict, vice, misery, and alienation.

[23] See a) to e) above. Another way of articulating where the Kantian diagnosis goes wrong would be to say that it focuses exclusively on one of *amour-propre*'s fundamental characteristics—its relative (comparative) nature—and ignores others, including *amour-propre*'s relativity in the second sense distinguished above (and discussed in c).

4

Why Inflamed *Amour-propre* Is So Common

Having acquired a systematic understanding of the sources of *amour-propre*'s dangers, as well as the various ways it can become inflamed, we are closer to our goal of determining whether, or to what extent, those dangers can be averted. Before undertaking this task in the following chapter, however, it is necessary to fill in an important gap in our understanding of the source of the evils for which Rousseau means to find a remedy. In Chapter 2 I examined how *amour-propre* makes possible a host of social and psychological ills that, in the absence of that passion, would be closed off to creatures of our kind. But the view that motivates Rousseau's project ascribes to *amour-propre* a much greater power to wreak havoc in human affairs than this analysis alone implies. It is impossible to appreciate the enormity of the problem that *Emile* and the *Social Contract* set out to solve if we think of enslavement, conflict, vice, misery, and alienation as merely possible features of human existence. As Rousseau makes clear in all his major works, these evils are not merely possible but probable—indeed, virtually unavoidable—consequences of social interaction for beings moved by *amour-propre*. It would be no exaggeration to say that Rousseau regards the fall from innocence and harmony depicted in the Second Discourse as the 'natural' course of development for human society. This does not mean that the fallen state is a necessary consequence of human nature but only that, in the absence of 'artificial' intervention that is either very wise or very lucky, it is by far the most likely outcome of human interaction. This state is, in fact, so difficult to avoid that many philosophers have taken it to be definitive of the human condition, the necessary effect of a permanently flawed human nature. The question that needs to be addressed before reconstructing Rousseau's solution to the ills produced by *amour-propre* is why those ills are not merely possible but ubiquitous, nearly unavoidable features of human existence. Why, in other words, are the evils made possible by *amour-propre* so widespread and intractable? Without an answer to this question it will be difficult to determine where and how education and institutional reform must intervene if they are to remedy those evils.

It is tempting to seek an answer to this question by scrutinizing the two genetic accounts of *amour-propre* that Rousseau provides—in the Second Discourse and *Emile*—in an attempt to locate the moment at which a still benign *amour-propre* becomes inflamed. If we could determine why this transformation takes place—why it is a 'natural' if not unavoidable occurrence—then, we are tempted to think, we would understand why those evils are not mere possibilities but pervasive features of human intercourse. If, in addition, we assume that inflamed *amour-propre* is nothing more than the striving for superior standing, then our investigation reduces to the task of determining at what moment, and why, humans begin to be motivated by the desire to be recognized as better than others. This is the strategy Joshua Cohen recommends in his broadly Kantian reconstruction of Rousseau's project. For Cohen, it will be recalled, 'the central question for an explanation of vice' is 'how ... a generic, not–intrinsically–inegalitarian concern to be treated with respect come[s] to be particularized as a desire and demand to be treated as a better'.[1]

Unfortunately, this simple strategy will not work. One implication of my argument in Chapter 3 is that because inflamed *amour-propre* is not a unitary phenomenon, there can be no single comprehensive answer to the question of why *amour-propre*'s harmful potential is so frequently realized. If we take seriously the idea that *amour-propre* can be inflamed in a number of ways, then scouring Rousseau's genealogies for the one moment where human development goes awry is bound to end in failure. This is not to say that those genealogies provide no help in addressing the question at hand but only that there is no simple, easily isolated answer to be found in them. In order to make progress on this complicated issue, I propose considering Rousseau's two genealogies of *amour-propre* one at a time, examining each for whatever help it offers in understanding why the fallen state seems to be humankind's default condition.

---

[1] Cohen, 111.

Social origins of inflamed *amour-propre*

It is natural to expect the Second Discourse, whose announced aim is a genealogy of inequality and vice,[2] to be the most helpful of Rousseau's texts in the present context. What one quickly discovers, though, is that it says frustratingly little that bears directly on the question of why human *amour-propre* is so likely to be inflamed. The most striking example of this is that when *amour-propre* first appears in the Second Discourse, it is already configured as a desire to achieve superior standing—to be regarded as the *best* singer or dancer (*DI*, 166/*OC* 3, 169)—and, contrary to what we might expect, Rousseau makes no effort to explain this crucial fact. It might be relevant that the immediately preceding paragraph makes reference to a different kind of according of preference, namely, attaching 'sentiments of preference' not to oneself but to objects of sexual love. But if there is some connection between this concern for preeminence—the preeminence of *others*—and the desire to be recognized oneself as the best singer or dancer, it remains, in these passages at least, completely unexplained. (I consider this connection further below, in discussing *Emile*'s more extensive treatment of the same theme.)

Despite the enormity of what Rousseau leaves unsaid, we can make some progress in reconstructing his position by bearing in mind the following point: from the fact that the desire for recognition first appears as a desire for superior standing it does not follow that *amour-propre* is already at its inception inflamed. To make this inference would be to assume that the desire for preeminent standing is sufficient to make *amour-propre* inflamed, and this assumption, as I have argued in previous chapters, is mistaken. Those arguments find further confirmation in the fact that, according to the story told here, the desire to be recognized as better than others establishes itself in society well before the latter enters its 'happiest and most durable epoch' (*DI*, 167/*OC* 3, 171), the so-called golden age of human development. What more conclusive proof could there be that the desire for preeminence is not equivalent to inflamed *amour-propre*—that the quest for superior standing is not by itself the source of the many ills *amour-propre* is capable of producing?

---

[2] The work's full title is *On the Origin and Foundations of Inequality among Men*. Rousseau characterizes it as a genealogy of vice at LCB, 28/*OC* 4, 936.

Four socio-economic conditions

In fact, the message of the Second Discourse appears to be that the desire for superior standing plays a role in generating the ills that plague human society only when accompanied by a number of other, 'accidental' conditions. The most important of these, in roughly 'chronological' order, are: 1) improved methods of production that enable humans to produce more than their subsistence requires, thereby introducing them to the pleasures that leisure and luxury, even in primitive forms, afford; 2) an ever expanding material division of labor—first manifested in the rise of metallurgy and agriculture—that increases individuals' dependence on others for the satisfaction of needs;[3] 3) the establishment of private property, especially in the means of production, such as land; and 4) an increased differentiation of individuals with respect to character, circumstances, and possessions that results from a combination of differences among those individuals in luck, effort, and natural endowment. The precise order in which these conditions are said to arise is far less important than the fact that, once introduced, each further stimulates the growth of the others, with the result that human development comes to be fueled by a self-perpetuating and increasingly complex interplay of social, economic, and psychological forces.

Even though these four phenomena quickly cease to be (or perhaps never were) causally independent of one another, there is a point to distinguishing them as Rousseau's genealogy does. For, although existentially interdependent, each contributes in its own way to transforming the (in itself benign) desire for superior standing into inflamed *amour-propre*. The increase in dependence occasioned by an expanding division of labor, for example, makes it possible for *amour-propre* to seek satisfaction in new ways that disrupt the harmony that prevailed when individuals 'applied themselves only to tasks that ... did not require the cooperation of several hands' (*DI*, 167/*OC* 3, 171). Rousseau's thought is that since enduring relations of

---

[3] Although Rousseau emphasizes the material division of labor in his claim that metallurgy and agriculture 'civilized men and ruined the human species' (*DI*, 168–9/*OC* 3, 171–3), he also alludes to the pernicious effects of the first class divisions: 'as soon as ... [men] learned that it was useful for a single person to have provisions for two, equality disappeared, property was introduced, labor became necessary, and the vast forests changed into laughing fields that had to be watered with the sweat of men, and in which slavery and misery were soon seen to sprout and grow with the crops' (*DI*, 167/*OC* 3, 171).

domination and servitude require dependence as their condition[4]—'what yoke could be imposed on men who need nothing?' (*DSA*, 7n/*OC* 3, 7n)—increased dependence offers humans the opportunity to seek novel and more pernicious forms of superior standing. For alongside the old strategies of striving to be the best singer or dancer, new opportunities for achieving preeminence arise, including the possibility of exploiting others' dependence for the purpose of subjugating them. It is easy to see that a peasant who produces only one of the many foods he needs to subsist is much more vulnerable to enslavement than his self-sufficient counterpart. The point that interests Rousseau, however, is that subjugation of this kind is rarely, if ever, motivated by purely economic ends. For in addition to the economic benefits it brings, establishing oneself as the master of others—especially once the roles of master and mastered become formalized and sanctioned by social institutions—presents itself as a highly alluring strategy for finding clear and enduring confirmation of one's high standing in the eyes of others. (In Marxist terms, Rousseau's point is that increased economic dependence is one of the conditions that make social classes, and hence exploitation, possible. Moreover, economic advantage is not the only, perhaps not even the primary, reason for wanting to be part of the class of exploiters: owning the means of production and living off the labor of those who do not is an especially visible way of achieving superior standing for others.)

In a similar way, the growth in productive forces, along with the advent of private property, makes *amour-propre* susceptible to other dangerous modifications. The former, for example, introduces leisure and luxury into the world, and both of these affect how individuals conceive of and pursue their standing for others. Leisure is relevant to this story because without it—without some respite from biologically necessary labor—it is hard to see how 'looking at others and wanting to be looked at oneself' could establish itself as a pastime of importance. As Rousseau notes, caring about who among us dances or sings the best is the province of 'idle and assembled' beings (*DI*, 166/*OC* 3, 169)—that is, of those who have enough time to gather in front of their huts once their working day is completed. (Of course, merely having the free

---

[4] 'Since the ties of servitude are formed only from the mutual dependence of men and the reciprocal needs that unite them, it is impossible to enslave a man without first having put him in the position of being unable to do without another' (*DI*, 159/*OC* 3, 162).

time to observe who is superior to whom would be inconsequential if there were not also significant differences to take note of; this is the contribution individual differentiation makes to the inflaming of *amour-propre*.)

Leisure's counterpart, luxury, also contributes to the process through which *amour-propre* becomes inflamed. The aspect of luxury that Rousseau emphasizes is its role in generating new needs, which increase the dependence of humans and, at the same time, their susceptibility to subjugation:

> men enjoyed very great leisure, and they used it to procure many kinds of commodities unknown to their fathers, and that was the first yoke they imposed on themselves without knowing it. ... For ... since these commodities, by becoming habitual, had lost almost all their pleasantness and had ... degenerated into true needs, being deprived of them became much more cruel than possessing them was sweet.
>
> (*DI*, 164–5/*OC* 3, 168)

But luxury, especially when conjoined with private property, has a more consequential effect on *amour-propre* as well: to beings who desire confirmation of their worth for others, owning more than one needs, and making that excess visible, offers itself as another way to gain public recognition of their superior standing.[5] As society's productive forces continue to grow, the possibilities for acquisition expand along with them, and in the absence of 'artificial' constraints on private accumulation, the desire for property easily turns into a feverish and limitless drive to own more and more, all for the sake of improving or holding on to the social status one currently enjoys. The result, Rousseau tells us, is a society dominated by the 'consuming ambition' of its members, by their 'fervor to raise [their] relative fortune ... in order to place [themselves] above others' (*DI*, 171/*OC* 3, 175). Despite the prominent role Rousseau's genealogy gives to the advent of private property—'all these evils are the first effect of property' (*DI*, 171/*OC* 3, 175)[6]—he also makes clear that it is *amour-propre*, not a straightforward desire for the necessities or comforts of life, that ultimately

[5] 'Luxury [is] impossible to prevent among men greedy for ... the consideration of others' (*DI*, 201/*OC* 3, 205).

[6] Similar claims attributing the world's ills to property can be found at *DI*, 161, 167/*OC* 3, 164, 171. It should be noted that elsewhere Rousseau appears to accord explanatory primacy to various other factors, among them: the division of labor (*DI*, 167–9/*OC* 3, 171–3), leisure and luxury (*DI*, 164–5/*OC* 3, 168), and, of course, *amour-propre* (*DI*, 166/*OC* 3, 169).

explains the rapid growth—perhaps even the origin[7]—of private property. The drive to possess acquires the importance for humans that it does only because the extent and value of a person's property is so readily perceived by others as an external sign of her worth as an individual.

All four of these developments, then—increasing productivity, the division of labor, private property, and the flourishing of individual differences—contribute in the same general way to the process through which *amour-propre* becomes inflamed: each plays a role in generating new possibilities for inequalities of various kinds to germinate and take root in society. By themselves, however, these developments would have little effect on human happiness. That they initiate a process of decline depends on the fact that an already awakened *amour-propre*, which includes an indeterminate longing to do better than others, is able to latch on to these new possibilities and use them to further its aim of achieving standing in the eyes of others. As Rousseau's genealogy would have it, *amour-propre* does not itself generate the practices and institutions that allow all sorts of 'artificial' inequalities to enter the world, but once those possibilities are there, it takes full and reckless advantage of them, thereby furnishing the fuel for the swift, inexorable growth of inequality that follows and that finally results in the enslavement, conflict, vice, misery, and alienation whose existence Rousseau is trying to explain. It is important to recognize that the *amour-propre* that first encounters the possibilities for inequality it later exploits is not yet inflamed (which is to say: even though it may seek superior standing of certain kinds, it is not yet configured such that it makes the evils of human society virtually unavoidable). Rousseau's position, in other words, is not that an already inflamed *amour-propre* appears in the human world, without explanation, and then lies dormant, awaiting, as it

---

[7] Immediately after lamenting the 'crimes, wars, murders, ... miseries, and horrors' that humans would have been spared if private property had been prevented, Rousseau unequivocally denies that property is the ultimate cause of those evils: 'For this idea of property, depending on many prior ideas that could have arisen only successively, did not take shape all at once in the human mind. It was necessary to make much progress ... before arriving at this last stage of the state of nature' (*DI*, 161/ *OC* 3, 164). Private property, then, must itself be explained as the result of other, more fundamental causes. Despite its announced intention, Rousseau's text does not provide a convincing explanation of why private property follows naturally from the division of labor, the cultivation of land, or any other development of the productive forces alone. This suggests that, even at its origin, private property might be more a product of *amour-propre* than *amour de soi*. What could better explain a person's urge to fence off a plot of ground and to announce before others 'this is mine!' (*DI*, 161/*OC* 3, 164) than the desire to have his worth reflected in pieces of the external world and to have that worth publicly confirmed by the constraints his ownership imposes on others' actions?

were, the development of the external conditions that allow it to unleash its destructive power. His view, rather, is that it is only under such conditions that the generic desire for superior standing—in itself a harmless manifestation of *amour-propre*—is transformed into the particular versions of that desire that, once aroused, lead inevitably to the evils of human society. It is only under the conditions brought about by increasing productivity, dependence, private property, and individual differences that the relatively harmless desire to be regarded as a superior dancer or singer, or as stronger or more handsome than others, is transformed into a limitless drive to accumulate wealth, to subjugate others, and to do harm to one's rivals—in short, to establish one's superior standing in whatever way possible and at virtually any cost.

Two additional conditions

The four conditions discussed thus far are what Rousseau himself emphasizes in recounting the developments through which *amour-propre* becomes inflamed. But if this is all there were to his account, finding a remedy for the ills of human society would encounter a serious problem: if the inflammation of *amour-propre* followed more or less directly from the combination of developed productive forces, the division of labor, private property, and the flourishing of individual differences, then countering the dangers of *amour-propre* would require doing away with (or at least severely limiting) some, or perhaps all, of these conditions. While it is no doubt true that Rousseau's ideal society would have less productivity, economic specialization, private wealth, and individual diversity than contemporary Western societies, his position is not so utopian as to require eliminating any of what he himself acknowledges to be the basic conditions of civilization. As he makes clear in a too frequently ignored footnote to the Second Discourse, the solution to civilization's problems does not lie in destroying societies, abolishing property, and returning to the forests to live with bears (*DI*, 203/*OC* 3, 207). For this reason it is worth asking if there are other, less prominent conditions that also play a role in Rousseau's account of how inflamed *amour-propre* arises once the basic features of civilization are in place.

A careful reading of the Second Discourse shows that there are, in fact, two such conditions, both of which have implications for the task of remedying the ills produced by *amour-propre*. The first is alluded to in a passage that immediately follows Rousseau's account of the origin of the division of labor, improved productive forces, and private property but precedes his description of the evils that follow in their train:

Here, then, are all our faculties developed, … *amour-propre* aroused, reason made active, and the mind having reached almost the limit of the perfection of which it is susceptible. Here … the rank and fate of each man established, not only on the quantity of goods and the power to serve or harm, but also on the mind, beauty, strength, or skill, on merit or talents. *And these qualities being the only ones that were able to attract consideration*, it soon became necessary either to have or to affect them.

(*DI*, 170/*OC* 3, 174; emphasis added)

The implication of the words highlighted here is that the specific nature of a given society affects the consequences *amour-propre* will have in it by delimiting the field of possibilities within which recognition can be pursued. Every society, in other words, makes certain options for recognition available to its members and forecloses others, and this plays an important role in shaping how individuals will seek to satisfy their desire for standing in the eyes of others. This suggests that part of what explains why events in the Second Discourse unfold as they do is that the society that arises 'naturally' from the beginnings of civilization (which is to say, in the absence of human intervention directed at realizing some consciously intended end) fails to provide its members with the kinds of opportunities for recognition that must be available if the pernicious effects of *amour-propre* are to be avoided.[8] More precisely, as the quote above makes clear, such a society offers no generally recognized way for its members to acquire standing for others that does not require them to outdo, and hence to compete with, their associates. Just as important, among the ways of 'standing out' it allows for, those that bring the most prestige are superficial and invidious forms of superiority, such as opulence and domination. Here again, it is important to remember that for Rousseau this 'natural' course of human development is not the only one possible; if other, healthier sources of recognition could be made available, the path leading from civilization to inflamed *amour-propre* might be avoided. The relevance of this point for Rousseau's project of finding an institutional solution to the problems of

---

[8] Cohen makes this point clearly, 121, 123.

amour-propre is apparent: one of the tasks of such a project will be to discover how the social world can be structured so as to provide its members with stable and less destructive ways of satisfying their fundamental need for the regard of others.

The second condition Rousseau's genealogy of vice presupposes beyond the four basic features of civilization is more difficult to pinpoint textually but is no less important: the original innocence, or naiveté, of human beings. Since this feature of Rousseau's account may be less evident than others, it is necessary to say a word about how and where it makes its appearance. One feature of the Second Discourse that stands out to even a casual reader is its insistence that the developments it narrates are not made necessary by either human nature or the nature of the world but instead the effects of accident, or chance. A similar theme is sounded in Rousseau's frequent remarks to the effect that the history he is recounting is the product of human will—the result of freely chosen actions—and, so, something for which human beings themselves are in some sense responsible. This point finds expression not only in the general claim that 'man has hardly any evils but those he has given himself' (*DI*, 197/*OC* 3, 202) but also, and more concretely, in the striking fact that most of the story's main turning points—the invention of luxuries, the origin of property, and the creation of the state—are depicted as the results of conscious human choices. But if, as Rousseau famously holds, human beings are by nature good,[9] what could lead them to produce voluntarily the conditions of their own debasement? Though it is easily missed, the Second Discourse repeatedly names the cause of the bad choices its characters consistently make: by inventing luxuries they imposed a yoke on themselves 'without knowing it' (*DI*, 164/*OC* 3, 168); in assenting to the first social contract they 'ran toward their chains in the [false] belief that they were securing their freedom' (*DI*, 173/*OC* 3, 177); when someone first fenced off a plot of ground and declared it his, the rest were 'simple enough' not to recognize the miseries they would have avoided by opposing him (*DI*, 161/*OC* 3, 164). And, in case any doubt remains, in looking back on the story he has just told, Rousseau lays the blame for human decline on 'the *blindness* of man, which, in order to feed his foolish pride and ... vain admiration of himself, makes him run eagerly after all the miseries of which

[9] The best account of this notorious thesis is Cohen's.

he is susceptible' (*DI*, 197/*OC* 3, 202; emphasis added). It is evident, then, that a further condition presupposed by Rousseau's genealogy is the original innocence, or naiveté, of those whose own free choices set in motion the process of their debasement. Moreover, as these passages make clear, this innocence consists in a kind of ignorance or blindness—a lack of knowledge of the nature and extreme fragility of true human happiness, as well as of the complex conditions, both internal and external, that make it possible.

Rousseau's recasting of Judeo-Christian myth so as to locate the source of human depravity in ignorance rather than sin[10] has important implications for how philosophy can contribute to averting the dangers intrinsic to human society. From the assumption that humanity's fall is due to a defect in understanding rather than will, it follows that intellectual enlightenment will play an important part in solving the problems created by *amour-propre*. The kind of enlightenment Rousseau's project requires is evident from the role ignorance plays in the corruption of humanity: if it is the inability to foresee the evil consequences of their choices that makes humans the agents of their own debasement, then avoiding the ills of *amour-propre* is a possibility for them only on the condition that they possess, and let themselves be guided by, knowledge of the nature and conditions of human flourishing. Not by coincidence, it is knowledge of precisely this sort that Rousseau regards as the first—perhaps even the only[11]—aim of philosophy, and it is easy to read both *Emile* and the Second Discourse as devoted to just this task. In any case, the implication of Rousseau's view that ignorance of the conditions of human flourishing makes humanity's fall practically inevitable is that, in addition to social and pedagogical reforms, philosophy will play a permanent and necessary role in any world in which the dangers of *amour-propre* are successfully checked.

[10] Despite this difference, Rousseau's account remains deeply rooted in Judeo-Christian myth. The original naiveté he emphasizes, for example, is also central to the story of the fall in Genesis. Insofar as they lack the (divine) knowledge of good and evil, Adam and Eve possess an ignorance similar to the one that plays a role in Rousseau's account. One crucial difference is that Adam and Eve know in advance that eating the apple is wrong but do it anyway; thus, ignorance is not the cause of their fall.

[11] This would explain Rousseau's apparent lack of interest in metaphysical and epistemological questions for their own sake. His 'Profession of Faith of the Savoyard Vicar', for example, addresses such issues but only insofar as they are relevant to religious doctrines bearing on questions about the human good and right action (*E* IV, 277/*OC* 4, 581); see also *RSW*, 23/*OC* 1, 1018.

Psychological origins of inflamed *amour-propre*

Let us turn now to *Emile*, the site of Rousseau's other genetic account of *amour-propre*, in order to see what implications it contains for understanding why the inflamed form of that passion is so likely to take root in human society. As we should expect given the difference in focus between it and the Second Discourse, *Emile*'s narrative concerns not the social and political conditions that encourage the inflammation of *amour-propre* but rather the psychological developments internal to each individual that tend to lead to the same result. As Rousseau himself announces in various places, the most important aim of Emile's education is to prevent inflamed *amour-propre* from gaining a foothold in the latter's character. How Rousseau thinks this is to be accomplished will occupy us in the following chapter; our concern now is to understand what forces are at work in the development of Everyman that make inflamed *amour-propre* so difficult to avoid. In other words, why, even in the absence of unfavorable social conditions, is the inflammation of *amour-propre* a constant threat?

Once again, it is bewildering to discover how little Rousseau says about this topic explicitly. Despite this, a careful reading of two significant passages of the text—one in Book I, the other in Book IV—makes it possible to reconstruct the beginnings of an answer to why 'artificial' intervention is almost always required in order to insure that *amour-propre* assume a benign rather than destructive form. The first of these passages explains how, early on and as a part of normal development, children become vulnerable to the temptation to find confirmation of their worth in *dominating* others. (It also shows how a different form of inflamed *amour-propre*, a disposition to fury and spite, can arise.) The second passage offers an account of why the *desire for superior standing*—indeed, the desire to be first—is, as it were, *amour-propre*'s default configuration. Taken together, these points constitute a strong case for the view that, regardless of the social conditions that obtain, there are psychological forces intrinsic to normal human development that encourage the inflammation of *amour-propre* in a number of ways. That there is more than one way the educational process can go awry is important to Rousseau's vision of the ubiquity of inflamed *amour-propre*. For even if one avoids instilling, say, a spirit of domination in a child, there remain many other pitfalls that must be avoided if the child's education is to succeed.

Fostering the will to dominate

I turn first to the passage from Book I, where Rousseau's topic is infancy and the specific problems it poses for Emile's education. To readers who know Rousseau primarily as the proponent of the natural goodness of man it will no doubt come as a surprise that he finds the first seeds of inflamed *amour-propre* already in the earliest stages of infancy, before any corrupting influences of society at large could have begun their work. Regardless of the kind of social order he is born into, Rousseau implies, the infant's 'first ideas are ... domination and servitude' (*E* I, 48/*OC* 4, 261), and the first danger his educator faces is a 'disposition ... to fury, spite, and anger' that, without proper attention, easily takes root in the newborn's character (*E* I, 66/*OC* 4, 287). Rousseau locates the source of these dangers in a basic condition of human infancy: the baby's complete dependence on others for the satisfaction of his elementary needs:

> Since the first condition of man is want and weakness, his first voices are complaint and tears. The infant feels his needs and cannot satisfy them. He implores the help of others through screams. ...
>
> From these tears ... is born man's first relation to all that surrounds him; here is formed the first link in that long chain of which the social order is formed. ...
>
> The first tears of infants are pleas. If one is not careful, they soon become orders. Infants begin by getting themselves assisted; they end by getting themselves served. Thus, from their own weakness, which is the first source of the feeling of their dependence, is subsequently born the idea of empire and domination.
>
> (*E* I, 65, 66/*OC* 4, 286, 287)

As in the Second Discourse, here, too, Rousseau underscores the role dependence plays in defining the human condition and in explaining the obstacles to well-being that are intrinsic to it. In the first stage of life, the dependence that characterizes human existence generally is even more acute due to the fact that, in contrast to adults, infants possess no language (beyond tears and screams) with which to communicate their need and ask for aid. Rousseau's focus here diverges importantly from that of the Second Discourse in that the danger that infantile dependence is said to introduce into the human world is not the loss of freedom (subjection to a foreign will) but a taste for empire and domination.

Before considering how the infant's dependence, joined with her inability to speak, engenders a taste for empire and domination, it is important to get clear about just what Rousseau is up to in this passage. Three significant claims can be distinguished. First, the desire to dominate others, far from being alien to human psychology, is common in human beings, even in the earliest stages of life. Second, this inclination, when present, is not original (innate) but learned. Third, since the conditions that favor its acquisition are basic to human existence, the desire to dominate is a permanent possibility for the species—one that is, as it were, built into the human condition. In order to make a plausible case for this view and to reconcile it with the thesis of humankind's natural goodness, Rousseau must be able to show how the basic conditions of infancy make it possible—indeed 'natural'—for a desire that is not original to human nature (the desire to dominate others) to establish itself in the characters of human beings. More precisely: since the essential claim of the natural goodness thesis is that 'there is no original perversity in the human heart—there is not a single vice to be found in it of which it cannot be said how and whence it entered' (E II, 92/OC 4, 322), Rousseau is committed to explaining how an inflamed inclination such as the desire for domination issues from a normal developmental process that presupposes no original predisposition to vice[12] (or to any of the other evils that inflamed *amour-propre* is taken to be responsible for).

The closest Rousseau comes to formulating such an explanation is in the following passage:

As soon as [infants] can consider the people who surround them as instruments depending on them to be set in motion, they make use of those people to follow their inclination and to make up for their own weakness. That is how they become difficult, tyrannical, imperious, wicked, unmanageable—a development that does not come from a natural spirit of domination but rather gives one to them, for it does not require long experience to sense how pleasant it is to act with the hands of others and to need only to stir one's tongue to make the universe move.

In growing, one gains strength, ... but the desire to command is not extinguished with the need that gave birth to it. Dominion awakens and flatters *amour-propre*, and habit strengthens it. In this way, whim succeeds need, and prejudices and opinion take their first roots.

(E I, 67–8/OC 4, 289–90)

---

[12] For Rousseau's view of the relation between vice (or evil) and corrupted dispositions, as well as a comparison of this view with Kant's, see Cohen, 134–5, n. 24.

Rousseau's argument, such as it is, focuses on explaining how infants learn to take pleasure in something—commanding others—that, unlike sucking at the breast or being held by the mother, does not satisfy one of their innate needs. The general idea seems clear enough: because they depend so thoroughly on others' aid for comfort and survival, infants have a strong incentive, stemming from *amour de soi*, to learn to harness the forces of the stronger creatures who surround them. In order to do so, they must find a way of communicating their condition of want to their potential benefactors, and since they lack the language adults use for this purpose, they are forced to resort to the only one available to them, the language of tears and screams. The basic fact that the infant must engage the forces of other persons in order to satisfy his needs means that each of his attempts to do so—every effort his *amour de soi* prompts him to make—includes, in effect, an attempt to command the will of another. Tears and screams are highly effective at eliciting the responses they aim at not only because they normally evoke compassion in adults but also because, continued for any length of time, they become extremely annoying. For both of these reasons tears and screams are ideal instruments of coercion and manipulation,[13] and learning this is easily within the grasp of even the very young.

So far all that Rousseau has established is that the neediness and weakness of infants, together with their ability to cry, conspire to teach them how to get their wills (their desires or wants) heard and obeyed by those who are in a position to aid them. This implies that from the very start infants begin to discover how to be effective in satisfying the needs of *amour de soi*, but it does not yet explain the pleasure they supposedly take in commanding others (as distinguished from the pleasure of having their bodily or emotional needs satisfied). Where does the pleasure in *being obeyed* come from, if it is independent of the ends of *amour de soi* and if, as the thesis of natural goodness postulates, dominating others is not an original aim of human

---

[13] Rousseau alludes to this aspect of a child's crying at *E* I, 48, 65/*OC* 4, 261, 286. More could be said about the role played by infants' lack of language in acquiring inflamed *amour-propre*. One such point is hinted at in Rousseau's remark that infants' inability to communicate their needs in words allows them 'no middle ground' between giving orders or receiving them—no opportunity, in other words, for mutually determined cooperation, or for what Jürgen Habermas calls communicative action (*The Theory of Communicative Action* (Boston: Beacon Press, 1981)). Other, psychoanalytically oriented interpretations of the significance of the infant's inability to speak his desires are tempting as well.

nature? In order to explain why in the normal course of development infants learn to find pleasure in commanding others, Rousseau is forced to introduce—to smuggle in, really—a piece of psychology missing from the account of human nature set out in the Second Discourse; that is, the explanation he suggests relies on a type of motivation that cannot be traced back to *amour de soi*, pity, or *amour-propre*.[14]

In the paragraph immediately preceding his explanation of the infant's will to dominate, Rousseau introduces this new psychological force under the name of 'the active principle' (*E* I, 67/ *OC* 4, 289).[15] As he characterizes it there, the active principle is a kind of life force, or impulse to vitality, that strives to 'animate' the surrounding world, to infuse as much of one's environment as possible with one's own spirit. One prominent manifestation of the active principle is the young child's urge 'to upset everything he sees, to smash and break everything he can reach' (*E* I, 67/ *OC* 4, 288). The idea here is that what the rambunctious child ultimately seeks is not to destroy the things around him but to see the world display the effects of his will. His true aim is not to smash and break but to have before himself a world that reflects back to him, and so confirms, the fact of his subjectivity. If the active principle is not intrinsically destructive, it is also not a drive to construct or produce (though it can manifest itself in constructing or producing). In other words, there is nothing utilitarian in the active principle (and this is what distinguishes it from *amour de soi*). To it the world appears not as a potential tool to be employed for the satisfaction of biological needs but as an inert, formable mass that offers itself to the active human subject as raw material for its (species-defining) project of making external things bear the imprint of its own subjectivity.[16]

---

[14] One might include among the natural drives recognized by the Second Discourse a propensity to preserve one's freedom, since sometimes Rousseau seems to ascribe such motivations to inhabitants of the original state of nature.

[15] There is little discussion in the secondary literature of this crucial aspect of Rousseau's psychology. Dent gives a careful and nuanced reading of these passages (emphasizing their connection to Melanie Klein's theory of object relations) without mentioning the active principle (70–9). One notable exception is Chitty, who (mistakenly, in my view) interprets the active principle as an extension of *amour de soi* (28–9).

[16] Though the debt is seldom acknowledged, the views of human nature underlying Hegel's and Marx's theories of alienation implicitly presuppose some version of Rousseau's active principle, insofar as they regard the externalization, or objectification, of subjectivity as a central human need.

What the crying infant discovers is that she can make use of the forces of adults not only to satisfy her needs to be fed, dried, and held but also to make the world bear the imprint of her whims and thereby satisfy her active principle. It is the latter discovery that explains why the infant's desire to command is not extinguished with the need that gave birth to it. Although the impulse to command others' wills sneaks into the world under the cloak of *amour de soi*, once it is there it achieves independence from that sentiment by offering the infant a distinctive form of gratification that retains its allure even after the needs of *amour de soi* have been satisfied.[17] Rousseau suggests, but does not emphasize, that the infant's condition can just as well produce in her a tendency to subservience (*E* I, 48/*OC* 4, 261). That is, depending on what kinds of adults surround her, the infant might learn that the only way to get her needs satisfied is to subjugate herself to the wills of those more powerful than she. In this case, the infant's lesson is that her own desires and needs have no claim on others, in contrast to the imperious child, who learns the same thing about others' desires and needs. What these attitudes share is the supposition that certain wills count for more than others.

It is important to see that there is nothing intrinsically vicious in the ultimate goal motivating the infant's first attempts to command others. There is no evil merely in wanting to make the world bear the mark of one's own subjectivity. Indeed, it would be closer to the truth to view this urge as a disposition to the *good* (though not in a moral sense), as becomes clear when one considers how grimly utilitarian human experience would be without the active principle's drive to instill the world with expressive significance. The reason for regarding an infant's taste for domination as the beginnings of a disposition to vice lies not in the ultimate purpose of his attempts to command—in his desire to 'make the universe move'—but rather in the specific means by which that aim is (of necessity) pursued by the incipiently imperious child, namely, by manipulating (by using as a mere tool) the wills of others.[18] Because of his inability to make the universe move by his own forces, the infant has little choice but to express

---

[17] A further provocative discussion of how passions can be transformed by acquiring new objects can be found at *RJJ*, 9–10/*OC* 1, 669–70.

[18] Such a child is not, at first, consciously 'manipulating' others (which requires a recognition of their subjectivity) but merely using them as he would a stick or a robot.

his active principle in a way that implicitly treats the wills of others as mere instruments for his own satisfaction.

Presumably, what makes this use of others a prototype of manipulation (and so a forerunner of vice[19]), in contrast to the use the infant makes of adults in satisfying her needs of *amour de soi*, is meant to be captured by Rousseau's remark that in the former 'whim succeeds need' as the source of the infant's pleas for assistance. It might be more exact to say that when the infant's demand is dictated by need rather than whim—by *amour de soi* rather than the active principle—those whose forces are harnessed in service of her ends would generally endorse, or consent to, their being used for such purposes, whereas in the contrasting case they generally would not.[20] (Here again, the infant's inability to speak may be of relevance. For the exchange of reasons that non-coercive agreement relies on requires being able to communicate one's own demands and to understand those made by others.) That the latter is a form of manipulation, and a predecessor of vice, rather than an appeal for help occasioned by genuine need is made clear by the fact that when it is whim that commands, success in getting others to obey depends on the true object of the infant's pleas being mistaken by—in effect, concealed from—those whose service she is attempting to enlist.

One important aspect of the genesis of the infant's taste for domination remains to be discussed: the connection between the desire to command others (and, by implication, the active principle from which it arises) and *amour-propre*. How is the desire to make others obey connected to the quest to find confirmation of one's worth by other subjects? In the passage cited

---

[19] It is important to bear in mind that Rousseau is attempting to explain how humans can come to take pleasure in commanding others—to acquire a 'taste' for domination—and that merely having such a desire or taste is not yet vicious. Rousseau has very little to say about the complicated issue of what beyond this desire must be present (and how it comes about) in order for vice or, alternatively, a *disposition* to vice to emerge. I am indebted to Daniel Viehoff for insightful remarks on this topic.

[20] This point is complicated by the fact that a good education surely includes sometimes indulging a child's desires even though no genuine need stands behind them. For without this, how will a child learn to accord the importance to his own desires that a healthy sense of self requires (that is, to regard them not as having unconditional authority but as deserving to be considered and responded to by himself and others)? Yielding to a child's desires under the appropriate conditions teaches him that his wishes have a prima facie claim to respect merely because they are his. Of course, knowing when these conditions obtain is one of the most difficult challenges of child-rearing. Although Emile's education can appear not to leave room for responding to the child's desires in this manner, Rousseau explicitly contradicts this at *E* II, 89n/*OC* 4, 316n, where he distinguishes real pleasures, which should be permitted so far as possible, from whims, which aim only at commanding other wills.

above Rousseau claims that dominion—the taste for, and success in, getting others to obey—'awakens and flatters *amour-propre*'. This suggests that the infant's first experience of commanding others is not only a point in his development at which *amour-propre* can easily become inflamed ('flattered') but also the point at which *amour-propre* is *born* ('awakened')—or, in Rousseau's formulation, the point at which '*amour de soi* turns into *amour-propre*' (*E* IV, 235/ *OC* 4, 523).[21] Implicit in the claim that the experience of domination can awaken *amour-propre* is the suggestion that the latter's basic aim—to find one's worth or standing confirmed in the external world—is already somehow implicit in the active principle itself, the original source of the pleasure the infant learns to take in getting others to obey. The best way to make this suggestion plausible is to think of the active principle's urge to make the world into a reflection of me (of my subjectivity) as an effort to demonstrate and thereby confirm my control, or sovereignty, over it. By refashioning the world to conform to me (to my wishes or whims or will), I prove—to myself, but also to anyone else who might be there—which of the two poles of the subject–object relationship has mastery over the other. The drive to command other wills, then, would be a derivative or extension of the active principle.

In this form, however, the active principle is not yet *amour-propre*: as long as I seek to prove my status only in relation to objects, the relativity to others that is essential to *amour-propre* is not yet present. This, however, is precisely what the infant's dependence introduces into her relation to the world: because the earliest expressions of the active principle are by necessity mediated by other wills—because the infant must rely on the cooperation of others to make the universe move—her first attempts to prove herself the master of *things* are inextricably bound up with achieving mastery over *persons*. Because of this the infant discovers, so to speak, a second external world—the realm of social or intersubjective phenomena—that presents itself as a further arena within which her quest for sovereignty in relation to what is not-she can be pursued. Moreover, the strategy of satisfying one's active principle by commanding other wills ensures that this quest will take on the very character it needs in order to count as *amour-propre*, namely, being relative to other subjects in both senses distinguished in

---

[21] Though this quote is from Book IV, I have argued throughout that Rousseau is mistaken, even by his own lights, in claiming that *amour-propre* first appears in adolescence.

Chapter 1. First, when a pattern develops in which the infant commands and someone else obeys, a hierarchy is established between the two that inevitably introduces *comparative standing* into their relationship. The fact that the infant can find her standing reflected in the world only by making herself the master of another's will means that for her achieving a confirmed standing becomes inseparable from positioning herself in relation to—in this case, above—another subject. Secondly, because it involves mastering another's will, this positioning herself relative to others also takes on the character of having her worth confirmed *in the eyes of another subject*. Once the infant is capable of recognizing that the adult who obeys her cries does so freely—that his submission is the effect of his own will—then she can see that her position of superiority has been conferred on her by another subject. The adult's submission presents itself therefore as an expression of the value accorded to her by another subject, which is to say, as a species of recognition. Thus, the infant's experience of commanding others *awakens* her *amour-propre* because it introduces her to the possibility of winning external confirmation of her subjectivity not by conquering things but through a kind of recognition from other subjects. The same experience *flatters* her *amour-propre* by accustoming her to seek recognition in asymmetrical relationships that affirm her superiority without demanding that she in turn acknowledge the sovereignty or worth of the person who recognizes her.

The claim that the infant's experience of commanding others tends to flatter (or inflate) his *amour-propre* can appear to be uncomfortably close to the thesis Rousseau is intent on denying, namely, that inflamed *amour-propre* has its source in nature. If a penchant for seeking confirmation of one's worth through manipulation and domination follows more or less directly from the active principle, combined with certain fundamental features of human infancy, what sense does it make to insist that inflamed *amour-propre* is not, as it were, inscribed in human nature? One possible answer is that in the account just given, nature is not the source of inflamed *amour-propre* because the developmental process that gives rise to it relies not only on the operation of ('blind', unconscious) natural forces but also on the willed responses of (conscious, free) human agents. In other words, since discovering the pleasure in commanding depends on the compliance of adults, it is not, strictly speaking, nature's effect. Although Rousseau sometimes has in mind precisely this conception of nature (forces that work independently of conscious human intervention), this answer is not fully satisfying. To see why, consider the kind of adult participation Rousseau's account relies on: providing infants with the experiences that teach them the pleasure of domination requires of adults only that they do what nature strongly inclines them to do: to respond with compassion to the cries of helpless members of their species. The problem this raises is not that it makes the adult responses that Rousseau's account relies on unfree (and so a part of nature after all). On the contrary, human adults for Rousseau *are* free even when they are predisposed by nature to behave in certain characteristically human ways—which is to say that along with their natural inclinations humans also possess the capacity to resist those inclinations and, so, (in the present case) to choose not to respond, or even to respond maliciously, to the infant's cries. The real problem raised by an account of the infant's penchant for domination that requires only that adults behave as nature predisposes them to is that it threatens to make inflamed *amour-propre* a necessary—or at least the standard—outcome of normal human development (standard in the sense that any other outcome would be possible only if adults repudiated their own nature by refusing to act on their natural inclination to do what they can to relieve the discomfort of children who depend on them). This, too, for Rousseau would make inflamed *amour-propre* 'come from nature', and though it involves a slightly different sense of that idea from the one suggested above, he is no less committed to denying this less literal version of the claim.

Rousseau's position can avoid this problem by distinguishing between the mere ability to take pleasure in domination, on the one hand, and an enduring tendency to seek some part of one's sense of self through domination, on the other. The former, which falls short of inflamed *amour-propre*, implies that one is familiar with the pleasure to be had in commanding others and that one is therefore to a certain degree always susceptible to its lure. This, on the view Rousseau is committed to, is a typically human characteristic, one that comes from nature in the second (but not the first) sense distinguished above. The latter, in contrast, makes use of the human capacity to take pleasure in domination and, by incorporating it into the strategy by which *amour-propre* seeks to satisfy its need for recognition, turns it into the more or less entrenched disposition of an imperious or tyrannical character. This is the very essence of inflamed *amour-propre*; it is, however, by no means a necessary or standard human trait, which is to say that it does not have its source in nature in either of the senses at issue here. It is easy to see why this 'spirit of domination' is not natural in the first of these senses, but what entitles him to claim it is not the standard outcome of human development?

Rousseau's response is implicit in his remark that it is only 'if one is not careful' that infants will move from 'getting themselves assisted' to 'getting themselves served' (*E* I, 66/*OC* 4, 287). The suggestion here is that the reason the spirit of domination, a species of inflamed *amour-propre*, does not have its source in nature is that it is not an inevitable outcome of human development—or, more precisely, because there are definite measures adults can take—feasible measures that do not require superhuman wisdom or effort—that can prevent the infant's normal experience of the pleasure of commanding from burgeoning into a domineering character. The idea underlying Rousseau's view is this: if adult caregivers respond to their charges' cries in the appropriate way—among other things, one must 'distinguish in [infants'] desires what comes immediately from nature and what comes from opinion' and 'limit oneself to the really useful without granting anything to whim or to desire without reason' (*E* I, 68/*OC* 4, 290)—and (presumably) if the world they inhabit offers other, more benign opportunities for finding affirmation, then the principal species of inflamed *amour-propre* that threatens to take root in early infancy can be successfully warded off by well-considered but not extraordinary human intervention.

The birth of fury and spite

Before proceeding to the second passage of *Emile* that helps to explain why inflamed *amour-propre* is so likely to take root in the human soul, it is worth pausing briefly to consider a further, independent point in Rousseau's discussion of the psychological dangers of infancy. In addition to the will to dominate I have just discussed, Rousseau (as cited above) includes among those dangers a 'disposition ... to fury, spite, and anger' that, like the will to dominate, has its source in the infant's helplessness and need. Here is the passage that precedes and explains this claim:

When the infant cries, he is uncomfortable; he has some need he does not know how to satisfy. One examines, one seeks this need, one finds it, one provides for it. When one does not find it or when one cannot provide for it, the tears continue.

One is bothered by them ... If he persists, one gets impatient, one threatens him; brutal nurses sometimes strike him. These are strange lessons for his entrance in life.

I shall never forget having seen one of these difficult criers struck in this way by his nurse. He immediately became quiet. I believed he was intimidated. I said to myself, 'This will be a servile soul ... .' I was mistaken. The unfortunate was suffocating with anger; he had lost his breath; I saw him become violet. A moment after came sharp screams; all the signs of the resentment, fury, and despair of this age were in his accents. ... I am sure that a live ember fallen by chance on this infant's hand would have made less of an impression than this blow, light enough but delivered in the manifest intention of offending him.

(*E* I, 65–6/*OC* 4, 286–7)

This passage provides a further example of how adult responses to an infant's earliest needs help to shape the character she will develop later in life, including the form her *amour-propre* will take once it is fully aroused in adolescence. Here the effect of the caregiver's behavior is to instill in the infant not a spirit of domination or subservience but a character marked by fury and resentment. The danger represented here is not that the infant will learn to think of herself as either a commander or servant of other wills but that the hostility she encounters in her first attempts to communicate her needs to others will instill in her such a deep sense of having been deprived of her due that later in life nothing the world can offer will be able to compensate for her early loss and no amount of respect or esteem from others will be enough to satisfy her that she has received the consideration she deserves. As Rousseau points out, the natural response to this perceived stinginess of the universe (which, as Rousseau describes the case here, has its roots in *real* deprivation in infancy[22]) is enduring rage, resentment, and despair, all products of an unshakable belief in the world's inability to provide the resources required to fill one's need for standing in the eyes of others. This attitude is a species of inflamed *amour-propre*, for even though it does not presuppose an inflated or deflated sense of the position one

---

[22] That the deprivation is real and not merely perceived is important to Rousseau's account. If perceived deprivation alone were sufficient to produce a disposition to spite and fury, and if (as Klein seems to hold) infants' experience of deprivation were common, or 'natural', even when, objectively speaking, there was none, then such a disposition would be both more common and less dependent on real circumstances than the thesis of the natural goodness of humans could allow. The parallels between Rousseau's view and Klein's theory of child development are fruitfully discussed by Dent, 243–5.

deserves, it implies that no level of recognition from others will ever be experienced as enough. In such a case the longing inspired by *amour-propre* is incapable of being quenched, and this results not only in unhappiness for the furious, resentful individual but also in unyielding hostility towards all who inhabit and constitute such an unreceptive, withholding world. Although this developmental pattern is common enough, it is no more 'natural' to human beings than the spirit of domination or submission. For here, too, the birth of inflamed *amour-propre* depends on the contingent responses of free adults—which is to say, on 'artificial' human intervention that could well have taken an alternate course and produced a different outcome.

Origins of the drive to superiority

The second major passage relevant to understanding the various psychological forces that tend to foster inflamed *amour-propre* is located in Book IV, the site of Emile's entry into adolescence. In this passage Rousseau provides the resources for explaining why the desire for superior standing—indeed, the desire to be first or best—is, as it were, *amour-propre*'s default configuration.[23] Before reconstructing this argument, it is necessary to recall from Chapter 3 that not every form of the desire to outdo others, or even of the desire to be best, qualifies as inflamed (which is to say: not every form of those desires tends to produce the evils that *amour-propre* makes possible). For this reason, showing merely that normal human development naturally gives rise to the desire to be best does not constitute proof that normal human development naturally gives rise to inflamed *amour-propre*. At the same time we know that the desire for superior standing, although not sufficient by itself to produce the world's ills, is one of the most virulent sources of *amour-propre*'s power to work mischief in human affairs. The implication of the argument I am about to reconstruct, then, is not that inflamed *amour-propre* is a natural or necessary feature of human existence but only that the basic conditions of the latter make it a permanent and frequently realized possibility.

---

[23] Kant, in his appropriation of Rousseau, reverses this axiom and assumes, without providing an argument, that desire for equal status is the default condition (*Religion within the Boundaries of Mere Reason*, eds. Allen Wood and George di Giovanni (Cambridge: Cambridge University Press, 1998), 6:27). In this respect, Rousseau's less optimistic position is superior to Kant's both for purely theoretical reasons (it makes its case for human goodness tougher to prove) and as a more accurate depiction of the human condition.

That Rousseau accords something like default status to the desire to be best is evidenced by a startling, unsupported claim early in Book IV:

Since my Emile has until now looked only at himself, the first glance he casts on his fellows leads him to compare himself with them. And the first sentiment this comparison arouses in him is the desire to be in the first position. This is the point where *amour de soi* turns into *amour-propre*.

(*E* IV, 235/OC 4, 523)[24]

This passage explicitly links the birth of *amour-propre* with a particularly acute form of the desire for superior standing, the desire to be in the *first* position. If this is the first sentiment that comparison with others arouses in the adolescent, it is easy to see why *amour-propre*, generalized throughout society, is so apt to produce the conflict, misery, and other ills that Rousseau ascribes to it and why educational measures are necessary if *amour-propre* is to be prevented from taking on a destructive form. What is not clear is what entitles Rousseau to regard the desire to be best as *amour-propre*'s 'natural' starting point.

Although, once again, Rousseau provides no explicit argument for this crucial claim, the elements of such an explanation are hinted at in the opening pages of Book IV. The theme emphasized again and again in these passages is that Emile's entry into adolescence is accompanied by two major psychological developments: the birth of the passions (which is, at root, the blossoming of *amour-propre*) and the awakening of sexuality. Not surprisingly, these two developments are related, even if it is not obvious precisely how. What is surprising, though, is Rousseau's claim that Emile's *amour-propre* is awakened only now, long after his initiation as an infant into the pleasures and temptations of domination and submission. In addition to contradicting what was explicitly asserted in Book I—that the infant's experience of domination 'awakens and flatters [his] *amour-propre*' (*E* I, 68/OC 4, 289)—this claim is also belied by the arguments developed in the same parts of Book IV in which it is made. For in attempting to explain how the adolescent's *amour-propre* is born—how it originates as a 'modification' of *amour de soi* (*E* IV, 213/OC 4, 491)—Rousseau finds himself forced to rehearse developments that take place in infancy and

---

[24] For help with the claim that '*amour de soi* turns into *amour-propre*,' see Ch. 1, n. 27 and the paragraphs in the text surrounding this note.

that therefore properly belong to the subject matter of Book I. In other words, Rousseau discovers in Book IV that he is unable to explain the birth of either sexuality or *amour-propre* without tracing each back to the experiences of infancy.[25] While it is clear that Rousseau's text asserts a deep connection between *amour-propre*, sexuality, and the desire to be first in the eyes of others, and that all these phenomena are recognized as being rooted somehow in infancy, unraveling the twisted strands of his account is difficult.

It may be helpful to recall that the same interconnected themes arose in the account of *amour-propre*'s origin in the Second Discourse, where the desire for standing in the eyes of others made its first appearance in the guise of a wish to be regarded as the best singer or dancer, which itself followed directly on the development of enduring sexual attachments that included preferring the object of one's love above all others (*DI*, 165–6/*OC* 3, 169). The suggestion there seemed to be that the desire to be first for others was parasitic on a more primitive, other-directed type of preference, namely, awarding first place in one's sentiments to a highly specific object of sexual love. The same claim reappears, more explicitly, in Book IV of *Emile*. In the middle of explaining where *amour-propre* (in 'the form we believe natural to it') comes from, Rousseau enters into a discussion of sexual love and explicitly traces the desire to be first for another back to the sentiments of preference that a lover feels for his beloved:

[When one loves,] one wants to obtain the preference one grants. Love must be reciprocal. To be loved, one has to make oneself lovable. To be preferred, one has to make oneself more lovable than another, more lovable than every other, at least in the eyes of the beloved object. This is the source of the first glances at one's fellows; this is the source of the first comparisons with them; this is the source of emulation, rivalries, and jealousy.

(*E* IV, 214/*OC* 4, 494)

The point made here seems plausible enough: if I love you above all others, I cannot be satisfied unless you feel the same way towards me,[26] and this

---

[25] See the four paragraphs immediately following the claim that *amour-propre* is born (in the adolescent) out of *amour de soi* and preceding his extended discussion of the birth of sexuality (*E* IV, 213–14/*OC* 4, 491–3).

[26] The same holds for esteem: 'We want to be esteemed by the people we esteem, and as long as I could judge men, or at least some men, favorably, the judgments they held about me could not be uninteresting to me' (*RSW*, 71/*OC* 1, 1077).

inspires in me an impassioned concern for how (in your eyes) I measure up to my possible competitors and whether (in your eyes) I surpass them. The problem with this explanation is that its reach is too short: it explains the desire to be first in terms of a prior preference for another but leaves that initial preference itself unaccounted for. What this argument, as it stands here, fails to explain is where the impetus to prefer someone else above all others comes from.

In the Second Discourse no such explanation is provided. That the natural sexual drive should lead individuals to focus their affections jealously on a single object (so as to prefer one person above all others) is left unexplained—or, rather, explained only lamely, as the result of habit and 'mutual frequentation' (*DI*, 165/*OC* 3, 169). In *Emile*, however, where it is not the history of the human race but the history of an individual that is at issue, it is possible to detect the hint of such an explanation, and, not coincidentally, it occurs at the very moment at which Rousseau finds himself compelled to return to the subject of infancy. Unfortunately, capturing the complex movement of ideas in this part of Rousseau's text requires a fair bit of stage-setting.

Ostensibly Rousseau revisits the topic of infancy in Book IV in order to explain the birth of *amour-propre* in general, which he takes to be equivalent to showing how *amour-propre* arises out of—as a 'modification of'—the infant's *amour de soi*. (Note, once again, how difficult it is to take seriously the claim that Emile's *amour-propre* first comes into existence in adolescence.) Here is the explanation Rousseau offers in response to the question of how an innate concern for one's own non-relative and (initially) merely physical well-being is transformed into a passion to achieve a good that is comparative and moral (mind- or opinion-dependent), namely, comparative standing in the eyes of others:

Amour de soi-même is always good and always in conformity with order. Since each person is specially entrusted with his own preservation [or, better, his own non-relative good], the first and most important of his cares is and ought to be to watch over it constantly. And how could he watch over it if he did not take the greatest interest in it?

Therefore, we have to love ourselves to preserve ourselves; and it follows immediately from the same sentiment that we love what preserves us. Every infant is attached to his nurse.... At first this attachment is purely mechanical. What fosters the well-being of an individual attracts him; what harms him repels him. This is merely a blind instinct. What transforms this instinct into sentiment, attachment into love, aversion into hate, is the intention manifested to harm us or to be useful to us. One is never passionate about insensible beings, which merely follow the impulsion given to them. But those from whom one expects good or ill by their inner disposition, by their will—those we see acting freely for us or against us—inspire in us sentiments similar to those they manifest toward us. We seek what serves us, but we love what wants to serve us.

(*E* IV, 213/*OC* 4, 491–2)

The most striking thing about this passage is that while it shows how love of others (of those who care for one's earliest needs) can grow out of the infant's original love of self (*amour de soi*), it does not, contrary to what we are given to expect, explain how *amour-propre* enters the infant's psyche. Nor does it go on to do so in any straightforward way. Instead, Rousseau's text appears to wander off from its supposed aim to end in a brief discussion of the spirit of benevolence to which children are said to be 'naturally inclined' (*E* IV, 213/*OC* 4, 492). Where in all of this is the birth of *amour-propre*? Perhaps the most that can be inferred from these meanderings with confidence is that tracing the origin of *amour-propre* (and its companion, sexuality) requires going back to infancy and to the intense dependence and love that are its chief characteristics. Although Rousseau does not pronounce the thought explicitly, the text's not fully transparent juxtaposition of infantile dependence, adolescent sexuality, the birth of *amour-propre*, and the infant's 'first love' strongly suggests that adult sexuality, as well as *amour-propre* itself, are in some way the effects of that earliest, all-important bond between the helpless infant and her first provider.

Here, I submit, are the missing parts of the story Rousseau is struggling to tell: the infant's first love for another person is crucial to the birth of *amour-propre* because of the way in which all love—including love of self—implies a valuation of the loved object on the part of the one who loves. This point is implicit in the distinction Rousseau draws between the infant's merely 'mechanical' attraction to what promotes his well-being and the love he feels for the persons who appear to benefit him voluntarily, 'by their inner disposition'. What explains the infant's love for those who *want* to serve him is that their demonstrated intention to attend to his needs stands as a sign that he occupies an important place in their sentiments.

Finding his needs freely administered to by someone else is the infant's first experience of being recognized by another as a subject of value. At first, being valued by others takes on so urgent a significance for the infant because of its intimate connection to the needs of self-preservation. The recognition of others becomes a matter of (literally) vital importance to the infant because, painfully aware of his utter dependence on adults, he 'knows' that finding their favor is, in his circumstances, a matter of life or death. (No doubt this very early perception of the connection between love and physical survival explains a good deal of the franticness with which, even as adults, many of us seek the good opinion of others.) But, like the will to dominate discussed earlier, the desire to be valued detaches itself eventually from the drives of *amour de soi* and establishes itself as an independent psychological force that promises a kind of satisfaction in its own right, distinct from the pleasures of physical well-being. This marks the true birth of *amour-propre* as an independent passion.[27]

Yet, despite its eventual independence, *amour-propre* is properly regarded as an outgrowth, or modification, of *amour de soi*, and this in two senses. First, as we have just seen, the attraction of *amour-propre*'s distinctive object, the good opinion of others, is initially undistinguished from and dependent on the infant's overriding concern to satisfy the self-preservative needs of *amour de soi*. Second, and no less important, *amour-propre* can be seen as merely taking up the basic imperative of *amour de soi*—to seek one's own good—and extending it to a new domain of (essentially intersubjective) goods that opens itself up to human beings whenever social bonds are established among them. Both species of self-love are forms of self-interestedness (or concern for self), but the good that *amour-propre* seeks—and hence the self it seeks to benefit—is of a fundamentally different type from *amour de soi*'s: insofar as a person is moved by *amour-propre*, the object of her concern is not her absolute (non-relative) good but rather her selfhood-for-others, which is to say, the standing she possesses for, and in comparison with, those of her own kind. As Dent formulates this

---

[27] To be precise, all that has been established here is that the infant comes to care about his standing in the eyes of others. This makes his self-love relative in one sense (it is his self as others perceive it that he is concerned with) but not yet relative in the further sense that *amour-propre* requires (that the standing he seeks is defined in comparison with others'). But for reasons I explain immediately below, in the developments described here the second sort of relativity appears simultaneously with the first; hence it is correct to speak already of the birth of *amour-propre*.

point: *amour-propre* is nothing but 'the form that our innate concern ... to do well ... for ourselves takes (our *amour de soi*) ... when we have regard to ourselves in our standing and place with other people.'[28]

Although these points clarify the developmental connection between the infant's first love for another and the birth of *amour-propre*, they do not yet explain why, engendered in these circumstances, *amour-propre* typically takes the form of a desire to be first or best. Rousseau's texts provide resources for reconstructing two distinct but compatible answers to this question. The first of these traces the reason that wanting to be best is the default configuration of *amour-propre* back to a basic feature of the sentiment from which that passion originates, *amour de soi*. The claim here is that the 'preferring ourselves to others' (E IV, 214/OC 4, 493) that is at the core of the infant's desire to be first derives from a preference for self that is already implicit in *amour de soi*. Even though Rousseau does not make this claim explicitly, it is suggested by the terms he uses to characterize the attitude to self and others that *amour de soi* implies. Consider the following description of the inhabitant of the (hypothetical) original state of nature, who is moved by *amour de soi* and pity but not yet by *amour-propre*:

as long as he does not resist the inner impulse of commiseration [or pity], he will never harm another man or even any sentient being, except in the legitimate case where, his preservation being involved, he is obliged to give preference to himself.

(DI, 197/OC 3, 126)

What this quotation makes clear is that even non-relative self-love incorporates a form of loving oneself *more than others* (or preference for self). Although this aspect of *amour de soi* manifests itself only rarely, it surfaces nonetheless in situations where a zero-sum conflict of basic interests arises among self-loving individuals: when my survival is incompatible with yours, it becomes clear that even in the absence of *amour-propre* there is a sense in which I love myself more than you. (The quotation mentions only cases in which preservation itself is at stake, but the same would also

---

[28] Dent, 56. Chitty makes a similar point when he says that '*amour-propre* is essentially a concern for the preservation of the self as it is conceived by others' (37n16), an insight he attributes to John Charvet, *The Social Problem in the Philosophy of Rousseau* (London: Cambridge University Press, 1974).

hold for less urgent zero-sum conflicts, as long as the pain that deprivation would cause me is at least equal to the pain that deprivation would cause you.) If the infant's *amour-propre* is merely *amour de soi* extended to a new conception of the self and its good, then it is only to be expected that the self-preference implicit in the latter will carry over to the former and characterize it as well. As soon as individuals begin to define their well-being in comparative terms—which is to say, as soon as they are moved by *amour-propre*—situations in which one person's good comes at the expense of another's are greatly multiplied, and this makes it 'natural' to assume the attitude that doing well for oneself implies doing better than everyone else.

It is important to see that this element of self-preference does not make *amour de soi* a relative sentiment in the sense in which I have used that term to describe *amour-propre*. For it remains the case that the good sought by *amour de soi* is defined absolutely rather than in relation to how well others fare with respect to similar goods. This means that, in contrast to *amour-propre*, there is nothing intrinsic to *amour de soi*'s aims that makes my level of satisfaction depend on the success or failure of those around me; in the case of *amour de soi*, it is only under rare conditions of external scarcity that my gain translates directly into your loss.

The second possibility for explaining why newly awakened *amour-propre* tends to take the form of a desire to be best is hinted at in the text even more obliquely than the first. Although Rousseau shows no signs of avowing this explanation himself, the passages I have been considering provide all the resources we need to reconstruct it ourselves. This explanation, unlike the first, picks up on a point from my earlier discussion of Rousseau's apparent wish to draw connections between *amour-propre*, sexuality, and the infant's desire to be first in the eyes of others. We know from that discussion that, in some moments at least, Rousseau wants to explain this desire as the consequence of the 'first place' that someone in love accords to his beloved. (When one loves, 'one wants to obtain the preference one grants.') Rousseau makes these claims while discussing adult (or adolescent) sexual love, but if we take seriously the constant juxtaposition of infancy and sexuality in the opening pages of Book IV, we need to ask whether the infant's first love for another might not anticipate and explain this feature of adult love. Our question, then, is whether the developmental story rehearsed above can help to explain why in his first love for another the infant is bound to accord 'first place' to the object of his affections and, as a consequence of that, to demand that he, too, be first in his beloved's eyes.

Is there, then, some feature of the infant's condition that accounts for his according 'first place' to another and for his wanting in return not just some measure of love or approval but passionate, exclusive love that allows no room for equal standing with others? Once again, the key to reconstructing Rousseau's position lies in taking note of the importance he ascribes to human dependence. Since nowhere is this dependence more acute than in infancy, it should come as no surprise if the reason for the infant's according 'first place' to the object of his love were traceable back to this 'first condition of man' (his 'want and weakness') (*E* I, 65/*OC* 4, 286). In this context the significance of the infant's thoroughgoing dependence lies in the immense importance his caregiver—let us call her 'Mom'[29]—is bound to assume for him. The infant's awareness of his near-complete dependence on Mom for everything he needs, including survival itself, means that she inevitably becomes 'the whole world' to him,[30] for without her beneficence there would be, quite literally, no world for him. If he is not in turn the whole world to her—or so it must seem to the helpless infant—his very existence becomes imperiled, and so the faintest hint that Mom's affections might have other objects as well is sufficient to evoke in him a profound anxiety that manifests itself in strident possessiveness and a fierce jealousy of all potential rivals for her love (including, especially, other family members). It is because of the vital importance she holds for him, then, that the infant demands to be the only one Mom loves or, at the very least, the one Mom clearly loves best (which is to say: this is why the infant seeks so desperately 'to obtain the preference [he] grants'). On this account, it is his *amour de soi* and extreme helplessness, working

[29] My use of 'Mom' in this context implies that Rousseau thinks it 'natural' that infants have a single primary caregiver and that that caregiver be his mother. In spite of remarks that appear to exclude Emile's parents from participating in his upbringing (e.g. *E* I, 52/*OC* 4, 267), Rousseau usually seems to accept these assumptions about the role of mothers. On the text's very first page he asserts that the child's 'first education belongs incontestably to women' (*E* I, 37n/*OC* 4, 245n), and he emphasizes the importance of mothers throughout most of Book I (e.g. *E* I, 46–7/*OC* 4, 257–9). Since Rousseau assumes rather than argues for the naturalness of these conventions, it would be worth asking whether they do in fact 'accord with nature' and whether different arrangements might affect his claim that wanting to be first is *amour-propre*'s normal starting point.

[30] These are the terms Sartre uses to characterize the attitude of the (adult) lover to his beloved: 'in love the lover wants to be "the whole world" for the beloved' (479).

WHY INFLAMED *AMOUR-PROPRE* IS SO COMMON   149

against the backdrop of the imagined consequences of abandonment, that, under entirely normal conditions, conspire to bring the infant to identify his well-being with occupying first place in the eyes of another, thereby making the achievement of such preeminence *amour-propre*'s default aim.

Locating the source of the desire to be first in the needy infant's attitude towards his mother—the element of exclusive preference is said to come from *his* regard *for her*—does not contradict Rousseau's earlier claim that the infant's love for his caregiver develops only in response to his perception of her love for him as demonstrated by her apparently intentional acts of beneficence.[31] It remains true on this account that love for another, as opposed to mere ('mechanical') attachment, is first evoked in the infant by his experience of the other's love for him. Even before his love is awakened, however, his neediness and dependence are acute, and his attachment to the external power that administers to his needs already possesses a furious intensity—that power already counts as 'the whole world to him'—even before it is transformed into love. Once that transformation occurs, the intensity of his original attachment is carried over to the love he feels for his mother (and is no doubt heightened by the fact that now his worth in the eyes of another is also at stake). That he feels love rather than mere attachment is due to the acts of another (or, more accurately, to his perception of them[32]), but his demand to be first in her love comes from his own, not necessarily mistaken fantasy of the consequences that losing his beloved's favor would have.

Let us pause now to see where this inquiry into the factors that tend to foster inflamed *amour-propre* has brought us. Its general conclusion is that although

[31] The Bible expresses the same point in relation to humans' love for God: 'We love him because he first loved us' (1 John 4:19).

[32] It might be wondered where the real difference lies if both factors—the mother's aid and the consequences of abandonment—are colored by the infant's perception or imagination: isn't the mother's benevolence as much a product of the infant's fantasy as his perception of what will happen to him if she is not there? (Something close to this thought lies at the heart of Klein's theory of development.) It might be countered that the first of these factors is more narrowly constrained by reality than the second since the infant's real experience of the mother's responsiveness to his needs is destined to impinge on his beliefs about her, whereas, for most infants at least, real abandonment is never experienced; (or, rather, the moments he experiences as abandonment—whenever his caregiver fails to anticipate, discern, or respond to his needs—do not in fact have the drastic consequences he expects). The plausibility of this response depends, of course, on the extent to which infants' fantasies are susceptible to correction by reality.

inflamed *amour-propre* is not a necessary consequence of human nature, there are several more or less fundamental conditions of human existence that tend naturally (in the absence of remedial human intervention) to produce that result. These conditions include both social circumstances (the division of labor, private property, advances in productivity) and features of normal human psychological development (the infant's dependence and inability to speak; the birth of *amour-propre* and love for others; the vicissitudes of *amour de soi* and the active principle). In Rousseau's view, his account of the source of human ills exonerates human nature—and, by extension, its creator—because in each case the circumstances that generate inflamed *amour-propre* are not necessary consequences of human (or non-human) nature but the effects, to a significant degree, of free human action that might have had, and could in the future have, different results. This is clearer perhaps in the case of the social conditions, where it is relatively easy to see the division of labor, the rules of property, and improved methods of production as contingent results of human actions and as subject to modification by further human intervention in the form of consciously devised social policies. But the same is true of the psychological conditions, which in each case produce inflamed *amour-propre* only in the event that free, adult human beings respond in certain avoidable ways to the circumstances of child-rearing: the spirit of domination takes hold of a child's character only if her caregivers fail to distinguish her needs from her whims and to respond appropriately to each; a child develops a disposition to spite and anger only if her cries for assistance are met with impatience and violence; and even though the desire to be first may be *amour-propre*'s 'natural' starting point, its degeneration into inflamed *amour-propre* can be forestalled by the right educational measures.

Even though this multidimensional account of the sources of inflamed *amour-propre* in some sense exonerates human nature, it does not in the end yield an optimistic view of human existence. For the number and complexity of the conditions that tend to inflame *amour-propre* imply that unless human beings can hit on just the right combination of judicious responses to those conditions, enslavement, conflict, vice, misery, and alienation are destined to be their lot. As I suggested above, however, regardless of how pessimistic Rousseau's position may be, it does assert that a solution to the problems posed by *amour-propre* is in principle possible in the world we inhabit (which is to say, possible within the constraints imposed by human nature itself, as well as by the basic features of the human condition). From the preceding account of the sources of inflamed *amour-propre* it is possible to discern the rough contours of the twofold task Rousseau faces in devising such a solution: in his social and political philosophy he must find a way of restructuring institutions that preserves the positive aspects of specialization, property, and efficient production while minimizing their tendency to produce the familiar ills of civilization; in his philosophy of education he must, above all,[33] find a way of forming children's characters that substantially reins in their drive to occupy the first position while granting it certain limited, benign modes of expression.

[33] This statement of the task of Rousseau's educational philosophy leaves out two of the three opportunities for remedial intervention I drew attention to above: distinguishing between an infant's needs and whims, and avoiding impatience and violence in response to his cries. But this reflects the fact that *Emile* focuses almost exclusively on the third problem (taming the desire to be first), which is the main concern of its lengthy Book IV.

PART III
Prescription

5

Social and Domestic Remedies

The aim of this chapter is to determine what solutions might exist to the numerous problems that *amour-propre* imposes on human existence. Equipped with a systematic understanding of *amour-propre*'s dangers, we are now in a position to consider whether, or to what extent, those dangers can be averted by the right kind of ('artificial') human intervention. Given what we now know about why *amour-propre* tends to engender enslavement, conflict, vice, misery, and alienation, what, if anything, can be done to avoid them? Answering this question requires reconstructing Rousseau's view of how the social and political world, together with the characters of those who inhabit it, must be configured if the dangers posed by *amour-propre* are to be avoided or minimized. In the first section of this chapter I discuss Rousseau's account of how good social and political institutions can hold the development of inflamed *amour-propre* in check. In the second section I examine how the same end is achieved by Emile's domestic education.

It should be clear by now that Rousseau does not endorse the most obvious response to these problems: simply extirpating or suppressing the passion responsible for them. As I have argued, Rousseau believes that the tendency to care about one's relative standing in the eyes of others is unavoidable in creatures with our natural capacities once they have established enduring social relations, which is to say: *amour-propre* is ineliminable in *human* beings. This implies that any attempt to avoid the evils of *amour-propre* by eradicating it from the characters of humans—by educating them, say, not to care about others' opinions of their worth—is destined to be both futile and oppressive. Moreover, as I argue in the following two chapters, Rousseau holds that even if the extirpation of *amour-propre* were possible, it would be undesirable, since success in this undertaking would destroy the very condition of nearly everything that makes human existence valuable.

It is necessary to underscore these points again here since, despite clear and abundant evidence that Rousseau rejects this strategy, it is not uncommon to find commentators who read him as making the eradication of *amour-propre* the goal of Emile's education. This view is implicit in the widespread belief that Emile's tutor aims at ridding his charge of all dependence on the opinion of others—at enabling him, in other words, to achieve a sense of his own worth (a sentiment of his own existence) without relying on affirmation from without.[1] It is also implicit in the commonly held view that Rousseau exhorts us to return to some version of the state of nature as depicted in the Second Discourse. But, as I have argued at length, these claims are neither philosophically tenable nor interpretively plausible.[2] Rousseau clearly recognizes that a being so perfectly self-sufficient with respect to his sense of his own worth would be a monster or a god—at any rate not a *human* being.[3]

Yet if we accept the ineradicability of *amour-propre*—together with its implication that dependence on others for the sentiment of one's own existence is unavoidable for humans—what stance are we to take to Rousseau's depressingly persuasive account of *amour-propre*'s dangers? It might be thought that the only response available to Rousseau is a lucid pessimism that, while asserting the intractability of *amour-propre*'s malignant powers, at least affords the consolation of clear insight into why the human condition is as desperate as it is—why we cannot help but pursue what is bound to be bad for us—rather than resorting to mystical non-explanations of the sort offered by the Christian thesis of original sin.[4] Although this way of reading Rousseau is both more interesting and more textually sound

---

[1] Allan Bloom, for example, in his introduction to *Emile*, claims that 'the primary intention of [Emile's] education is to prevent *amour de soi* from turning into *amour-propre*' (*E*, 10) and that the tutor's aim is to make Emile 'intellectually and morally self-sufficient' (*E*, 27).

[2] 'I would find someone who wanted to prevent the birth of the passions almost as mad as someone who wanted to annihilate them; and those who believed that this was my project ... would surely have understood me very badly' (*E* IV, 212/*OC* 4, 491); see also *E* IV, 215/*OC* 4, 494.

[3] 'Every attachment is a sign of insufficiency. If each of us had no need of others, he would hardly think of uniting himself with them. Thus from our very infirmity is born our frail happiness. A truly happy being is a solitary being. God alone enjoys an absolute happiness. But who among us has the idea of it?' (*E* IV, 221/*OC* 4, 503). And recall Rousseau's own unsuccessful attempt to rid himself of the desire for affirmation from others (*RSW*, 71, 73/*OC* 1, 1077, 1079).

[4] A further possibility is that although the problems engendered by *amour-propre* are in principle eradicable, they are no longer so *for us*. Rousseau himself suggests this possibility: 'It is to the task of discovering what it would be necessary to do in order to prevent [men] from becoming [evil] that I dedicated my [*Emile*]. I did not claim that such a thing was absolutely possible in the present order' (LCB, 29/*OC* 4, 937). This possibility, while offering no more hope to us than the more pessimistic

than the one dismissed above, it fits badly with the fact that two of his central texts—*Emile* and the *Social Contract*—appear, at any rate, to propose social, political, and educational remedies to the problems so masterfully depicted in the Second Discourse and elsewhere. It is possible, of course, that this appearance is deceptive. It might be, for example, that the various remedies Rousseau seems to recommend are so obviously impracticable in themselves or so clearly in tension with one another that they demand to be read as arguments for the impossibility of averting *amour-propre*'s dangers. At times Rousseau seems to encourage such a reading, nowhere more prominently than in the opening pages of *Emile*, where he emphasizes the necessity of choosing between 'two contrary forms of instruction': domestic education, which forms children into men (*hommes*) and public education, which makes them into citizens (*citoyens*) (*E* I, 39–42/*OC* 4, 248–52). Although Rousseau provides plenty of indications that he takes Emile's education to negotiate successfully the tension between being a man and being a citizen[5]—at its end, for example, the 'man' Emile is prepared for citizenship by his tutor's recital of a condensed version of the *Social Contract* (*E* V, 458–69/*OC* 4, 836–52)[6]—interpretive considerations alone cannot settle the question of most interest here, namely, whether Rousseau's texts give us good reasons to believe that such a resolution is possible. Rather than attempt to determine in advance how seriously Rousseau's remedies are meant to be taken, I propose that we first assume them to be offered in earnest in order to see what a straightforward examination of their merits reveals about the possibility of a human world where the harmful potential of *amour-propre* is for the most part held in check.

The solutions Rousseau offers to the problems of *amour-propre* fall into two broad categories: those focusing on the restructuring of social and political institutions and those that concern the education, or formation, of individual character. That Rousseau envisages a two-pronged approach

reading, would at least be compatible with the goodness of God's creation since fallenness, though practically irreversible once it occurs, would not be a necessary outcome of human history.

[5] In fact, Rousseau's claim is that 'one cannot make both [man and citizen] *at the same time*' (*E* I, 39/*OC* 4, 248; emphasis added), which explains why Emile's formation into a man precedes, but does not preclude, his formation as a citizen. I expand on this and related issues in the final section of this chapter.

[6] See also *E* IV, 455/*OC* 4, 833: 'Now that Emile has considered himself in his physical relations with other beings and in his moral relations with other men, it remains for him to consider himself in his civil relations with his fellow citizens.'

to the ills of inflamed *amour-propre* is underscored by the fact that, with only a bit of overlap, he consigns these solutions to separate books: the first to the *Social Contract*, the second to *Emile*.[7] The thought behind this dual approach is that although both factors—a society's basic institutions and how the individuals within them are privately raised—influence which forms the quest for recognition will take in a given society, neither by itself is sufficient to forestall the dangers of inflamed *amour-propre*. In other words, making *amour-propre* benign requires not only that certain social and political institutions be in place but also that individuals come to those institutions with the appropriate desires, ends, and self-conceptions.

It is important not to misconstrue what distinguishes these two projects. Despite *Emile*'s subtitle—*On Education*—the difference is not precisely between measures that shape the subjectivity of individuals, on the one hand, and those that shape external, 'objective' social conditions, on the other. For, as Rousseau clearly recognizes, social institutions, too, play a major role in forming their participants' characters. To cite just the most prominent example of this principle: the particular ways individuals seek to satisfy their *amour-propre* vary widely depending on what opportunities for recognition their social institutions encourage and permit. A society that limits disparities in wealth will generate different recognitive aspirations in its members from one whose economic system feeds on and celebrates the desire to be 'filthy rich'; a social order based on inherited class privileges will encourage individuals to find their sense of self differently from one that recognizes each person as entitled by nature to the same basic rights as all others. This means that social and political institutions have an educative function in the broadest sense of the term. In this case, though, where does the difference between Rousseau's two projects lie?

The answer is not simply that *Emile* has *more* to say about character formation than the *Social Contract*—though, of course, it does—but rather that it concerns itself with a specific kind of education that falls outside the bounds of social and political theory. The first thing to note in this regard is that Emile's education begins in infancy and ends with adulthood, whereas the formative measures at issue in the *Social Contract* endure over the course

---

[7] It would be foolish to insist that these tasks are as neatly divided between the two texts as I suggest here. Apart from a certain unavoidable overlap between them, Rousseau's vision of a rational social and political order is also expounded in works other than the *Social Contract*, including *PE*, *LWM*, *PCC*, and *GP*.

of individuals' lives and are directed mainly at those who are already full members of their society's institutions. The thought here is that since it is only as adults that humans take their place in the social world—as citizens, as producers, as buyers and sellers—the formative consequences of social institutions will affect individuals who are, in one sense, already formed. In other words, when humans first enter the social world as full participants, they bring with them beliefs, aspirations, and self-conceptions that are the results of long and complex learning processes undergone during their 'formative' years. It is this 'first education' that *Emile* takes as its object (*E* I, 37n/*OC* 4, 245n), and this marks the principal difference between the educational projects undertaken in the two parts of Rousseau's remedial response to the problem of inflamed *amour-propre*.

It is not, however, merely because *Emile* addresses the education of those who are not yet full members of society's institutions that it falls outside the domain of social and political theory. There are other, weightier reasons as well, and they come to light in the distinction Rousseau draws between domestic and public education. The main idea behind this distinction is that whereas public education is 'common' (undertaken by the community and the same for everyone) and seeks to produce 'citizens',[8] domestic education is 'individual' (*particulière*) and seeks to produce 'men' (*E* I, 40/*OC* 4, 250). On this formulation of the distinction, domestic and public education differ along two dimensions, each of which marks an important difference between the two types of education.

The more important of these dimensions concerns the endpoint, or goal, of the education in question—specifically, whether its aim is to produce citizens or men. Of these two goals, one clearly derives from social and political theory: forming a child into a citizen entails instilling in him the character traits he needs in order to be able freely to endorse or affirm the general will—or, what is the same, to take the good of his political community as his own. Achieving this goal, Rousseau thinks, requires that social institutions 'take [man's] absolute existence from him in order to give him a relative one and transport the *I* into the common unity, with the result that each individual no longer believes himself one but a part of the unity and is no longer perceptible (*sensible*) except within the whole'

---

[8] Prime examples of public education are the educational institutions of Sparta and those Plato recommends in the *Republic* (*E* I, 40/*OC* 4, 249–50).

(*E* I, 40/*OC* 4, 249). In contrast to this, Emile's domestic education finds its goal independently of social and political theory. Its aim is not to make Emile into a bearer of the general will but to form him into a man—that is, into someone who exists 'for himself' rather than merely 'for others', someone whose being as a self has sources independent of his membership in a communal body (*E* I, 39–40/*OC* 4, 248–50). (In addition to this rather vague description, being a man is said to include 'being oneself', 'acting as one speaks', being 'decisive in making one's choice', and 'sticking to' the choices one makes (*E* I, 40/*OC* 4, 250).) It is this difference in goals that gives rise to the possibility contemplated by Rousseau at the beginning of *Emile* that the two forms of education might be incompatible. What is of interest now, though, is not whether the two can be reconciled but what the tension between them says about the necessity of waging a two-pronged attack on *amour-propre*'s harmful potential. As I argued in the Introduction to this book, Rousseau's insistence that Emile's education be domestic rather than public is an expression of his view that there are ideals that ought to govern human lives beyond the principal educative aim of political theory, namely, making individuals into reliable willers of the general will. This is because attending only to this aim is compatible with forms of education that make citizens into vehicles of the general will at the expense of their individuality, their integrity, their (relative) independence as a source of their own being as a self. One of the purposes of Emile's domestic education is to rule out this possible outcome.

The second dimension along which domestic and public education differ is closely related to the first and may even follow from it. This difference concerns not the goal of education but the kind of social space in which it takes place. Here again it is important not to misdescribe the difference at issue. In spite of the fact that *Emile*'s project lies outside the domain of social and political theory, it would not be correct to say simply that one of these educations is social while the other is not. This is because Emile's domestic education is clearly social in at least a broad sense of that term: it depends on an enduring, substantive relationship between two individuals. But if Emile's education is social in this broad sense, it is still domestic rather than public. For it takes place within the confines of a private and very small association that educates in relative independence from the watch and influence of society at large. The question is: why must Emile's education be domestic in this sense? One reason, no doubt, is that if it were not—if it were organized by the state and designed to be implemented en masse—it would inevitably tend to favor the interests of society over those of individual selves and end up producing citizens at the expense of creating men. But there is a further reason as well, one with profound implications for my project here: Emile's removal from the larger society during his formative years is crucial to his tutor's efforts to prevent inflamed *amour-propre* from gaining a foothold in the young boy's character. The idea behind this prominent and perplexing feature of Emile's education is that living in society can only intensify and multiply the temptations to which *amour-propre* gives rise and, so, thwart domestic education's aim of molding the passion to count as someone for others in such a way that it furthers rather than impedes human flourishing. Grasping the full significance of the privacy of domestic education is too large a task to be undertaken now; I return to this topic later when examining more closely how this part of Rousseau's remedial strategy is designed to help solve the problems created by *amour-propre*. For the moment it is sufficient simply to note the domestic, or private, character of Emile's education and to recognize it as marking an important difference between Rousseau's project in *Emile*, on the one hand, and that of his social and political theory, on the other.

Social and political remedies

The first step in articulating Rousseau's view of how social and political institutions can be structured so as to check the development of inflamed *amour-propre* is to acknowledge that his main political writings, above all the *Social Contract*, appear not to take the problems posed by *amour-propre* as a major concern. When Rousseau formulates the fundamental problem of political philosophy,[9] for example, he names freedom (and its opposite, enslavement) as his main concern, not the need for recognition. Nevertheless, once one has traced the problem of *amour-propre* through *Emile* and the Second Discourse, it is not difficult to see that significant

---

[9] The fundamental problem to be solved by the social contract is said to be: 'To find a form of association that defends and protects the person and goods of each associate with all the common force, and by means of which each, uniting with all, nevertheless obeys only himself and remains as free as before' (*SC*, I.6.iv).

aspects of that problem are also addressed by the social and political measures endorsed in the *Social Contract*.[10] Indeed, the basic outline of Rousseau's socio-political strategy for holding *amour-propre* in check can be read more or less directly from the Second Discourse's account, reconstructed in Chapter 4, of the social conditions under which inflamed *amour-propre* comes to dominate human life. According to that account, four features of civilization in general—increased productivity, the division of labor, private property, and the flourishing of individual differences—contribute to the inflammation of *amour-propre* by allowing inequalities in wealth and power to take root in human society, which are then exploited by *amour-propre* in its quest to achieve standing relative to others. In addition to these four factors, two background conditions aid the spread of inflamed *amour-propre*: the absence of other, less destructive ways of acquiring a socially recognized standing and ignorance of the nature and conditions of human well-being. Because the latter problem is addressed primarily by the educational project of *Emile*, Rousseau's socio-political response to the evils of *amour-propre* are guided by just two main goals: countering the socially pernicious inequalities that the process of civilization tends to bring with it, and promoting institutions that make stable and benign forms of social recognition available to all. Since the first of these goals cannot reasonably be achieved by simply eradicating inequality—this would also abolish the conditions of civilization more generally—Rousseau's remedy focuses on imposing substantial limits on both the extent and kinds of inequality that society can permit. Its guiding principle is to minimize the opportunities available to *amour-propre* for seeking satisfaction through forms of superior standing that tend to impede the society-wide achievement of peace, happiness, virtue, freedom, and unalienated selfhood.

Limiting social inequality

Rousseau's approach to the problem of inequality is best illustrated by two examples, one of which points to a kind of inequality his social philosophy rules out altogether, while the other illustrates limits imposed on a kind of inequality that Rousseau thinks cannot be fruitfully eliminated but

---

[10] An excellent discussion of this topic that goes beyond my own is found in Viroli, 191–6. On other issues, too, Viroli's book is an exceptionally sophisticated and reliable treatment of Rousseau's political thought.

only held in check. One type of inequality the *Social Contract* appears to be committed to prohibiting entirely is what Marx, in his extension of Rousseau's project, calls *class* inequality.[11] As Marx conceives it, class is an economic category defined by the relation individuals have to the means of production: one class owns (or controls) the material resources necessary for production, while the other does not; (or, to be exact, its members own no productive forces beyond their own labor power). The problem with class inequality for Marx[12] is not that it implies disparities in wealth or resources that are objectionable in themselves but rather that it institutionalizes a fundamental asymmetry in an important species of social power and, so, makes the relations between classes into relations of subjugation or domination (or, as Marx would say, exploitation). More precisely, the very condition that distinguishes the classes in capitalism—ownership of the means of production—is what compels one class to labor regularly for the benefit of the other (that is, to produce according to terms that yield surplus value only for the property-owning class). This represents an asymmetry in power because one class, which is free from the compulsion to work, reproduces—and enriches—itself by organizing, commanding, and profiting from the labor of the other.

Even though Rousseau lacks Marx's precisely defined concept of class, the division of society into those who own productive forces, such as land, and those who do not is an important part of the increase in human dependence that the Second Discourse chronicles and laments (*DI*, 167/ *OC* 3, 171). A class system, unlike the material division of labor, represents for Rousseau (as for Marx) a species of dependence that is both inimical to freedom and avoidable, and for this reason he is committed to its abolition. Moreover, the same principle Marx relies on in criticizing class inequality is endorsed more or less explicitly in the *Social Contract* and implicitly in the Second Discourse's account of the origin of human enslavement. In the former Rousseau asserts that 'no citizen should be so opulent that he can buy another, and none so poor that he is compelled to sell himself' (*SC*, II.11.ii); in the latter he suggests the same point when he singles out private property in land (a productive force) as the true source of

---

[11] For a discussion of this theme in Rousseau, see Andrew Levine, *The Politics of Autonomy* (Amherst, Mass.: University of Massachusetts Press, 1976), ch. 5.

[12] Or one of them, since alienation from the species essence is also a consequence of class inequality.

the 'crimes, wars, ... miseries and horrors' that plague the human race.[13] It is important to note that what Rousseau calls for is not so much the elimination of economic dependence as its equalization, for whenever there is a material division of labor of some kind, individuals will rely on the cooperation of others in order to satisfy their needs. In the absence of class divisions, however, mutually dependent laborers encounter one another on relatively equal footing, and the structural basis for relations of domination is dissolved. The example of class, then, illustrates a general principle of Rousseau's social philosophy: since the dangers of dependence are vastly multiplied when it is conjoined with inequality—one could even say that the former becomes truly dangerous *only* in the presence of the latter[14]—the economic dependence necessary for civilization can be both preserved and rendered benign (or at least tolerable) by equalizing as much as possible the basic terms of social cooperation.

Of course, class inequality is relevant to Rousseau's treatment of *amour-propre* because it is the source not only of economic benefits (surplus value) but also of social esteem: occupying a position in society that empowers one regularly to command and profit from the labor of others is a compelling way of demonstrating the exalted standing one has both for and relative to others. The first principle, then, that Rousseau's social philosophy adopts from his analysis of *amour-propre* is that good institutions must be structured such that the main opportunities they offer for achieving social standing do not depend on the systematic subjugation of others; in a good society the strategies social members standardly pursue for winning recognition must not presuppose fundamental asymmetries in social power that, in effect, enable some to find esteem (and enrichment) at the expense of others' freedom.

---

[13] 'The first man who, having enclosed a plot of land, took it into his head to say *this is mine* and found people simple enough to believe him was the true founder of civil society. What crimes, wars, murders, what miseries and horrors the human species would have been spared by someone who, pulling up the stakes or filling in the ditch, had cried out to his fellow men: beware of listening to this impostor; you are lost if you forget that the fruits belong to all and the earth to no one!' (*DI*, 161/*OC* 3, 164).

[14] For Rousseau the converse also holds: inequality without dependence would have no serious consequences for human well-being. The fact that Rousseau places greater emphasis on reducing inequality than on eliminating dependence reflects his view that the latter is more fundamental to civilization than the former. This finds textual expression in the fact that while Rousseau hypothesizes a golden age—where there is dependence but no significant inequality—he fails to imagine a society marked by inequality but not dependence.

The second example of how Rousseau's social philosophy responds to economic inequality involves a type of inequality he thinks ought to be held within certain bounds but not eliminated altogether. The point at issue here is expressed in the following statement: 'Do you, then, want to give the state stability? Bring the extremes as close together as possible; tolerate neither opulent people nor beggars. These two conditions, naturally inseparable, are equally fatal to the common good' (SC, II.11.iin). This type of inequality differs from the previous one in that it concerns inequality in wealth rather than class. Even if class differences in the Marxian sense are done away with, significant disparities in wealth are possible and even likely, assuming that such 'natural' factors as luck, determination, and innate talent are not completely divested (by 'artificial' means) of their power to affect individuals' fortunes. Rousseau's rather general recommendation that society's extremes be brought 'as close together as possible'[15] is meant to authorize a wide variety of state policies, tailored to specific circumstances, whose aim is to hold in check the natural tendency (in the absence of government regulation) for the gap between rich and poor to grow ever wider (SC, II.11.iii). Three policies of this sort that Rousseau explicitly endorses are progressive taxation (PE, 30–1/OC 3, 271), taxes on luxury goods (PE, 35/OC 3, 275–6), and restrictions on inheritance (OC 3, 945).

The most important reason Rousseau has for regulating material inequality is akin to his reason for outlawing economic classes: great disparities in wealth endanger the *freedom* of the less advantaged.[16] Such disparities intensify the economic dependence of the poor and so increase the likelihood that they will have to submit to the wills of others in order to satisfy their needs. Beyond this, however, there are reasons for minimizing the gap between rich and poor that follow from Rousseau's analysis of the dangers of *amour-propre*. Seen from this perspective, regulating inequalities in wealth has the purpose of placing substantive boundaries on the extent to which the desire for preeminent standing can infect a society's economic life, transforming the pursuit of property into a feverish, limitless drive to acquire goods for the sake of enhancing social status. It is in this context that

---

[15] Elsewhere Rousseau offers an even vaguer formulation of this idea: laws regulating economic inequality ought to produce a situation where 'all have something and no one has too much (*rien de trop*)' (SC, I.9.viiin). For more concrete suggestions, see PE, 19–38/OC 3, 258–78.

[16] See SC, II.11.i, where equality is named as one of the two principal objects of law for the reason that freedom depends on it.

Rousseau advocates 'high taxes ... on those objects of luxury, amusement, and idleness[17] that are visible to all and are all the more difficult to hide as their sole use is display' (PE, 36/OC 3, 276). It is unlikely that such measures could completely prevent private property from functioning in society as an indicator of its owner's worth in comparison with others', but they might reasonably be expected to limit the most extreme and damaging forms of the mania to accumulate property so familiar to Rousseau (and to us). Moreover, it should not be thought that policies aimed at redu-cing the possibilities for ostentatious consumption and acquisition would function merely as external constraints on individuals' behavior without affecting their desires and ideals—that they would, in other words, combat the undesirable consequences of inflamed *amour-propre* while leaving their inner source unaffected. This is because the character of the social world one inhabits, including the concrete opportunities for seeking recognition it encourages or precludes, plays a role in shaping not just behavior but desires and ideals as well. In a society that made minimizing the gap between rich and poor a first priority—in a society where it was difficult to distinguish oneself much through conspicuous consumption or fabulous wealth—individuals would be less likely to think of their standing for others as rooted in what or how much they own; they would be less likely, in other words, to confuse the value of things with the value of persons, and that would represent a significant victory in the struggle against not just extravagant behavior but inflamed *amour-propre* itself.

Institutional sources of respect and esteem

The second major class of Rousseau's socio-political remedies focuses on devising institutions that make a sufficient range of stable and benign forms of recognition available to all. If one of the conditions that favor the inflammation of *amour-propre* is the general lack of non-destructive opportunities for acquiring a recognized standing, then it ought to be possible to curb much of the mischief *amour-propre* is capable of unleashing simply by establishing healthier alternatives to the forms of recognition individuals are led to seek in a society (such as the one depicted in the

---

[17] The examples mentioned are: 'liveries, carriages, mirrors, chandeliers, furniture, fabrics and gilding, courtyards and gardens of mansions, theatrical performances ... , [and] the idle professions, such as buffoons, singers, actors' (PE, 36/OC 3, 276).

Second Discourse) that has not yet been reorganized by reason's principles. Once the problem is viewed in this light, it is easy to see the *Social Contract* as playing a central role in Rousseau's strategy for remedying the evils of *amour-propre*. For one of the main accomplishments of the legitimate state as Rousseau envisages it is to guarantee all its members a substantial form of social recognition: the *equal legal respect* accorded to citizens of a republic. In other words, this part of Rousseau's solution makes the political community itself a major source of the recognition individuals seek as a consequence of *amour-propre*.

In a true republic—in any state ruled by the general will (*SC*, II.6.ixn)— law is the source of three types of recognition, each of which counts as a form of respect rather than esteem since each prescribes a mode of treating individuals that in its own way proclaims the equal worth of all citizens. The first of these is enshrined in what is usually called equality before the law or, as Rousseau puts it, in the equality of citizens as *subjects* (*SC*, I.6.x). This type of recognition derives from the fact that legitimate laws must be universal in the sense of applying equally to everyone: no individual citizen stands outside their reach. A state that upholds the universality of law in this sense confers a kind of equal standing on its members by insisting, as it were, that no individual is 'above' the law.

The second type of legal respect a republic affords its members consists in the equality they enjoy as the collective *sovereign*, or author, of the law: legitimate laws not only 'apply to all' but also 'issue from all' (*SC*, II.4.v). The most obvious sense in which the laws of a republic come equally from all is that all citizens are accorded the same rights of political participation: equal say in the assembly, equal right to vote, and equal access to political offices. There is, however, a further respect in which legitimate laws come equally from all citizens. The laws of a republic originate in the wills of its members not only in the sense that all citizens participate in framing them but also in the sense that, insofar as they are grounded in the general will, they are obliged to protect the fundamental interests of each citizen.[18] Here legitimate laws recognize the equal worth of citizens by proclaiming, in effect, that every individual's fundamental interests have the same standing as anyone else's. This species of recognition comes closest to the Kantian

---

[18] For more on the role that fundamental interests play in Rousseau's conception of law and the general will, see Neuhouser, *Foundations*, 77, 166, 185-9.

ideal of moral respect discussed in Chapter 2, namely, the idea that in forming principles that all are obligated to obey, each individual's interests deserve to count for as much as every other's. In the true republic, finding this form of respect is supposed to depend not on the possibly arbitrary deeds and dispositions of other individuals[19] but on the impersonal and more reliable guarantee furnished by the rule of law itself.

There is a third species of recognition provided by the republic that is not reducible to the forms of respect implicit in the ideals of equal subjection to the law and equal sovereignty. This is the recognition of an individual as a bearer of rights, or—to use Hegel's later terminology—as a 'person'.[20] The idea here is that citizens of the legitimate state must have a recognized standing beyond those of 'equal subject' and 'equal sovereign'. In a republic, laws also recognize citizens as free agents (or persons), and the importance of their individual agency is expressed in a system of established rights[21] that impose constraints on permissible legislation and assure each person a determinate and equal sphere of 'civil freedom' in matters where the general will is silent (SC, I.8.ii). The rights associated with civil freedom are essentially guarantees that others—both the state and other individuals—will not interfere with one's own freely chosen actions, including the free disposition of one's property,[22] provided those actions are consistent with the general will's defining ends (which is to say: consistent with the conditions under which the fundamental interests of all citizens can be secured).[23] In this third form of legal recognition what is at issue is not that everyone's interests count the same but rather that a certain fundamental interest of each person—the freedom to author one's private actions to the extent that such freedom is consistent with the freedom of all—is accorded an essential, non-fungible value, which amounts to a

---

[19] As Rousseau acknowledges, one of the factors that make reliable and satisfying recognition hard to come by is that 'the judgments of the public are often ... the effect of chance' RSW, 71/OC 1, 1077.

[20] I explain Hegel's conception of personhood in Neuhouser, Foundations, 24–5, 27–9, 100–1, 164–5.

[21] As defined by the main aim of civil society, namely, 'assuring the goods, the life, and the freedom of each member through the protection of all' (PE, 9/OC 3, 248).

[22] Civil freedom includes 'proprietorship of everything [one] possesses' (SC, I.8.ii).

[23] See SC, I.8.ii, where civil freedom is said to be 'limited by the general will'. This proviso limiting the extent and validity of citizens' rights is the only point behind Rousseau's frequently misunderstood claims, against Locke, that such rights come not from nature but convention (SC, I.1.ii), that the social contract requires a 'total alienation' of all associates' rights (SC, I.6.vi), and that 'the right each individual has over his own land (fond) is always subordinate to the right the community has over all' (SC, I.9.vii).

recognition of every individual as having the status of a free and inviolable end in itself.

If my earlier criticism of Kantian interpretations of Rousseau is correct—if the problems of *amour-propre* are too complex to be disposed of by moral respect alone—then the recognition individuals achieve as citizens of a republic cannot exhaust Rousseau's answer to those problems. It is reasonable to expect that the difficulties arising out of humans' need for esteem (as opposed to respect) might be reserved for the second part of Rousseau's project of reform, his program for domestic education. While this is for the most part true, it is still worth asking whether his socio-political program has anything to contribute to the task of satisfying *amour-propre*'s yearning to be valued by others for one's distinctive qualities and achievements. In fact, Rousseau's analysis of *amour-propre* can be seen as providing the impetus for a new and distinctive project in the realm of social philosophy: if political institutions can serve as a significant source of recognition for citizens (in the form of respect), how might social institutions more generally be arranged so as to afford members ample opportunities to find *esteem* in ways that avert the dangers of inflamed *amour-propre* and contribute positively to society's functioning? It must be said that in this area Rousseau never fully exploits the possibilities his own theory opens up. (That was left to Hegel, who theorized the family, civil society, and the state as distinct social spheres that, by encouraging social members to occupy particular, socially useful roles within those institutions, allowed individuals to find diverse and satisfying forms of social esteem.[24]) Still, it is possible to find in Rousseau's texts certain tentative moves in the same direction. For example, it is a constant theme in many of his writings that life in the state—more precisely, distinguishing oneself as a brave and virtuous citizen—offers individuals an opportunity to win esteem, even 'glory', for qualities and achievements that promote the collective good.[25] Even here, though, Rousseau fails to go much beyond the ideas he absorbed from his youthful reading of the ancients to think creatively about the distinctive forms political honor might take in a modern, democratic state.

Somewhat more innovative is Rousseau's treatment of the modern nuclear family—or, more precisely, marriage—to which a large part of

---

[24] For details, see Neuhouser, *Foundations*, especially 14, 92, 98–9, 108–10, 143–4, 156.
[25] Examples of this prominent theme are found at *DSA*, 23–4/*OC* 3, 26; *PE*, 14–16, 21–2/*OC* 3, 253–5, 261.

Emile's final book is devoted. The point of following Emile even after he has emerged from adolescence is that his education is not complete until he has entered into a lifelong, monogamous, heterosexual union based on his exclusive, passionate love for a particular woman, Sophie. (The other important topic of Book V is Emile's simultaneous entry into the state and assumption of the duties of citizenship.) Sex, love, and marriage are vast and tortured topics in Rousseau's corpus, above all in *Julie, or the New Heloise*, his epistolary novel of romantic love that became the eighteenth century's most widely read work of fiction. Despite the complexity and messiness that attend these themes in Rousseau's works (which reflect their complexity and messiness in reality), the place they occupy in his socio-political response to inflamed *amour-propre* is—at least in *Emile*—relatively straightforward.[26] First, sexual love is relevant to *amour-propre* because it is an especially intense and intimate confirmation of one's value for another subject, and as such, Rousseau supposes, it is an urgent and universal human need. (He takes it to be a need for both men and women, even if not the same kind of need for each.) That is, sexual love addresses the individual's need to be esteemed by another for her very particular qualities. (Rousseau gets this general point right, even if he tends to think, both here and in *Julie*, that it is the beloved's virtuous character that is, and ought to be, the primary object of a lover's esteem.) Beyond simply functioning as a source of esteem in general, though, sexual love responds to the specific desire to occupy 'the first position' in the eyes of others (*E* IV, 235/*OC* 4, 523), which, as explained above, Rousseau regards as a deep and persistent yearning of human beings. The peculiar achievement of romantic love is that, by taking a single person as its object, it transforms the general desire to be first for others into the specific desire to be first for *one* other person. In doing so, romantic love makes the longing to be first satisfiable in principle for everyone, and so, from the perspective of society as a whole, its power to produce misery and discord is significantly reduced, even if not eliminated altogether.[27] Marriage, whether sanctioned by church or state

[26] My remarks here do not begin to do justice to Rousseau's intriguing attitudes to sexuality. Two books that address this topic insightfully are Elizabeth Rose Wingrove, *Rousseau's Republican Romance* (Princeton, N. J.: Princeton University Press, 2000) and Joel Schwartz, *The Sexual Politics of Jean-Jacques Rousseau* (Chicago: University of Chicago Press, 1984).

[27] There is a downside to this exclusivity, of which Rousseau is fully aware (*DI*, 165/*OC* 3, 169): romantic love implies that one object cannot easily be substituted for another when the first proves unattainable. Thus, when the exclusive affections of two persons are directed at the same

(or both), represents the institutionalization of romantic love. As such, it supplies external incentives for keeping the bond between lovers intact and for maintaining its exclusivity, especially at those inevitable moments of a relationship when sexual passion alone might be insufficient to do so. More important from the perspective of the problem of *amour-propre*, however, is that the institution of marriage adds a new layer of recognition to the more intimate standing for another that is intrinsic to the relation of love. In addition to reinforcing the bond of love itself, marriage secures *society's* recognition of each spouse's supreme and exclusive standing for one other person. In reciprocated romantic love, each lover enjoys this standing in the eyes of the other, but when such a relation is officially recognized by society, this merely private attestation to a person's worth acquires a public confirmation—a kind of objective status—as well. Marriage, in other words, transforms each spouse's being 'first for another' into a being 'first for another for everyone', and because of this it counts as part of Rousseau's socio-political response to the dangers of *amour-propre*.

The remedy of domestic education

Insofar as *Emile* forms part of Rousseau's systematic treatment of *amour-propre*, its principal aim is to investigate how the right kind of domestic education can prevent inflamed *amour-propre* from gaining a foothold in the character of a young child. In explaining the ubiquity of inflamed *amour-propre* in Chapter 4, I alluded to several measures adults can take to avoid awakening angry, greedy, domineering, or submissive dispositions in infants: responding solicitously to their needs but not to their whims; providing them with plenty of opportunities for finding benign forms of recognition; and taking care not to humiliate them when they express their needs (or whims) by the only means available to them, loud and annoying cries. In the remainder of this chapter I attempt to formulate the main principles that underlie Rousseau's apparently formless and meandering

object, or when love is not reciprocated, the result is jealousy, conflict, and misery of the gravest kind. This, I suspect, is the kind of danger (or possibility for unhappiness) that Rousseau thinks cannot be abolished from human life without at the same time eliminating one of the greatest goods available to humans—or, as he puts it, one of 'the sweetest sentiments known to men, conjugal love' (*DI*, 164/*OC* 3, 168).

description of Emile's educational regimen after infancy, especially during the critical period of adolescence.

Getting a grasp on the underlying principles of Emile's education requires returning to the distinction with which the present chapter began between two contrasting goals of education—the formation of men and the formation of citizens—and to Rousseau's well-known dictum that it is necessary to choose one or the other as one's pedagogical goal since 'one cannot make both at the same time' (*E* I, 39/*OC* 4, 248). It is important to give appropriate weight to the final three words of this frequently cited quote, for if one fails to see that what Rousseau denies is only the possibility of *simultaneously* forming children into both men and citizens, it is impossible to account for the obvious fact that part of Emile's education—taking up a sizable portion of Book V (*E* V, 448–75/*OC* 4, 823–60)—consists in preparing him to assume his place as a member of the state. This instruction for citizenship is easily reconciled with the well-known fact that Emile's education is designed to make him into a man, once one realizes that his formation as a citizen (in Book V) takes place only *after* his formation as a man (in Books I–IV). The end result of *Emile*, then, is not a man *instead of* a citizen but a man-citizen whose education has proceeded in two stages: the first is governed exclusively by the ideal of a man, while the second provides the product of the first stage with what he needs in order also to be a citizen (and husband), thereby unifying the two educations and accomplishing *Emile*'s explicitly stated goal of 'removing the contradictions' between them (*E* I, 41/*OC* 4, 251).[28]

Because the first of these stages itself falls into two parts—namely, before and after *amour-propre*'s full awakening in adolescence—Emile's education as a whole can be divided into three phases. First, in Books I–III, Emile is raised exclusively 'for himself' (*E* I, 39/*OC* 4, 248), or 'in his relations with things' (*E* IV, 214/*OC* 4, 493). This means that his education takes

---

[28] These contradictions are described principally in terms of the opposition between existing 'for oneself' and existing 'for others', where the former consists in being an 'absolute whole, related only to itself' and the latter in having a 'relative' existence in which 'one's value is determined by one's relation to the whole' (*E* I, 39–40/*OC* 4, 248–9). Since educating Emile to be only a man would entail suppressing rather than cultivating his *amour-propre*, it cannot (if my basic thesis in this book is correct) be what Rousseau means to recommend. My interpretation of his project is confirmed several paragraphs later, when the goal of *Emile* is described as an education in which 'the double object [is] ... joined in a single one by removing the contradictions of man,' enabling him, in effect, to exist both for himself and for others (*E* I, 41/*OC* 4, 251).

place outside society and is devoted primarily to the appropriate formation and expression of *amour de soi* (and to preserving for as long as possible the dormancy of *amour-propre*), all in accordance with the 'natural' ideals of individual integrity and self-sufficiency (or independence). In the second phase—in Book IV—Emile's education as a man is continued, but with one crucial difference: the onset of puberty, with its awakening of sexual passion, makes it impossible to prolong *amour-propre*'s dormancy. With the latter stirred, Emile can no longer be content with existing only for himself, and his education—still carried out in isolation from all social relations—must concentrate on forming his *amour-propre* (and, secondarily, his pity) so that, once he finally enters the institutions of marriage and the state, he will possess the psychological resources he needs in order to exist 'for others' while also preserving, as far as possible, the integrity and self-sufficiency he learned as a child. In the final phase, in Book V, the exclusive bond between pupil and tutor is loosened, Emile is instructed in the roles of husband and citizen, and he steps into the social world at last, equipped as well as one ever can be to negotiate the tension between being-for-self and being-for-others that, for Rousseau, defines the human predicament.

The first phase: Forming amour de soi *and maintaining* amour-propre's *dormancy*

It is, of course, the second phase of this education that is most relevant to Rousseau's theory of *amour-propre*. Yet the success of this phase depends on certain achievements of the first, which deserve to be mentioned briefly here. The main principle behind the first phase of Emile's education could be summed up as follows: 'until the guide of *amour-propre*, which is reason, can be born, it is important that a child do nothing because he is seen or heard—nothing, in a word, in relation to others—but only what nature asks of him' (*E* II, 92/*OC* 4, 322). In accordance with this maxim, Emile is encouraged throughout Books I–III to develop his natural capacities, to explore the world, and even to learn a trade (carpentry), all in the absence of the evaluating gaze of other subjects. In learning, playing, and working in isolation from others, Emile learns to affirm himself in his newfound strengths and abilities without needing the approval of others and, so, in accordance with ('true' or 'natural') values that have not been distorted by fashion, arbitrary opinion, or society's whims. This means, for example, that Emile is given free rein to indulge and enjoy his native drive to know—the 'curiosity natural to man concerning all that pertains to his interests'—while remaining free of the socially perverted variant of this drive, an 'ardor to know founded only on the desire to be esteemed as learned' (*E* III, 167/*OC* 4, 429). It also means that in judging the results of his carpentry, say, Emile consults 'natural' (exclusively object-relative) standards, such as simplicity, harmony, and utility, rather than other subjects' opinions of what is good or pleasing, which are perpetually liable to distortion by an undue concern for what fashion dictates and what social approval requires. The most important result of this 'education from things' (*E* I, 38/*OC* 4, 247) is that before the passions of adolescence force him to give weight to the opinions of others, Emile will have developed a substantial reservoir of self-esteem as well as the capacity to evaluate himself according to transparent, non-fluctuating standards and independently of others' judgments. By the end of this phase Emile will have learned, as Rousseau puts it, to 'make use of his reason, not someone else's'; to 'give nothing to opinion ... [or] authority'; and, most important, to 'think well of himself without regard to others' (*E* III, 207–8/*OC* 4, 486–8).[29]

The second phase: Forming amour-propre *(and pity)*

The decisive phase of Emile's education—the shaping of his *amour-propre* in adolescence—is also the hardest to reconstruct. This is in part because the formation of *amour-propre* interacts in complicated ways with the development of the second other-related passion of human beings, pity.[30] But the difficulty in grasping the educational strategy of Book IV is no doubt also due to the fact that, as Chapters 2 and 3 demonstrate, Rousseau has set himself an exceedingly complex task. Because the dangers posed by *amour-propre* are themselves so varied, it is not surprising that in Book IV the goal of devising a unified, easily graspable educational remedy proves so elusive.

As Rousseau formulates it, the primary goal of Book IV with respect to shaping Emile's *amour-propre* is to instill in him a correct understanding of

[29] In other words, Emile is being raised to become a 'person whose rank does not depend in his own estimation on the one it pleases others to accord him' (*RSW*, 74/*OC* 1, 1080).

[30] The formation of pity occupies an important place in Emile's education in Book IV, and attempts to shape his *amour-propre* are incomplete without it. In the present context, however, I concentrate on the latter topic.

the 'rank' he occupies relative to others—or more precisely, the rank he takes himself to deserve, or to be entitled to:

as soon as *amour-propre* has developed, the relative *I* is constantly in play, and the young man never observes others without returning to himself and comparing himself with them. The issue, then, is to know in what rank among his fellows he will put himself after having examined them.

$$(E \text{ IV}, 243/OC 4, 534)^{31}$$

Not surprisingly, the rank that Emile is to learn to claim for himself is equality with all other human beings (as such). (This confirms that the Kantian interpretation examined in Chapters 2 and 3 gets an important part of Rousseau's remedial strategy right; it does not, however, imply that egalitarian *amour-propre* is a sufficient answer to the problems Rousseau is concerned with, nor that seeking superiority is in every instance pernicious.) While the core of this ideal is surely some version of what I earlier called equal moral respect—the idea that no one is by nature entitled to a better life than others or that no one's interests deserve more consideration than others' in determining the laws that obligate us commonly—equality actually appears in an intriguing variety of guises in the lengthy and convoluted educational regimen proposed in Book IV. In the following paragraphs I attempt to impose a modicum of order on Rousseau's presentation of this educational regimen, one that helps it to be seen as a coherent and effective response to the problems of *amour-propre* as reconstructed here.

The two educational principles with which Book IV begins concern, first, the temporal order in which the adolescent's new passions are allowed to emerge and, second, the principal psychological resource—the pupil's imagination—that this educational phase will make use of in shaping those passions. Rousseau makes a point of insisting that the emergence and formation of pity precede the stirring of *amour-propre*. His thought is that since after the latter has occurred, the adolescent will necessarily care about securing a favorable place in relation to others, having first acquired a capacity to pity his potential rivals—to empathize with their pains and sorrows—will make it easier for him to mollify and restrict the aims of his drive for relative standing,[32] which in the absence of such empathy

---

[31] See also *E* IV, 219, 235/*OC* 4, 501, 523.

[32] Pity has the capacity 'to soften the ferocity of … *amour-propre*' (*DI*, 152/*OC* 3, 154).

can easily assume exaggerated, pernicious forms. In other words, if pity is aroused and fortified before *amour-propre* enters the scene, it is capable of turning the adolescent's emerging character 'towards beneficence and goodness' (*E* IV, 221/*OC* 4, 504) before it can be moved in the opposite direction by an inflamed drive to outdo or harm.[33]

Part and parcel of awakening pity is providing it with an object—how can one pity without pitying something or someone?—and it is here that imagination becomes important. On Rousseau's view, human passions—or drives, as Freud will call them—have a purely biological source, which, however, provides them with no determinate direction until they are guided by 'ideas' (broadly construed) supplied by the imagination. In the absence of ideas 'the blood ferments and is agitated, a superabundance of life seeks to extend itself outward,' but in such a way that 'one desires without knowing what' (*E* IV, 220/*OC* 4, 502). The role of imagination, then, in forming, or habituating, the passions—making them 'second nature'—is to fix their objects, which, in the present case, amounts to determining to whom and on the basis of what Emile's pity is to be directed. This is the sense in which the imagination 'determines the passions' bent', and it explains why influencing the imagination is crucial to Emile's education in Book IV: 'it is the errors of imagination that transform the passions into vices' (*E* IV, 219/*OC* 4, 501). Conversely, it is the imagination, properly directed, that transforms passions into good character.

One reason imagination is so important in the formation of pity—beyond the fact that all passions require ideas to fix their objects—is that sensitivity to the pains of other creatures depends on a capacity for imaginative identification, that is, on the ability to 'transport ourselves outside ourselves and identify with the suffering animal' (*E* IV, 223/*OC* 4, 505–6). To experience pity, for Rousseau, is to 'put [oneself] in the place of the sufferer' (*E* IV, 221/*OC* 4, 504) and then, on the basis of this imaginative act, '*to feel oneself in one's fellows*, to be moved by their complaints and to suffer their pains' (*E* IV, 222/*OC* 4, 504; emphasis added).[34] Thus, the

---

[33] This principle, interpreted through the lens of sexuality rather than *amour-propre* more generally, runs: 'The first act of his nascent imagination is to teach him that he has fellows (*semblables*) [so that] the species affects him before the female sex' (*E* IV, 220/*OC* 4, 502).

[34] As many have pointed out, this seems to contradict Rousseau's earlier account in the Second Discourse (*DI*, 152–4/*OC* 3, 154–7), according to which pity, at least in its primitive form, precedes the capacity for reflection required by imaginative identification as described in *Emile*. I am indebted to Jonathan Rick for helpful conversations on this topic.

tutor's task in forming Emile's pity is twofold: to stimulate the latter's hitherto latent faculty of imagination[35] so that he is able in general to experience others' sufferings as painful and then progressively to extend the scope of his newly acquired sensitivity so as to encompass all human beings or, as Rousseau puts it, 'humanity' itself.

The principal means of achieving these ends is to furnish the adolescent's imagination with an abundance of 'objects on which the expansive force of his heart can act—objects that swell the heart, that extend it to other beings' (E IV, 223/OC 4, 506). In extending the adolescent's pity to all of humanity, the tutor focuses on evoking *experiences* of others' misfortunes—Emile must 'see', 'hear', and 'feel' the calamities he is to be moved by—that impress on him the pervasiveness and universality of human suffering. This includes 'unsettling and frightening his imagination' (E IV, 224/OC 4, 508) with pictures of the miseries to which all humans are subject: the certainty of death and vulnerability to pain, sickness, and need. It also includes acquainting him with a variety of miseries that only some humans actually experience, while simultaneously driving home to him the large role that fortune—arbitrary, undeserved good luck—plays in determining who at any particular moment happens to be suffering them. Finally, extending Emile's pity to humanity requires getting him to see (and to hear and to feel) that all human beings—even the poor and the low, who can appear to be inured to their suffering—*feel* the miseries to which they are subjected. Emile must be brought to 'see … the same sentiments in the hod carrier and the illustrious man' (E IV, 225/OC 4, 509) and to attach the same weight to a human being's pains regardless of her position in society. Already before *amour-propre* has entered the picture, then, the education of Emile's passions involves instilling in them—fashioning them so as to incorporate—an ideal of human equality. Indeed, the sense of equality his properly formed pity provides him with is but a prototype of the one he will need in adulthood in order to consider his actions from the moral point of view (or to judge legislation by the standards of the general will): since there are pains in the world other than my own, and since every human feels his pains as acutely as I do mine, all human suffering

---

[35] Since 'it is the errors of imagination that transform the passions into vices' (E IV, 219/OC 4, 501), a prominent theme of Books I–III is the need to keep Emile's imagination dormant until, in Book IV, his social passions—pity and *amour-propre*—have been formed.

has a claim on my pity and—at least from any point of view I can expect others to share—equal importance in deciding how to act.

The sense of equality that informs Emile's pity before he is fully affected by *amour-propre* is able to serve as a necessary counterbalance to the immediate tendency of the latter, once awakened, to seek superiority, even 'the first position', in relation to others (*E* IV, 235/*OC* 4, 523).[36] In the next step of his education, coincident with the emergence of *amour-propre*, Emile is brought face to face with a feature of human life that stands in tension with his newly acquired ideal of moral equality: the basic and, to him, startling fact of social inequality[37]—the existence of 'artificial' inequalities in wealth and power, which, though highly variable with time and place, are intrinsic to human society (*E* IV, 236/*OC* 4, 524). It is, of course, no accident that Emile's exposure to social inequality coincides with the awakening of his *amour-propre*, which, according to the Second Discourse, is the psychological source of that phenomenon.

Beyond merely acquainting his charge with the ubiquity and variety of social inequality, the tutor's aim is to get Emile to attach the proper significance to the real disparities in wealth and power he finds around him (all in service of the ultimate goal of teaching him what 'rank among his fellows' he occupies). In this the main point is to bring Emile to appreciate the superficial and arbitrary character of most actually existing inequality. More precisely, he is to learn that even if social advantages are (to some extent) unavoidable, they are also for the most part arbitrarily distributed—which is to say: existing disparities in wealth, class, and power rarely correspond to differences in genuine merit (*DI*, 131/*OC* 3, 131–2). Superior wealth, class, and power are, in other words, mostly undeserved, and appreciating this distinction—between occupying a favored place in society and deserving to be there—is crucial to the proper formation of *amour-propre*.

A further goal of this part of Emile's education is to impress on him not only that inequalities in wealth, class, and power are mostly undeserved but also that having them (or having them alone) seldom brings genuine satisfaction. Emile must learn to look beneath the public mask worn by the

---

[36] This default tendency of *amour-propre* is explained in the second half of Ch. 4.

[37] These socio-political inequalities are what the Second Discourse calls moral inequalities (*DI*, 131/*OC* 3, 131), a concept I discuss in Ch. 1. I avoid Rousseau's term here in order to prevent confusion with the Kantian conception of equality, which I have called throughout 'moral equality'.

socially successful in order to 'read their hearts' and see that their riches and power are frequently accompanied by insecurity, obsession, jealousy, and pain. (History, it turns out—especially biographies of the 'illustrious' that enable readers to 'see' the hearts of the personages they describe and the events in which they took part (E IV, 237–40/ OC 4, 526–30)—is the best way to reveal these truths to the adolescent.) Learning that superior wealth, class, and power often stand in the way of true happiness—the standard Emile has learned by now to take most seriously—is to have the effect of evoking in him pity for the well off rather than envy or the desire to emulate them, both of which can easily turn into an inflamed drive to compete or injure in order to occupy a favored position for others.

Once Emile has learned to judge the true value of the more superficial forms of superiority, such as wealth and prestige, the formation of his *amour-propre* still requires one major intervention.[38] Emile must learn that even those who enjoy superiority with respect to genuine human goods—happiness, wisdom, esteem from oneself and others—do not in any robust sense *merit* their advantages. (I discussed this claim in detail in Chapter 3.) This lesson is especially important for Emile, who, having had the good fortune to receive an exemplary education, will most likely occupy a favored position of precisely this sort and, so, be especially vulnerable to the type of pride (*orgueil*) or vanity (*vanité*) that Rousseau is concerned here to prevent. As we saw in Chapter 3, the danger to be averted in this situation is not that Emile might delight in his favored place, or even desire it, but rather that he might 'attribute his happiness to his own merit' and therefore believe himself *worthy* of his good fortune (E IV, 245/ OC 4, 536–7) and, by extension, believe the unhappy and unesteemed *deserving* of their lot. To believe oneself worthy of one's happier position—whether because one takes it to be the result of one's own doing or a manifestation of one's superior nature—is not only to be grievously self-deceived but also to be fundamentally mistaken about one's true 'rank' in the human species. Such an overestimation of self represents a serious danger to the formation of both men and citizens, for it is incompatible with sincerely and reliably taking up the perspective on others that morality and political justice require, namely, regarding all individuals as equally worthy of happiness (at least in the sense that each person's fundamental interests

---

[38] 'One more step, and we reach the goal' (E IV, 244/ OC 4, 536).

must count for as much as anyone else's). It is somewhat surprising, then, that the only concrete pedagogical measures that Rousseau suggests here for avoiding this outcome are sketchy (and, where concrete, rather harsh):

Do not get lost in fine reasonings to prove to the adolescent that he is a man like others. ... Make him feel it, or he will never know it. ... [M]y pupil is to be intentionally exposed to all the accidents that can prove to him that he is no wiser than we. The [humiliating] adventure with the magician[39] would be repeated in a thousand ways.

(*E* IV, 245/*OC* 4, 537)

Recommendations as general as these encourage the suspicion that the educational measures espoused in Book IV are not quite up to the demanding task of ensuring that the adolescent will avoid the whole range of possible varieties of inflamed *amour-propre* so forcefully described in the diagnostic part of Rousseau's project. Even if one acknowledges that *Emile* is not intended as an instruction manual for potential educators—that it aims instead at setting out the general principles a successful domestic education must somehow translate into practice—the complexity of the problem it seeks to combat makes it difficult to tell whether Rousseau has successfully shown, even in principle, that sufficient educational measures are available to the domestic tutor for preventing the inflammation of *amour-propre*. The suspicion that is hard to dispel, in other words, is that Rousseau's powerful case for the malignant potential of *amour-propre* ends up formulating so enormous a problem that his remedial project cannot fully solve it. Despite this possible failing, Rousseau's response to the problem of inflamed *amour-propre* does exhibit some of the systematicity it aspires to, insofar as it is possible to see the *Social Contract* and *Emile*, taken together, as offering a number of remedial responses to each of the ways *amour-propre* is susceptible to becoming inflamed. A brief recapitulation of these responses organized according to the five categories employed in Chapters 2 and 3 will serve as this chapter's conclusion:

a) In order to counter the *ferocity and power* with which *amour-propre* can seize individuals when deprived of a standing for others, domestic education endeavors to prolong the dormancy of that passion for as long as possible, giving pity an opportunity to be fostered and expanded into

---

[39] *E* III, 172–5/*OC* 4, 436–40.

the character trait of benevolence, which is then able to counteract the selfish and destructive motives that *amour-propre*, once awakened, can give rise to. Even before this, the infant is guarded against early experiences that fan the flames of *amour-propre*—instill in her dispositions to 'fury, spite, and anger' (*E* I, 66/*OC* 4, 287)—through humiliation or by otherwise damaging her sense of herself as worthy of others' respect or esteem. Along with these domestic measures, good social and political institutions help to reduce *amour-propre*'s 'feverish' quality by providing their members with diverse opportunities for finding recognition, including the very important forms of equal respect intrinsic to the rule of law in a republic.

b) The pervasive and dangerous tendency of *amour-propre* to seek *superiority* is combated already in infancy, when adults take care to respond empathetically to their infants' cries while also distinguishing need from whim and thereby preventing a spirit of domination from gaining an early foothold in the child's character. Later manifestations of the drive for preeminence are rendered benign by a domestic education that instills various versions of the ideal of human equality in the adolescent, especially by training his pity in ways that enable him to feel the pains of all human beings and to accord them equal moral weight. This is complemented by instruction in the true significance of social inequalities, namely, that they rarely reflect differences in merit and are seldom conducive to genuine happiness. Political institutions reinforce these psychological measures by ensuring the moral equality of citizens and by outlawing or severely restricting the most destructive forms of artificial inequality, those in property, class, and social power. At the same time, the state fosters social institutions that allow individuals to act on certain forms of the never completely eradicable desire for superiority in ways that pose minimal dangers to peace and happiness. (The nuclear family, based on romantic love, is an example of such an institution insofar as it domesticates each person's desire to be 'in the first place', transforming it into the desire to be first in the eyes of one specific other, one's mate.[40])

---

[40] This raises a question of the first importance: is it possible for the nuclear family, grounded in gender difference, to fulfill the recognitive mission Rousseau assigns to it without requiring a gender inequality that violates the more fundamental ideal of moral equality for all humans?

c) Since the drive for recognition implies a fundamental dependence on others for their judgments of one's worth, the *threats to freedom, integrity, and unalienated selfhood* that this poses must be countered by political institutions that provide for everyone a stable and dependable source of recognition (equal moral respect) that is independent of the often arbitrary and fluctuating opinions of particular individuals. Since the moral respect provided by the republic cannot satisfy all an individual's recognitive needs—since it leaves the need for esteem, with its implicit demand for preeminence, unaddressed—domestic education must develop in children, before they have learned to give weight to the opinions of others, a significant reservoir of self-esteem (including a confidence in their own judgments of the good) that gives solidity to the self when the esteem one deserves from others is difficult to find.

d) The principal means for preventing *amour-propre* from seeking to *appear*, rather than to *be*, worthy or excellent comes from a domestic education that removes children for as long as possible from the evaluative gaze of others, thereby allowing them to learn to judge themselves and their activities on the basis of 'objective'[41] standards that they themselves understand and see the value of rather than by standards that depend on fashion or caprice.

e) Chronic dissatisfaction stemming from inflated expectations as to how much or what kind of recognition one deserves is avoided by shaping a child's self-conception in such a way that she acquires a true (or reasonable) understanding of the position she deserves relative to others, both as a human being and as a particular individual with specific skills and excellences. On the one hand, children must be spared early experiences of (unnecessary[42]) humiliation and disrespect, which can produce greedy or stingy dispositions that no amount of actual recognition can ever satisfy. On the other hand, care must

[41] It is, of course, no easy matter to give content to the idea of 'object-relative' values, as distinguished from those that come from (other) subjects. Simplicity, harmony, and utility are, as mentioned above, three values Rousseau thinks of as belonging to the former class.

[42] As Emile's 'adventure with the magician' demonstrates, Rousseau is not averse to using techniques of humiliation when he sees no other way to prevent inflamed *amour-propre* from gaining a foothold in the child's character.

be taken in adolescence to ensure that once the 'relative I' comes into play, strivings for superiority are tempered by a robust sense of the moral equality of all humans, especially with regard to the weight accorded to their pains, their happiness, and their fundamental interests.

PART IV

Elevating Humankind by Curing the Malady from Within

6

The Standpoint of Reason

The final two chapters of this book treat what is both most original and most speculative in Rousseau's account of *amour-propre*. Their subject matter forms the heart of Rousseau's theodicy of self-love, for they aim to explicate his claim—or suggestion, really—that, despite its many dangers, *amour-propre* is a necessary condition of nearly everything that elevates human life and makes it a thing of value. For, as I indicated at the beginning of this book, Rousseau's suggestion is that rationality, morality, and freedom—indeed, subjectivity itself—would be impossible if it were not for *amour-propre* and the relations to other subjects it impels human beings to establish. In the course of articulating this view it will become apparent not merely that, but also why, Rousseau chooses not to follow his Stoic forebears and recommend the extirpation or suppression of a passion that is responsible for so many of the evils that plague human existence. As we shall see, Rousseau holds that the only response to the problems of *amour-propre* consistent with realizing the best of human potential is to undertake its cultivation—that is, to mold it in such a way that the desire to count as a being of value for others sheds the greatest part of its destructive character and serves instead the ends of human flourishing.

Revealing *amour-propre*'s positive potential

Rousseau's 'justification' of *amour-propre*—his account of its beneficial, even redemptive potential—falls into three main parts. The first involves the claim that *amour-propre* is directly the source of a number of human goods that are valuable in themselves, independently of whatever other goods they might also help to bring about.[1] According to this line of thought, even if

---

[1] See Cooper, 123.

it were possible to extirpate *amour-propre* from the human soul, doing so would be undesirable because the passion to acquire standing in the eyes of others is responsible for much of the richness of human existence; without *amour-propre*, a large part of what gives human lives meaning and value would be lost. Even if stamping out *amour-propre* succeeded in eliminating human misery, conflict, and degradation, it would also abolish, along with them, the basis for countless irreplaceable goods, such as love, friendship, and affirmation from others. Rousseau's acute perception of the dangers posed by *amour-propre* does not prevent him from seeing just as clearly that there would be little to give human existence zest and urgency without the projects and relationships that *amour-propre* induces us to pursue. This is why the Second Discourse's history of the human species is so relentlessly ambivalent about the developments it depicts.[2] For, to mention just one example, at the same moment that the birth of *amour-propre* opens the door to jealousy, fury, and passionate conflict, it also makes possible 'the sweetest sentiments known to men: conjugal and … paternal love' (*DI*, 164/ *OC* 3, 168). Finally, this point suggests a new way of viewing the project examined in the preceding chapter, namely, as an attempt to find ways of preserving the various human goods made possible by the passion for social esteem while avoiding the destructive consequences of inflamed *amour-propre*.

The second component of Rousseau's theodicy of *amour-propre* depends on finding instrumental value in the desire for the good opinion of others. This part of his view rests on the familiar thought that *amour-propre* can be cultivated so as to motivate individuals to pursue their quest for recognition through socially constructive avenues. The idea here is that human beings can be brought up (and the social world organized) in a manner that encourages them to seek esteem from others by becoming useful and (externally) virtuous members of society. In other words, through education and social reform the desire to count in the eyes of others can be harnessed and placed in the service of collectively beneficial ends. This point comes up again and again in Rousseau's texts: 'the universal desire for reputation … trains … talents and powers' and produces virtue, the sciences—even philosophy itself (*DI*, 184/ *OC* 3, 189); it gives rise to 'estimable qualities' in individuals who desire approval from others

---

[2] Rousseau's ambivalence is frequently overlooked, despite its pervasiveness. See, e.g. *DI*, 162–7, 183–4, 216/ *OC* 3, 165–71, 189, 217; and, most decisively, note IX at *DI*, 197–204/ *OC* 3, 202–8.

(*E* IV, 214/*OC* 4, 494); and it encourages citizens to sacrifice for their country by making them sensitive to the reward of honor (*PE*, 22/*OC* 3, 261).[3] This power to make human beings want to please and benefit others plays an important, if ultimately ambiguous, role in Rousseau's understanding of *amour-propre*'s positive potential. I return to it in the following chapter when considering the complex issue of how *amour-propre* makes it possible for humans to be motivated by the demands of duty and reason. For now it is sufficient to note that part of Rousseau's desire to preserve and cultivate *amour-propre* derives from his recognition that, given the right circumstances, the need to win others' esteem can become a force that promotes rather than impedes the human good.

Although not to be overlooked, neither of these points is controversial or original. It is widely recognized, for example, that part of Rousseau's political solution to the problems of *amour-propre* involves getting citizens to satisfy their need for social esteem by holding public office and serving the republic in other visible ways. Rousseau's most innovative thoughts on the positive potential of *amour-propre* are to be found instead in the third part of his account, and for this reason it will be the focus of both this chapter and the next. It is probably no accident that it is here, where Rousseau's thought becomes most original, that it is also the hardest to pin down. This means that articulating this part of Rousseau's justification of *amour-propre* will require a good deal of reconstructive work on a selected set of suggestive but elusive passages in a variety of texts.

The view hinted at by Rousseau's scattered remarks can be formulated generally as the claim that, indirectly, *amour-propre* furnishes humans with a substantial part of the subjective resources they require if they are to become rational beings, attain moral excellence, and realize themselves as free. In other words, subjects who lacked *amour-propre* (and who would therefore not be *human* subjects) would also lack a substantial portion of the cognitive and conative capacities necessary for rationality, morality,[4] and self-determination; indeed, they would not be subjects, or selves, at

---

[3] For similar claims see *DSA*, 23–4/*OC* 3, 26. This aspect of Rousseau's position is explored in O'Hagan, 171–2.

[4] Rousseau hints at this claim when he says that 'the dangerous disposition out of which all our vices are born' is to be transformed into 'a sublime virtue' (*PE*, 20/*OC* 3, 260). Chitty provides an excellent account of the role *amour-propre* plays in making human beings moral (chs. 1 and 2). My reconstruction of Rousseau's position is close to his in important respects.

all, at least not in the way human beings as we know them are subjects, or selves.[5] According to this claim, *amour-propre* is only indirectly the source of reason, virtue, and freedom because there is no direct connection between the ends that *amour-propre* impels humans to seek and the aspiration to be rational, virtuous, or free; humans do not become rational, moral, or self-determining because doing so satisfies, in any straightforward sense, their desire to have value in the eyes of others. Rather, in seeking to satisfy their passion for recognition, beings with *amour-propre* are led to establish relations to others that have the effect, unbeknownst to those beings themselves, of developing in them cognitive and conative capacities that open up new possibilities—for reason, morality, and freedom—that would otherwise be unavailable to them. In other words, the third part of Rousseau's justification of *amour-propre* emphasizes the latter's *formative* potential, or, as Hegel would put it, the ways in which *amour-propre* effects the *Bildung* of rational, moral, and self-determining subjects.[6]

In reconstructing this thesis I begin by setting aside what Rousseau has to say about morality, freedom, and subjectivity in general in order to focus on the claim that *rationality*—the capacity to adopt and to be appropriately moved by the standpoint of reason—requires *amour-propre* as one of its conditions. Proceeding in this way makes good sense for two reasons. First, concentrating on a single aspect of Rousseau's view makes it possible to investigate at least one of his claims at the level of detail that is necessary if we are to be able to grasp and evaluate his position adequately. Second, Rousseau's claims that morality, freedom, and subjectivity depend on *amour-propre* are all parasitic on his claim that reason, too, depends on it. This is because reason, though not identical to these other phenomena, plays a necessary and central role in each. According to Rousseau, there can be no virtue or freedom[7]—and no selfhood in the appropriate sense—without the exercise of reason.

---

[5] Neither 'subject' nor 'self' is a technical term for Rousseau. I treat them as interchangeable designations of the phenomenon I refer to, beginning in Ch. 2, in terms of the self's 'moral presence' or 'being' and that I discuss later in this chapter in conjunction with the claim that the social contract brings into existence a public 'self' (*moi*). Rousseau never articulates an account of the self, even though the concept is central to his thought. His sketchy remarks on alienation, for example, are an indication of his under-theorization of this topic.

[6] I discuss Hegel's understanding of *Bildung* and its connection to social life in Neuhouser, *Foundations*, 148–65.

[7] Rousseau makes the connection between virtue and freedom explicit at *OC* 3, 483, §7.

The close connection Rousseau draws between reason, on the one hand, and morality, freedom, and subjectivity, on the other, suggests that 'reason' here bears a distinctive meaning and that our first task should be to ask what reason in the relevant sense consists in. Unfortunately, Rousseau never answers this question directly, nor does he use the term 'reason' completely univocally.[8] Despite this, there is a specific and historically influential conception of reason that informs, if only implicitly, the vision of human flourishing articulated in the *Social Contract* and *Emile*. In my view, the best place to look for this conception of reason is in the *Social Contract*'s account of the general will. I shall proceed, then, on the supposition that analyzing the principles that are said to guide the general will is the key to discovering what Rousseau takes the content—or, better perhaps, the *standpoint*—of reason to consist in. Along with this, the *Social Contract*'s description of how the citizen (as opposed to 'natural' man) is constituted, and of the frame of mind he must adopt in the making of law, ought to give us a picture of what Rousseau thinks is involved subjectively in submitting oneself to—in recognizing as authoritative—the demands of reason.[9] Reason as it is considered here, then, is a practical faculty—it determines which actions I (or we) ought to undertake—and it coincides with the deliberative stance taken up by the citizen who strives to legislate for his state in accordance with the general will. Hence reconstructing Rousseau's conception of reason depends on articulating what it is for a citizen to adopt the standpoint of the general will. This means that Rousseau's justification of *amour-propre* aims to reveal what role nature—or providence?—relies on this passion to play in forming individuals' subjective capacities and dispositions so that they are suited to participate in a legitimate, or rational, social order and to do so in a manner consistent with humanity's highest potential.

[8] Especially in *Emile*, Rousseau often uses 'reason' very loosely. (It is a reference to 'reasoning' that is the occasion for his notorious remark that he does not 'always give the same meanings to the same words', *E* II, 108n/*OC* 4, 345n.) In other passages the term carries a specific meaning that links reason closely to morality (e.g. *E* I, 67/*OC* 4, 288; *E* II, 89/*OC* 4, 317; and throughout Book IV). It is in this sense that I employ the term here.

[9] Some interpreters have denied that reason, or reasoned debate, plays as central or as unambiguous a role in Rousseau's political philosophy as I maintain here. See, e.g. Arash Abizadeh, 'Banishing the Particular: Rousseau on Rhetoric, *Patrie*, and the Passions', *Political Theory* 29 (2001), 556–82.

Reason and the general will

I begin reconstructing Rousseau's conception of reason by recalling the well known passage of the *Social Contract* that, in effect, identifies reason with the standpoint of the legislating citizen:[10]

This passage from the state of nature to the civil state produces a very remarkable change in man, by substituting justice for instinct in his conduct and giving his actions the morality they previously lacked. Only then, when the voice of duty replaces physical impulse and right replaces appetite, does man, who until then considered only himself, find himself forced to act on other principles and to consult his reason before heeding his inclinations.

(*SC*, I.8.i)

It is evident from these remarks that Rousseau takes membership in the state—and so, subjection to the general will—to be centrally involved in both reason and morality. (And, as the immediately following paragraphs make clear, freedom, too, depends on being a member of the legitimate state.) As Rousseau depicts it here, reason's capacity to guide human conduct depends on its ability to replace what is variously described as impulse, appetite, and instinct as the motivating force of action. Moreover, we are told, reason is able to do this only by introducing into conduct the idea of right (or duty or justice) and by recognizing the principles of right as a higher authority than mere inclination. What this passage does not say much about, however, is what reason's consulting and obeying the principles of duty consists in. Some progress in this direction can be made by supposing that the 'other principles' referred to here—the principles the man of reason consults in order to know his duties—are those that define the general will. This connection between duty and the general will is made explicit at various places in Rousseau's texts, most plainly in his definition of virtue as the 'conformity of the particular will to the general [will]' (*PE*, 13/*OC* 3, 252). Statements such as these support my suggestion that the key to reconstructing Rousseau's conception of practical reason

[10] See also *PE*, 5/*OC* 3, 243, where Rousseau refers to law as 'public reason'; and GM, [189]/*OC* 3, 326, where he describes law as 'a public ... act of the general will'.

lies in understanding what it is to will from a universal perspective or, equivalently, to adopt the standpoint of the general will.[11]

The first step in this reconstruction is to inquire into the content of the general will as Rousseau conceives it: what is it that the general will wills? what ends does it endorse and seek to realize? Although Rousseau's characterizations of the general will are far from transparent, his answers to these questions are less confused than commentators tend to think. In introducing the term in the *Social Contract*, Rousseau characterizes the general will as the will that directs the collective body, or self (*moi*), that comes into existence when previously unassociated individuals agree to be governed by the social contract (*SC*, I.6.x; III.1.xx; IV.1.i).[12] In calling this collective body a self, Rousseau means to claim that the political community formed by the social contract is an entity whose identity, or unity, depends on its having a species of self-consciousness analogous to that possessed by individual human selves. Whether collective or individual, a self for Rousseau is self-conscious in two respects: first, it knows itself as a numerically distinct being that persists over time; and, second, it has a sense or understanding of what its own good consists in, together with a concern to realize that good.[13] In other words, a central part of what it is to be a self for Rousseau is to have, and to be motivated by, a conception of one's own good that is grounded in one's understanding of the kind of being one essentially is.

The will that Rousseau attributes to the political community as a consequence of its selfhood, then, can be nothing more than the collective body's concern to realize those ends it takes to constitute its good as the kind of being it is. This is precisely what Rousseau tells us later in the *Social Contract* when he says that the aim of the general will is simply to 'direct

---

[11] The discussion that follows supplements my attempts elsewhere to explain the general will in Neuhouser, *Foundations*, 55–81, 184–94.

[12] Despite Rousseau's temporal language, it is best to understand the social contract not as an actual event that creates a new entity (the state) but as a theoretical construct that articulates the principles that inform any legitimate political order. In light of this, it would be more accurate to say that the general will is what directs the collective body that exists wherever individuals let their actions be regulated by the provisions of the social contract.

[13] Rousseau's debt to Stoic conceptions of selfhood is evident; see Gisela Striker, *Essays on Hellenistic Epistemology and Ethics* (Cambridge: Cambridge University Press, 1996), 281–97.

the forces of the state according to the end for which it was instituted' (*SC*, II.1.i). In this passage the state's end is characterized only vaguely as 'the common good,' but—contrary to what interpreters frequently claim—the ends that define the good of the political association are clearly spelled out elsewhere, for example, in the description of the fundamental task the social contract is invoked to solve:

'Find a form of association that defends and protects the person and goods of each associate with all the common force, and by means of which each one, uniting with all, nevertheless obeys only himself and remains as free as before.' This is the fundamental problem to which the social contract provides the solution.

(*SC*, I.6.iv)

The task of the general will, then, is to direct the activities of the state towards the end for which it was instituted—the very end that explains the willingness of unassociated individuals to subject themselves to it—namely, the securing of a definite set of basic goods for each member of the association. The general will's aim, as Rousseau formulates it in an earlier text, is to 'secure the goods, life, and freedom of each member through the protection of all' (*PE*, 9/*OC* 3, 248).[14] Since Rousseau regards these particular goods—life, property, and freedom—as central to all forms of human flourishing,[15] the end at which practical reason aims could also be described as the systematic satisfaction of the essential, or fundamental, interests of all individuals qua human beings.

---

[14] This characterization of the general will's ends is consistent with Rousseau's claim elsewhere that the 'two principal objects' of the general will are freedom and equality (*SC*, II.11.i). For, as he goes on to say in the same passage, equality is willed by the general will only because, and to the extent that, freedom requires it.

[15] In the Second Discourse Rousseau calls life and freedom 'the essential gifts of nature ... that everyone is permitted to enjoy', the renunciation of which would 'offend both nature and reason' and 'debase one's being' (*DI*, 179/*OC* 3, 184). A similar claim is made in the *Social Contract* with respect to freedom: 'To renounce one's freedom is to renounce one's quality as a man. ... There is no possible compensation for someone who renounces everything. Such a renunciation is incompatible with the nature of man' (*SC*, I.4.vi). The right to property is less clearly asserted than the rights to freedom and self-preservation (the latter of which includes personal security). I suggest that the right to property is derivative of the other two rights: each individual is entitled, minimally, to as much property as his freedom and self-preservation require and is prohibited from owning more than is consistent with the freedom and self-preservation of all. This would imply that Rousseau recognizes only two fundamental human interests, which accords with the view I present in Neuhouser, *Foundations*, 185ff. It also helps to explain why in the passage from the Second Discourse just cited Rousseau explicitly makes the right to property less fundamental than the rights to life and freedom. On this topic, see *SC*, I.9.i–ii; and *PE*, 23–4/*OC* 3, 263.

Defining the standpoint of reason

This account of reason's ends helps to clarify what is involved in assuming the standpoint of reason as Rousseau conceives it, which is to say: the perspective the individual citizen adopts when deciding on the laws that ought to govern her own (legitimate) political community. From what has been established thus far it is clear that taking up the standpoint of the rational legislator involves asking oneself how a proposed law will affect the fundamental interests of all citizens, including one's own. More precisely, the legislating individual asks of herself: is this proposed law consistent with the freedom, survival, and basic well-being[16] of everyone who will be governed by it?

In order to discover more about what occupying this standpoint entails, it will be helpful to look at two passages in which Rousseau expands on the nature of rational deliberation. The first of these is found in an early, originally unpublished draft of the *Social Contract*, the so-called Geneva Manuscript:[17]

> [T]he general will is in each individual a pure act of the understanding, which reasons *in the silence of the passions* about what man can demand of his fellow man and what his fellow man has the right to demand of him. But where is the man who *is able to separate himself from himself* in this manner and to *look at ... the species in general* in order to impose on himself duties whose connection with his particular constitution is not visible to him? ... What is more, since the art of *generalizing ideas* in this way is one of the most difficult and belated exercises of human understanding, [how] will the ordinary man ever be in a position to derive his rules of conduct from this manner of reasoning?
>
> (GM, 157–8/OC 3, 286–7; emphases added)

If nothing else, this passage makes clear that for Rousseau knowing one's duty involves more than unreflectively heeding one's 'inner voice' or blindly following the impulses of pity. Rather, we are told, discerning the general will is an act of the understanding that takes place in the silence

---

[16] I speak here of basic well-being rather than self-preservation, since it is reasonable to take Rousseau's references to the latter to include, beyond mere biological survival, the basic goods (such as decent health care and housing) necessary to achieving a minimal standard of well-being.

[17] Parts of the GM's description of the general will are lifted directly from Diderot's 'Natural Right', published in 1755 in volume V of the *Encyclopedia* (OC 3, 1413–14, n. 3).

of the passions. This means that adopting the standpoint of reason requires the ability to put to the side, at least momentarily, the demands of one's own particular desires and interests. It requires, in other words, the ability to effect a distance or inner separation from oneself that temporarily mutes the promptings of impulse and appetite.[18] It is not implausible to think of this distancing as a form of abstraction—a bracketing of a certain given content of the self—which Rousseau regards as one of the hallmarks of reason.[19]

A further feature of the standpoint of reason comes to light in Rousseau's talk of 'the species in general' and 'the generalization of ideas'. His thought here seems to be that when consulting the principles of duty, the individual abstracts from his own particular desires in order to assume a point of view that is in some sense universal. This means that the perspective from which he endorses or rejects a proposed law will take as its determining criterion the good of all (some version of that idea) rather than his own particular desires, interests, or happiness. The idea is not just that the legislating individual *looks at* the object of deliberation from the general point of view made possible by the silencing of his passions; he also takes what he sees from that point of view as *authoritative*—he recognizes the good of all as the basis for imposing on himself principles of action that have no direct grounding in his own particular desires (and hence seem to conflict with the natural self-interestedness of creatures like us).

Rousseau says more about the kind of generalization reason requires in the second of the two passages that describe the citizen's deliberative stance. In this well-known (though puzzling) passage Rousseau depicts the frame of mind the citizen must adopt if he is to succeed in discerning the general will's content:

Why is the general will always right (*droite*), and why do all constantly will the happiness of each, if not because there is no one who does not apply (*s'approprie*) this word *each* to himself, and does not think of himself as he votes for all? Which proves that the equality of right and the notion of justice that this equality produces,

---

[18] 'Reason turns man back upon himself; it separates him from all that bothers and afflicts him' (*DI*, 153/*OC* 3, 156). In the same passage *amour-propre* is said to be 'engendered' by reason and 'fortified' by reflection.

[19] For the connection between abstraction and the generalization intrinsic to reason, see, e.g. *E* III, 207/*OC* 4, 487. Rousseau also emphasizes the importance of abstraction for language and thought at *DI*, 147–9/*OC* 3, 149–50.

derive from each man's preference for himself and consequently from the nature of man; that the general will to be truly such must be general in its object as well as in its essence; that it must come from all in order to apply (*s'appliquer*) to all; and that it loses its natural rectitude as soon as it is directed at any individual, determinate object.

(*SC*, II.4.v)

The repeated contrast here between each and all—*chacun* and *tous*—helps to clarify the sense in which reason involves the generalizing of ideas. It makes clear that the sense in which the 'species in general' enters into reason's deliberations is best expressed not in terms of the good of *all* but as the good of *each*; to will generally, we are told, is to will 'the happiness of each'. It is not, then, the aggregate 'happiness' (as Rousseau misleadingly calls it here) of some group with which the general will is concerned but rather the good—more specifically, the fundamental interests—of each individual member. (Happily, this is precisely what we should expect, given my earlier account of the ends that guide the will of the collective self to which the social contract gives rise.) This means that the generalizing of ideas that reason requires consists not so much[20] in taking on the standpoint of some supraindividual collective—in judging legislation from the vantage point of the species' (or community's) interests as a whole—as in adopting the perspective of an abstract 'each' that stands in for every particular member of the association in question. The general will is general, then, in a sense that approximates Kant's understanding of the universality of a rationally legislating will: in deciding whether to endorse or reject a proposed law, Rousseau's citizen subjects his will to a kind of universalizability test, asking in effect whether one's opinion on the law could be shared by every other citizen who will be bound by it,

---

[20] Viewing legislation from the perspective of the good of the whole may, however, play some limited role in framing the citizen's deliberations. This is suggested by some of Rousseau's formulations, such as his claim that the general will 'always tends to the preservation and well-being *of the whole* and of each part' (*PE*, 6/*OC* 3, 243; emphasis added). In considering how to defend the state from foreign attacks, for example, the citizen will no doubt think of the community as a collective self with its own legitimate interest in preserving itself. Nevertheless, the perspective that considers the good of the whole (collectively) always remains subordinate to the 'good of each' standpoint in two respects. First, the former perspective is constrained by the latter in the sense that no policy aimed at, e.g. preserving the state as a whole, is admissible if it compromises the fundamental interests of any individual citizen (*PE*, 17/*OC* 3, 256–7). Second, the value that any collective good possesses is parasitic on the value of securing the fundamental interests of individuals; what ultimately justifies the preservation of the state as a whole is that it alone guarantees the security and freedom of each.

if each were to judge the proposed law only insofar as it affects his own fundamental, 'human' interests.

There is a further issue addressed by this passage, though what it says on this topic is considerably more puzzling than the conceptual contrast between 'each' and 'all'. The issue concerns how it is subjectively possible for humans, who are by nature self-interested creatures, to impose principles of reason on themselves, and the interpretive puzzle is how the talk of appropriating, or applying, the word 'each' to oneself helps to explain this possibility. It is clear that Rousseau invokes the idea of applying the word 'each' to oneself when legislating for all in order to explain how the natural human preference for self, inherent in both *amour-propre* and *amour de soi*,[21] can be reconciled with reason's demand that we, sometimes at least, give priority to others' interests over our own. It is just as clear, moreover, that Rousseau wants to claim that this very self-interestedness, reconfigured in some way, can supply the motivational force rational agency depends on. In other words, his question here is how the human being's preference for self can be harnessed so as to move her in a direction precisely opposite to its natural tendency—to produce a will that seeks not preference and individual gain but the equality that justice demands.

Let us first get clear on the nature of this equality. Since our aim is to grasp what is entailed in assuming the standpoint of reason, our main concern should be to understand how the deliberating citizen must think of himself, especially in relation to his fellow citizens, in order to be able to will the equality that justice demands. We are concerned, in other words, with the kind of *self-conception* the standpoint of reason presupposes—a self-conception that is meant to be captured, presumably, by the talk of appropriating the word 'each' to oneself. The answer to this question follows directly from the idea of the general will as articulated above. Implicit in the general will's ends is a demand for equality of the following

---

[21] The claim that preference for self is inherent in *amour de soi* may seem to contradict Rousseau's claim that the latter, in contrast to *amour-propre*, is non-comparative. There is, however, no such contradiction. Self-preference is foreign to *amour de soi* in the sense that no comparison with others is ever built into the ends it seeks, in contrast to *amour-propre*, for which standing relative to others is always at issue. Nevertheless, a kind of self-preference is implicit in even non-relative self-love. Although *amour de soi* does not imply hostility or even indifference to the good of others, it does direct its possessor to prefer his good to another's when circumstances make a choice between the two necessary. Rousseau associates this sense of self-preference with *amour de soi* at *DI*, 127/*OC* 3, 126, and the same is implied at *E* IV, 352/*OC* 4, 687–8.

sort: each citizen must acknowledge that no one's good has a higher value—a right to count for more in public deliberations on what will be law—than anyone else's. This demand expresses itself in two ways. First, it requires each citizen to recognize that his own fundamental interests have the same status as everyone else's. A proposed law that would compromise the freedom or self-preservation[22] of a single compatriot must be regarded as no less objectionable than a law that would harm oneself in the very same way. A second implication of reason's commitment to the equality of all is expressed in the demand that, in their roles as legislators, citizens accord a *higher* value to the fundamental interests of others than to their own particular (and non-fundamental[23]) interests. This means that citizens must be able to endorse laws that harm some of their own particular interests when such laws are necessary in order to safeguard the fundamental interests of all. (A law that mandates progressive taxation in order to secure the autonomy and basic well-being of everyone is an example of this type of legislation (*PE*, 33/*OC* 3, 273). Rousseau's claim is that in such a case those who are better off must be able to acknowledge the priority of others' fundamental interests over their own particular interest in being able to enjoy all of what the market recognizes as theirs.)

How, then, must the citizen conceive of herself in order to occupy, and to will from, the standpoint of reason? My discussion of equality points to two features of the self-conception this standpoint presupposes. First, the citizen must have a conception of herself that makes her fundamental interests—her life and freedom—the most basic features of her identity. These two interests must be regarded as most basic in the sense that they are taken to have lexical[24] priority over all other goods. They must be seen, in other words, as an individual's overriding interests, the satisfaction of which

---

[22] Recall that I am interpreting 'self-preservation' widely, to include the basic goods necessary for achieving a minimal standard of well-being. See n. 16 above.

[23] This qualifier is necessary since individuals' fundamental interests in freedom and self-preservation count as particular interests for Rousseau, even though they are shared by and essential to all human beings. Rousseau uses 'particular' interchangeably with 'private' (*SC* I.5.1) and defines a particular interest as one that 'tends only to [one's] particular [or private] advantage' (*SC*, III.2.v). Particular, or private, interests are the interests one has in the state of nature—that is, when regarded as a separate individual, unattached to others through sentiment or obligation. Thus, a particular will is identical to a purely self-interested, or egoistic, will. This point is especially important since Hegel attaches a different meaning to 'particular'; see Neuhouser, *Foundations*, 41–3, 87–92.

[24] Lexical priority means that in determining the content of the general will, all fundamental interests must be satisfied before other, non-fundamental interests are taken into account. This term derives from John Rawls, *A Theory of Justice* (Cambridge, Mass.: Harvard University Press, 1971), 42–3. Rawls's

may not be renounced or traded away for any other goods.[25] Conceiving of oneself in this way is necessary if one is to be able to will laws that require one's non-fundamental interests to give way to fundamental interests (both one's own and others') whenever the two conflict. It is precisely this understanding of what is essential to her own being that enables a citizen to assent to laws that take away a sizable portion of her wealth in order to fund public education, community-owned radio stations, and publicly financed political campaigns.[26] In this context, Rousseau's description of the citizen as appropriating the word 'each' to herself acquires a specific and coherent meaning: in legislating for all, the citizen takes the qualities that characterize each to be the central features of her own identity—or, as Rousseau would also express it, she regards what is common and essential to every human being as her own most important interests.

This, however, cannot exhaust the sense in which the citizen thinks of himself as 'each' when occupying the standpoint of reason. For taking one's own life and freedom as one's most important interests does not yet explain the citizen's ability to accord overriding importance to the fundamental interests of everyone. Yet such a concern for the interests of others is necessary to the citizen's point of view, since reason requires him to endorse laws that harm some of his own non-essential interests in order to secure the fundamental interests of others. (The better off, for example, will need to assent to laws that equalize material wealth to the extent that realizing the freedom of everyone requires it—to the extent, in other words, that 'no citizen is so rich that he can buy another and none so poor that he is forced to sell himself' (SC, II.11.ii).) One way of expressing this requirement would be to say that the citizen must not only accord supreme importance to the 'essentially human' within himself but

---

account of the original position is but a version of Rousseau's idea of conceiving of oneself as 'each' and thinking of oneself as one votes for all.

[25] For evidence that this is how Rousseau views the status of fundamental interests, see n. 15 above. This way of understanding the sense in which fundamental interests are most basic is weaker than one possible alternative, according to which life and freedom are *conditions* of the value of all other goods—those things in the absence of which all other goods lose their value. On the view I attribute to Rousseau, it is never permissible to sacrifice one's freedom for any good (except, perhaps, for one's life), but in conditions where freedom is impossible, a comfortable servitude counts as better than a miserable one.

[26] This assumes that access to education as well as to news and political campaigns that are not beholden to private interests is essential to maintaining one's freedom. This seems plausible if, as Rousseau believes, freedom requires that political decisions be based on full information and undistorted communication (SC, II.3.iii).

also regard the humanity of every individual as of equal value to his own. A second necessary feature of the citizen's self-conception, then, is a sense of his essential equality with all other members of his species. More precisely, the citizen must be committed to what I called in Chapter 2 the equal moral status of all human beings—that is, to the belief that no individual's interests deserve to carry more weight than anyone else's in determining the rights and obligations of all.

These two aspects of the citizen's self-conception are perhaps more closely related than they initially appear to be. Indeed, there is some plausibility in thinking that their relation approximates mutual implication. For once an individual comes to locate her own most important goods in her life and freedom—in qualities she shares with all other human beings—it seems to be only a very short step to the conclusion that those things are to be accorded a similar value wherever they are found. But even if this is so, Rousseau's description of the subjective makeup of citizens makes it clear that he does not think of their concern for the fundamental interests of others as having its primary source in something as removed from human feeling as the force of logical entailment. As his talk of 'applying th[e] word *each* to himself' and then 'thinking of himself as he votes for all' suggests, he takes this concern to derive, instead, from a kind of affective *identification* with others that enables the citizen to will their good out of love for himself. This suggestion places us at the heart of an intriguing but difficult issue—how self-love enters into rational motivation—to which I return in Chapter 7.

The 'public' character of reason

There is a final aspect of Rousseau's conception of reason in need of consideration. It is hinted at throughout Rousseau's texts but is most evident in those places where he refers to the laws of the legitimate state as 'public reason' (*PE*, 5, 10/*OC* 3, 243, 248; GM, [178]/*OC* 3, 310; *J*, 430/*OC* 2, 524). This talk of public reason is fully in line with Rousseau's conception of the state as 'a moral and collective body', or 'self', that possesses a unitary life and will (*SC*, I.6.x). For if the state is a public person with a general will, it seems to follow that the reason that guides its will must be public as well. This, however, raises an important question: in what precise sense is reason for Rousseau public, or intersubjective, in nature? Is the standpoint of reason one an individual citizen could occupy all by herself, or does it presuppose certain relations among subjects that an individual is in principle unable to establish by or within herself?

As it has been characterized thus far, the standpoint of reason appears to be accessible to a single individual in one important sense: even if reason would have no domain of application in a world without a plurality of subjects (since there would be no conflict among fundamental interests for reason to adjudicate), and even if (as Rousseau believes) relations to other subjects are necessary for individuals to develop the mental capacities that reasoning presupposes, nevertheless the process of reasoning itself—deliberation about what is right—appears to be something an already formed human being can engage in within the confines of his own consciousness. For in consulting reason about the principles one ought to live by, all that seems to be required is a kind of thought experiment that the individual should be capable of undertaking on his own: he need merely envisage the enactment of a proposed principle of action and then consider how such a measure would affect the fundamental interests of every individual. Moreover, since what counts in this procedure are the interests humans share rather than those that differentiate them, it seems plausible that a single individual, simply by consulting the humanity within himself, could in principle discern what reason prescribes without the input of other subjects. In other words, the simple fact that reason by its nature takes into account the interests of others does not imply that an individual reasoner, equipped with the requisite imagination and sensitivity, is incapable of figuring out for himself how those interests are likely to be affected by a proposed law.

At the same time, Rousseau seems to hold that public deliberation—'voicing opinions, making proposals, dividing, discussing' (*SC*, IV.1.vii)—is essential to the process by which the content of the general will is determined in a legitimate state (*SC*, II.3.iii).[27] Of course, this alone does not settle the issue of whether reason is inherently intersubjective in the

---

[27] There is room for disagreement on this point. While Rousseau is unambiguous in criticizing representative democracy and in requiring legislative assemblies open to all citizens, it is less clear that he believes deliberation (as opposed to mere voting) to be necessary, or even desirable. Although Rousseau frequently uses the term, Bernard Manin argues that 'deliberation' always means 'decision' rather than the process of reasoning and will formation that precedes decision ('On Legitimacy and Political Deliberation', *Political Theory* 15 (1987), 345–7). Although Manin's argument is frequently

strong sense at issue here. There are many respects in which the exchange of ideas with others could improve the deliberative process without implying that the standpoint of reason was in principle accessible only to a 'we' and not to a solitary 'I'. For one thing, the testimony of others—especially of those to be affected by a particular law—is likely to uncover legitimate objections to the proposed measure that the limited imagination of a single individual can easily overlook. A further reason for requiring public deliberation is that in the real world, determining what will promote or compromise the fundamental interests of all often requires more experience and wisdom than a single individual can have on her own. A good deal of knowledge, both of the world and of human nature, is required to determine how, for example, a proposed revision in the welfare system will affect the freedom of all citizens. In thinking through issues this complex, many heads will usually be better than one. Finally, apart from improving the outcome of the decision process, public deliberation might play a crucial part in furthering the *freedom* of individuals, since participating in (or witnessing) the actual process through which the general will is formed makes it more likely that a citizen will be able to recognize the rationality of the laws that bind her and, so, to be free in her subjection to them.

None of these considerations implies, however, that the perspective of the general will is in principle unavailable to the solitary reasoner. The picture they convey, rather, is one in which the participation of others serves to provide the individual with more and better 'input' for his own reasoning process but where it is still, in an important sense, the individual who looks out from reason's point of view and determines what it prescribes. It is in this vein that Rousseau describes the process of deliberation in the assembly as one in which, after discussion has concluded, citizens look within themselves, each for himself, to determine whether a proposed law 'conforms or not to the general will that is theirs' (*SC*, IV.2.viii). That individuals have access to the standpoint of reason seems to be implicit as well in one of the *Social Contract*'s defining principles, namely, that the legitimate state must not only *be* rational; it must also, in its basic outline, be *visible* as such to all its members from their perspectives. (This, I take it, is one implication of the fundamental principle that consent

persuasive, it is hard to square with everything Rousseau says, e.g. at *SC*, IV.1.vii. Moreover, at *SC*, IV.2.iii, Rousseau uses 'deliberation' in the more usual sense of the term.

to the original contract must be unanimous.) These points make clear that Rousseau's conception of reason not only assumes that individuals are able to occupy and view the world from a universal standpoint; it also accords a kind of *authority* to individual reasoners, an authority central to the ideal of individual autonomy that informs the social contract tradition before Rousseau, as well as the tradition of German idealism after him. At the core of this ideal is the thought that the validity of moral laws depends on the consent or insight (in some form) of the individuals who are subject to them—or, as social contract theory formulates the idea, that individuals are obligated only by laws or political procedures that they themselves can recognize as justified. This idea reverberates, too, in Rousseau's description of citizens' legislative behavior in the assembly, according to which, after taking part in public debate, each looks within himself to decide whether a particular law 'conforms ... to [*his*] general will'. In other words, regardless of how publicly reason's deliberation is carried out, there is still a sense in which the ideal of rational autonomy implies that each individual ought ultimately to be able to 'see for himself'—by his own lights—the rational character of the laws that the body as a whole agrees on.

So, if after public deliberation it is their own reason that citizens consult, is there any substantive sense in which submitting to legitimate laws is a submitting to *public* reason? The best way to answer this question is to determine precisely what is at issue for Rousseau in those passages that emphasize the public character of reason. Interestingly enough, most of these passages also make it clear that the standpoint of reason is available to individual citizens in the sense just discussed. One such passage speaks of the citizen as having 'his own reason' but goes on to add that 'his own reason should be suspect to him, and he should follow no other rule than public reason, which is the law' (*PE*, 5/*OC* 3, 243). In another place the supraindividual character of reason is expressed in the statement that 'no one allows that the reason of each man is the unique arbiter of his duties' (*PE*, 21/*OC* 3, 260).[28] This same theme is expanded on in the very passage, referred to above, in which Rousseau depicts each citizen in the assembly as having and consulting his own general will. Citing this passage in full

---

[28] In the same vein, Rousseau says that law is 'the celestial voice that tells each citizen the precepts of public reason and teaches him to act on the maxims of his own judgment' (*GM*, [178]/*OC* 3, 310).

will help to clarify how Rousseau takes reason to be both accessible to individuals and inherently public at the same time:

The citizen consents to all the laws, even to those that are passed in spite of himself. ... The constant will of all the members of the state is the general will. ... When a law is proposed in the assembly of the people, what they are being asked is not precisely whether they approve the proposal or reject it, but whether it conforms or not to the general will that is theirs. Each one states his opinion (*avis*) on this by voting, and the declaration of the general will is drawn from the counting of the votes. Therefore when the opinion contrary to mine prevails, that proves only that I was mistaken, and what I thought to be the general will was not.

(*SC*, IV.2.viii)

The general message of these passages appears to be that while reason's point of view is in some sense accessible to an individual reasoner (and must be if it is to be binding on him), its power to generate obligation for both oneself and others depends on something more than the individual's opinion or will. Although an individual citizen is capable of assuming a suitably general perspective from which to assess the rationality of proposed laws, what he finds when he adopts that perspective 'should be suspect to him' (which is to say: his own reason is not 'the unique arbiter of his duties'). In other words, part of what constitutes the citizen's suspicion of his own reason is the recognition that it is not *his* but *public* reason (or law) that has the final say in determining what he ought to do.

The challenge here is to spell out what role Rousseau takes the wills of others to play in generating rational obligation and to do so in a way that is consistent with his view that individuals themselves possess a kind of moral authority (in the sense that the validity of moral laws depends on some form of their consent or insight). Whatever the answer to this question turns out to be, it is plausible to think that it will be bound up with the foundational claim expressed in Rousseau's well-known statements at the beginning of the *Social Contract* concerning the source of obligation, namely, that 'right does not come from nature [but] is founded on conventions' (*SC*, I.1.ii) and that 'conventions alone [are] the basis of all legitimate authority among men' (*SC*, I.4.i). In singling out convention—literally, the coming together, or agreement, of human wills—as the source of all right and all human authority, Rousseau clearly does not mean to claim that morality has no objective content apart from what any given group of human beings declares it to be. On the contrary, he insists repeatedly that it is possible, and not uncommon, for an actual assembly of citizens to fail to discern the general will correctly and so, in effect, to be mistaken about what is right (*SC*, II.3.i, IV.2.ix–x; *PE*, 8/*OC* 3, 246). Beyond this, as if to eliminate any doubt that might remain, Rousseau declares unambiguously that 'whatever is good... is so by the nature of things and independently of human conventions;[29] ... there is without doubt a universal justice that emanates from reason alone' (*SC*, II.6.ii). If, then, the coming together of actual human wills cannot simply decide the content of justice, in what sense is it grounded in convention?

There are two distinct senses in which Rousseau takes agreement among human wills to be the source of all right and obligation. Each of these senses points to a different respect in which reason is intersubjectively constituted, and both have to be brought together if Rousseau's position is to be understood. According to the first, it is the idea of convention itself—of what all human beings could rationally agree on—that furnishes the basic content for the principles of 'universal justice'. This means that the correct account of what right consists in follows directly from an analysis of the conditions under which the wills of rational human beings are able to 'come together' and reach agreement on the principles that ought to govern their cooperation. The concept of the general will as defined above is Rousseau's attempt to spell out the principles that follow from these conditions. According to this concept, the content of the justice that 'emanates from reason alone' and inheres in 'the nature of things' is arrived at by figuring out which principles all human beings would agree to be bound by if each were motivated first and foremost by the desire to secure her own fundamental interests in life (or basic well-being) and freedom. Thus, even though the idea of agreement among a plurality of human wills is central to the concept of right, the ideal, or hypothetical, character of

---

[29] This statement appears to contradict the claim that 'right does not come from nature [but] is founded on conventions' (*SC*, I.1.ii). But 'the nature of things' is not the same as 'nature'. The latter is to be understood as a realm that by definition excludes human will, so that there is in principle no place for right or justice—for laws that bind human wills—in 'nature' in this sense. The former expression is broader in scope and allows for talk about 'the nature of' all phenomena, including the nature of freedom and will. The nature of freedom and will is independent of human conventions in the sense that there is objective truth about freedom and will (and the laws that govern them) that does not depend on any *actual* agreement or convention among real human beings (though, as I explain later in the text, it gets its content from a version of the notion of ideal or hypothetical agreement). See also *RSW*, 23/*OC* 1, 1018, where Rousseau speaks of a 'moral order' that is 'dictated by Heaven'.

this agreement makes it possible both for actual groups of humans to err in their deliberations about what right prescribes and for lone individuals, equipped with a proper understanding of the basic nature and equality of all human beings, to reason soundly about the same.

The second sense in which the agreement of wills grounds right and obligation is more difficult to grasp. It is also more directly related to the point made in the passages cited above in which the final authority of right is said to reside in public reason (or law) rather than in the reason of any individual. Rousseau says there, it will be recalled, that an individual's judgment concerning the content of the general will is not the final arbiter of what is right but is, instead, subject to correction by the contrary opinion of a majority of his fellow citizens. These and similar statements are best understood as pointing to a particular frame of mind that Rousseau takes to be intrinsic to rational agency: part of what it is to be a rational agent—to regard oneself as bound by what reason demands—is to adopt an attitude of suspicion towards one's own judgments of right. Adopting this attitude is, in effect, acknowledging that a principle's appearing to me as right when I assume the perspective of reason does not suffice to give that principle rational authority. There exists, in other words, a logical gap between my own reasoned opinion (*avis*) that a certain law is right and the law's validity—its authority to obligate rational wills. Moreover—or so Rousseau asserts—this authority can be established only by a will that is public, or intersubjectively constituted, in some sense yet to be determined. An alternative way of formulating Rousseau's claim would be to say that, properly understood, the standpoint of reason is not simply the universal point of view an individual adopts when attempting to figure out what the general will wills but rather that point of view, *together with* the recognition that one's own opinion of what is right, no matter how convincing to oneself, does not by itself—independently of all relations to the actual wills of others—possess the authority of law.

It is important to be especially careful in specifying the sense in which Rousseau takes the authority of reason to depend on an actual collective will. We have already seen that he considers the basic content of justice (as defined by the concept of the general will) to be independent of any actual human decision or agreement. So whatever the sense in which reason's authority depends on a collective will, it must be compatible with Rousseau's view that the most general principles of reason (as, for

Hobbes, the laws of nature[30]) are fixed and possess a certain validity independently of actual human agreement. This observation is borne out by a closer examination of the context within which Rousseau makes his provocative—and potentially misleading—statement that 'when the opinion contrary to mine prevails [in the assembly], that proves only that I was mistaken, and what I thought to be the general will was not' (SC, IV.2.viii). Just before the paragraph in which this statement appears, Rousseau emphasizes that consent to the social contract itself—to the basic terms of political association—must be unanimous, and that in the absence of this original consent, majority opinions of whatever sort have no authority over individuals. This makes it clear that later, when a citizen's opinion is said to be mistaken if it conflicts with the majority's, Rousseau means to be discussing a very specific aspect of the authority of reason. What is at issue for Rousseau here is not the content or validity of reason's basic principles but rather the application of those principles in a specific situation. In other words, the rift among citizens that Rousseau describes is a dispute not over fundamental values but over what, concretely, their own shared principles commit them to do. The issue to be settled by the assembly's decision, then, is how to translate a set of generally recognized moral principles into concrete directives—positive laws—that assign specific obligations (and rights) to the agents who are bound by them. A dispute of this nature can arise because although citizens know that the general will enjoins them to safeguard and promote the freedom and basic well-being of all, it is rarely easy to determine simply from this formula which specific actions those demands entail.

I suggested earlier that Rousseau should be understood here as drawing our attention to a particular feature of the frame of mind that characterizes the standpoint of reason, namely, an attitude of suspicion towards one's own (individual) judgments of right. But this attitude towards oneself—towards

---

[30] For Hobbes the laws of nature are fixed independently of convention in the sense that they can be deduced, and understood as good, on the basis of certain convention-independent truths about human nature, including a claim about human beings' overriding interest in self-preservation. The authority they possess prior to the social compact is the authority to 'oblige *in foro interno*'; that is, 'they bind to a desire that [the laws of nature] should take place.' This seems to mean that we are required, so far as is compatible with our own preservation, sincerely to desire—and, so, to strive to bring about—a situation (that of established political authority) in which the laws of nature are generally followed: *L*, xv.36–9.

one's own reason—can just as well be described as an attitude one takes to others: part of being a rational agent is adopting a certain attitude of respect towards the opinions of other rational beings. (This attitude of respect is one especially important version of what Hegel will later call recognition, which, following Rousseau, he regards as essential to establishing the authority of reason.) This respect consists in according appropriate weight to the moral judgments of others. It requires one to grant a certain, though by no means absolute, authority to the opinions of others, including those that diverge from one's own. To do so is to recognize other rational agents as having a claim to know what is right—to be competent in interpreting or applying the basic principles of right—equal to that which I accord to myself. This is precisely what it means not to take oneself to be 'the unique arbiter of [one's] duties', and the opposite of this attitude—the tendency simply to take one's own understanding of the good as finally authoritative—is what one could call, with Hegel,[31] 'moral self-conceit' or the 'willfulness' of individual conscience. It may be easier to appreciate Rousseau's point by recasting it as a claim about how the rational citizen thinks of herself, and of her own access to the general will, in relation to the assembly of all citizens of which she is a part. As a member of the assembly whose task is to translate the principles that define the general will into specific laws binding on everyone, the individual citizen views herself as but one participant in a collective quest to determine what is right. This means that, although she takes herself to be capable of forming, on the basis of her own judgment, a reasoned *opinion*[32] as to what the general will prescribes, she does not regard this opinion as possessing, of itself, the authority of law—which is to say, she does not regard her opinion as possessing, of itself, the power to obligate others. Rather, the opinion of any single citizen acquires this authority if, and only if, it corresponds to the consensus that results from the free exchange of the opinions of all. In the absence of such confirmation by the opinions of others—when the opinion contrary to her own prevails—the citizen adopts an attitude that is

---

[31] Neuhouser, *Foundations*, 248–50.

[32] Rousseau consistently refers to citizens' votes as expressing opinions (*avis*) about the general will (e.g. *SC*, IV.2.viii) rather than knowledge, or even judgments. The point of this, I believe, is to differentiate opinions, which are statements about how a certain thing *appears* to one on the basis of one's own reasoning, from judgments, which assert that a thing *is* and, so, make a claim to objective validity (i.e. to holding for all rational beings).

the practical analogue of concluding that she was 'mistaken' and that 'what [she] thought to be the general will was not': she relinquishes in this case her own claim to determine what duty requires, and she recognizes the general opinion as her authority instead.[33]

Readers of Rousseau frequently take him to be saying something stronger and more sinister in this passage than the view I am attributing to him. But in saying that I must regard myself as 'mistaken' when 'the opinion contrary to mine prevails', he manifestly does not mean that the opinion of any majority is always correct,[34] nor, as we have seen, that there exist no valid general criteria for what is right apart from what the majority of any group declares it to be. Rousseau's purpose, rather, is to draw our attention to a point about the nature of rational obligation in general, a point that is said to follow as 'a consequence of the [original] contract itself' (SC, IV.2.vii). At one place Rousseau expresses his point as the familiar claim that once the social contract has been entered into, 'the vote of the majority always obligates all the rest' (SC, IV.2.vii). But if, as we already know, there are universal principles of justice that have their source in reason independently of actual human agreement, why is something beyond these principles—something as mundane as the actual vote of a majority—necessary to generate obligation? Rousseau addresses this question, though obliquely, when he says:

All justice comes from God; ... but *if we knew how to receive it* from such a lofty source, we would need neither government nor laws. There is without doubt a universal justice that emanates from reason alone; *but to be admitted among us, this justice must be reciprocal.*

(SC, II.6.ii; emphasis added)

Rousseau's most important reason for saying that government, law, and reciprocity are required if principles of justice are to obligate human beings is not the same one Hobbes famously appeals to in support of a similar claim (namely, that obeying the laws of nature is detrimental to an individual's self-preservation, and so contrary to reason, unless he has assurances that others will do the same) (L, xv.36). Rousseau's claim, in contrast, derives

---

[33] This point was inspired by a discussion with Christine Korsgaard many years ago.
[34] This is confirmed in the next paragraph, SC, IV.2.ix.

from a view about the inherent *indeterminacy* of the principles that reason by itself prescribes. Recall here that the context in which Rousseau's claim appears is his discussion of a dispute within the citizen assembly over how the general principles of justice are to be applied—that is, translated into positive laws that spell out, concretely, what each is obligated to do. Rousseau's underlying assumption—which, too, has its source in Hobbes[35]—is that although it is easy enough to recognize the rational force of the general will's basic principles, it is much more difficult to discern clearly, and to agree upon, which specific obligations those principles entail. This implies that if the principles of justice are to be received and acknowledged by human beings—if they are to be the source of real obligations in human society—those general principles must first be interpreted, or applied. And since God himself is not available to perform this task,[36] it must be undertaken by the very beings whose duties are at issue.

This, of course, raises the question of who should interpret those principles—or, more precisely, of who should be the final authority when disputes of interpretation arise. The answer, Rousseau claims, is inscribed in the terms of the social contract itself and, so, in the very conditions that make rational obligation in general possible: the actual consensus of those bound by the principles in question is the final authority on their proper application. Before I say more about what this answer implies, let us see why it follows from the logic of the social contract. If we accept Rousseau's assumption about the indeterminacy of the principles of justice, together with his account of the original position of the parties to the social contract, majority consensus is the only rule for settling interpretive disputes those parties could rationally agree to. The argument for this rests ultimately on Rousseau's understanding of the contracting individuals as essentially free. Freedom in general, for Rousseau, is defined as 'obeying only oneself' (*SC*, I.6.iv), or 'not being subjected to the will of others' (*LWM*, 260/*OC* 3, 841),[37] and the specific version of this that the *Social Contract* ascribes

[35] *L*, xvii.4.

[36] Even where God is thought to supply humans with very concrete ethical commands, human interpretation is no less necessary. God says, 'Love thy neighbor as thyself,' but who exactly is my neighbor, and how much am I to love myself? He commands, 'Thou shalt not kill,' but is capital punishment killing?

[37] For more on Rousseau's conception of freedom, including ambiguities in his concept of natural freedom, see Neuhouser, *Foundations*, 68–9, 185–7, 319n.11.

to the contracting parties—the freedom individuals are taken to possess by nature—consists in the absence of all relations of (*de jure*) authority among them (*SC*, I.4.i). In other words, in the state of nature, prior to political association, no human being has the right to command nor the duty to obey the will of any other. It is because any legitimate contract must preserve this freedom to the greatest degree possible, and to the same extent for all individuals, that the rule of law is a necessary feature of the civil order the contracting parties agree to. For Rousseau, this implies not only that all citizens must be equally subject to the laws of their state but also that they must have equal say in authoring them (*SC*, I.6.vi–x, II.4.v). Any inequality in either of these roles would violate the contract's need to preserve in equal proportions the freedom—in this case, the moral authority—of all individuals.

Given this, along with the enduring need to apply, or interpret, the principles originally agreed to, some form of majority consensus based on the free exchange of the opinions of all is the only acceptable answer to the question of where final authority in interpreting the general will resides. One way of reformulating Rousseau's point is to say that it follows from the very idea of self-given law—from the idea of self-imposed obligation—that an individual who subjects herself to the rule of law must, as a condition of belonging to such an order, relinquish her right to be the final arbiter of what she is permitted or obligated to do (*SC*, I.6.vii).[38] Moreover, relinquishing this right cannot be a matter of agreeing merely to comply externally with the majority's interpretation of the general will. (This much prudence alone is normally able to accomplish.) Beyond this—or so Rousseau's language implies—the citizen must regard the collective consensus as 'correct' and her own divergent opinion as 'mistaken'. This means two things. First, the rational agent considers the majority view correct from a *practical* point of view: in deciding how to act in the situation at hand, she recognizes the practical validity of the prevailing opinion in that she takes it to be the authoritative judge of what reason obligates her, and all her fellow citizens, to do. In other words, she lets her actions be determined by the opinion of others but only because she recognizes that opinion as the legitimate mouthpiece of reason—which is to say, the only earthly candidate for that role that could be freely assented to by all.

---

[38] I am indebted to Jason Hill for suggesting this formulation.

Secondly, the rational agent also regards the collective consensus as correct in a theoretical sense: he takes his disagreement with the majority as substantial evidence for the possibility that their opinion expresses the spirit of the general will more faithfully than his own. This is not to say that the citizen must view the group's consensus as infallible or as immune to future revision, nor that he must abandon all further attempts to challenge it by rational argument. It does mean, at the very least, that he looks on his own opinion with even greater suspicion than before. Beyond this, though, Rousseau's position also seems to require that the rational subject admit the truth (or objectivity) of the dominant opinion in the following sense: he recognizes that this opinion currently comes closest to meeting the only empirical criterion for truth in matters of right[39] that reason can acknowledge. This is to say: the actual consensus of the assembly is the view collectively endorsed by competent moral agents, through a free exchange of reasons that excluded no one, and until that consensus is disrupted, it remains the best candidate for the truth about justice that his community possesses.[40]

As we have just seen, taking seriously Rousseau's utterances regarding the public character of reason leads us to a view according to which subjection to reason is also necessarily a subjection to 'opinion' (to the normative judgments of other subjects). What Rousseau sometimes describes (and decries) as the 'yoke' of opinion (*E* IV, 260/*OC* 4, 558) is very closely related, then, to the phenomenon he describes (and celebrates) as 'the yoke of reason' (*E* IV, 315/*OC* 4, 637). If, as the Second Discourse maintains, surrendering to the rule of public opinion is one of the greatest dangers of human existence, it is also a necessary condition of freedom (since without reason there can be no freedom in the social state). One of Rousseau's deepest insights is that *amour-propre* is centrally involved in both of these phenomena; explaining in more detail how the 'yoke of reason' is but a reconfiguration of the 'yoke of opinion' is the main task of the following chapter.

---

[39] Hegel will extend this claim to truth in general.

[40] Thus, Rousseau's position approximates the account of moral objectivity Rawls finds in Kant: 'moral convictions are objective if reasonable ... persons who are sufficiently intelligent and conscientious in exercising their powers of practical reason would eventually endorse those convictions, when all concerned know the relevant facts and have sufficiently surveyed the relevant considerations. To say that a moral conviction is objective, then, is to say that there are reasons sufficient to convince all reasonable persons that it is valid or correct' (*Lectures on the History of Moral Philosophy*, ed. Barbara Herman (Cambridge, Mass.: Harvard University Press, 2000), 245).

Public reason, individual sovereignty, intersubjective recognition

This position on the overriding authority of majority decisions seems to conflict with my earlier claim that, in embracing the basic tenets of social contract theory, Rousseau accords a kind of autonomy to individuals, according to which the validity of moral laws depends on the consent or insight of those who are subject to them. This aspect of Rousseau's position finds expression, however, in the important but often neglected qualification he attaches to the end of the passage I have just been examining. Immediately after saying that 'when the opinion contrary to my own prevails, it proves only that I was mistaken,' Rousseau goes on to add: 'This presupposes, it is true, that all the characteristics of the general will are still in the majority. When they cease to be, there is no longer any freedom regardless of the side one takes' (SC, IV.2.ix). This addendum reconfirms my earlier claim that Rousseau does not simply equate the actual decision of a majority with the general will (since it is possible for the characteristics of the general will to have ceased to reside in the majority). In addition, though, it makes clear that it is not the majority opinion of just any group he belongs to that generates obligations for the rational agent. What Rousseau's crucial but exceedingly vague remark adds to his view is the qualification that a majority consensus generates obligations for a rational agent only if the community as a whole, including the procedures by which it reaches consensus, meets certain criteria, all of which concern features of a community that tend to make its majority decisions reliable indicators of the general will. Some of these features are purely formal characteristics of the consensus-building process, such as full access to relevant information (SC, II.3.iii), the free exchange of reasons (SC, IV.1.vii), equal and universal rights of participation (SC, IV.1.vii), and measures to restrain the influence of special interest groups (SC, II.3.iii−iv). But apart from these, there is a less tangible standard the community must meet as well, a standard Rousseau formulates by asking whether 'the characteristics of the general will are still in the majority'. By this he means to ask whether the *spirit* of the general will—a vital concern for the common good and the fundamental interests of each—sufficiently animates the community's life and permeates the dispositions of its members that one can plausibly view their deliberations as good-faith attempts to discern what their own shared principles of justice entail.[41] In effect, this qualification makes it a condition of a rational agent's being obligated by the majority decisions of his community that she have a certain enduring attitude towards the community that has the authority to bind her will—an attitude that might be described as ongoing consent or, more accurately perhaps, as *trust*: a confidence in the general moral health of the community whose judgments she takes as authoritative. In other words, the rational citizen's conclusion that she is mistaken when the opinion contrary to hers prevails, is predicated on her underlying conviction that her community is in fact sincerely motivated by the basic ideals of justice and that, for the most part at least, it comes tolerably close to realizing them.

To this it might be objected that Rousseau's view does after all locate the ultimate source of rational obligation in the individual, since, so it seems, he alone is the final judge of whether it is true of his community that 'the characteristics of the general will are still in the majority' and, so, the final judge of whether the majority's pronouncements are binding on him. While it is true that Rousseau's qualification accords more authority to the individual's conscience than his other remarks suggest, it would be mistaken to think that it alone can generate obligation. Although in this passage Rousseau says that there is no longer any *freedom* when the general will ceases to reside in the majority, the same could also be said of *obligation*. For in the absence of those features that make a community and its interpretations of the general will worthy of its citizens' trust, the conditions that make rational obligation possible do not obtain. This is because obligation entails being bound to laws that apply to more than just oneself and being subject to a power beyond one's own will that has the authority to interpret and enforce those laws.[42] An individual's taking something to be right, no matter how sincerely or reasonably, is never sufficient to generate obligation for others nor even, since genuine obligation requires a plurality of subjects, for oneself. To act as though it did is to claim for oneself the right to give law

[41] 'When the social bond is broken in all hearts, … the general will becomes mute' (*SC*, IV.i.v).

[42] The view of obligation I find in Rousseau has significant parallels with the account Robert Brandom attributes to Hegel in 'Some Pragmatist Themes in Hegel's Idealism', *European Journal of Philosophy* 7 (1999), 164–89.

for everyone, and this, to be sure, is inflamed *amour-propre* at its most presumptuous.

Before proceeding to consider how *amour-propre* is involved in constituting rational agents, it is worth pointing out two features of Rousseau's conception of reason that are relevant to that task, both of which concern the intimate relation between reason and recognition. The first is that, for Rousseau, recognition among subjects makes up the core of justice's *content*: to submit oneself to reason's authority is to let one's will be governed by principles that, by treating the fundamental interests of all as equally important, implicitly accord to each of one's associates the status—a type of relative standing—of a moral equal. This means that letting the principles of justice constrain my actions is itself an instance of recognizing the worth—the equal worth—of my fellow human beings. By the same token, when I inhabit a community in which those same principles are observed by others in relation to me, their actions constitute a recognition of my status as a subject worthy of respect. Recognition is, one might say, the very substance of reason.

The second point concerns the connection between recognition and the nature of reason's *authority* (rather than the content of its basic principles). As I have argued, a commitment to rationality involves according a certain authority to the actual judgments of one's associates with regard to what, specifically, our shared principles of justice permit and obligate us to do. This, too, can be seen as a form of recognition (of the equal legislative authority of all rational beings). At the same time, rational authority is more complex than this description implies. For there is, on Rousseau's view, no single ultimate source of that authority: neither the individual's conscience nor the actual consensus of the community enjoys unqualified sovereignty in the empire of reason. Instead, rational authority resides in a network of relations of *reciprocal* recognition among subjects. For while submission to reason requires accepting the legislative authority of others, it also rests on a background judgment on the part of the individual who submits to that authority that, on the whole, her community satisfies the basic criteria of moral legitimacy. Since obligation exists only when both of these conditions are met, rational authority, for Rousseau, is possible only *intersubjectively*—that is, as a network of relations of recognition among individual subjects, in which the sovereignty of each and the subjection of each to the whole are simultaneously acknowledged. Or, to put the point in Hegelian terminology: rational authority is an inherently 'spiritual' phenomenon, one that comes to be only through a supraindividual subject whose structure is that of an 'I' that is a 'we' and a 'we' that is an 'I'.[43]

---

[43] G. W. F. Hegel, *Phenomenology of Spirit*, trans. A. V. Miller (Oxford: Oxford University Press, 1977), 110. I return to this tension—or dialectic—between individual and community in Ch. 7.

7

Amour-propre's Role in Forming Rational Subjects

The preceding chapter distinguishes three features of the frame of mind individuals must acquire in order to assume the standpoint of reason. First, reason requires one to step back from one's own particular desires and interests and to take as authoritative an appropriately universal perspective (one that considers only the fundamental interests of each individual). Second, reason requires individuals to conceive of themselves as the moral equal of each of their associates, acknowledging that no one's fundamental interests have a right to count for more than anyone else's and that, for the purpose of framing laws, the fundamental interests of others take priority over their own non-fundamental interests. And, third, the individual must relinquish his claim to have ultimate authority over his own will and locate that authority instead in the opinions of others (in the prevailing consensus of his community, subject to the appropriate constraints).

With this account of the standpoint of reason in place, my task now is to determine what role *amour-propre* might play in making it possible for human beings to adopt such a standpoint. As we shall see in what follows, *amour-propre* plays a crucial role in bringing about each of these features of rational agency. More precisely: *amour-propre* is a necessary, though not sufficient, condition of the formation of human beings into rational subjects. In exploring *amour-propre*'s contribution to rational agency it is important to bear in mind two respects in which, on its own, it is insufficient to produce rational subjects. First, the formation in which *amour-propre* participates must be complemented by the appropriate education of pity and *amour de soi*. As the Second Discourse suggests (*DI*, 218/*OC* 3, 219) and Book IV of *Emile* makes explicit, *amour-propre* is not the only motivating force on which the capacity for rational agency depends. Secondly, the mere presence of *amour-propre* in human beings—even accompanied by pity and *amour de soi*—by no means ensures that rational formation will ensue. Unlike Hegel, Rousseau does not believe that there is a dialectic internal to the drive for recognition that makes one particular developmental outcome—rational, self-determining subjectivity—a necessary or probable result of human interaction.[1] For Rousseau both luck and contingent human intervention are required if *amour-propre* is to realize its potential to transform merely natural beings into rational subjects. With these two qualifications in mind, I turn to reconstructing the crowning piece of Rousseau's theodicy of *amour-propre*, his vision of the relation between rationality and the human drive for recognition.

Cognitive resources

Unfortunately, Rousseau's texts offer very little explicit discussion of how *amour-propre* contributes to the formation of human beings into rational agents. Rousseau hints at such a claim when, in discussing how to make Emile the ruler of his passions, he declares: 'it is always from nature itself that the proper instruments to regulate nature must be drawn' (*E* IV, 327/*OC* 4, 654). Apart from several other equally general statements,[2] however, he says almost nothing to help his readers understand how, more specifically, reason's dependence on *amour-propre* is to be envisaged. A slightly more informative clue is provided by the passage cited in the previous chapter in which Rousseau describes the 'remarkable change in man' that must occur if the state of nature, where appetite determines conduct, is to yield to the civil state, where reason and duty regulate human action: 'Only ... when ... right replaces appetite, does man, *who until then considered only himself*, find himself forced to act on other principles and to consult his reason before heeding his inclinations' (*SC*, I.8.i; emphasis added). The clue provided here is this: in order for reason

---

[1] A hint of the Hegelian view may, however, be present in the Second Discourse's depiction of the birth of *amour-propre*; see n. 9 below.

[2] Rousseau makes a similar statement in referring to how evils of the state of nature are to be overcome: 'let us endeavor to extract from the ill itself the remedy that will cure it' (*GM*, 159/*OC* 3, 288). In another place he declares his aim to 'transform into a sublime virtue the dangerous disposition out of which all our vices are born' (*PE*, 20/*OC* 3, 260). For other references to the positive value of *amour-propre*, see *E* IV, 244, 246, 248, 252, 262–4/*OC* 4, 536, 538, 541, 547, 560–2.

to become the regulator of human action, a way must be found for the isolated beings of the state of nature to be drawn out of their solipsistic existence—where each 'regards himself as the sole spectator who observes him' (*DI*, 218/*OC* 3, 219)—and to learn to act instead on principles that require them to take into account and, so, to acknowledge the perspectives of their fellow beings. It is reasonable to assume that Rousseau considers *amour-propre*, with its inherent concern for how things appear to others, to be the resource provided by nature that can make the required expansion of perspectives take place.[3] The question is, How, precisely, does it do so?

Let us begin with the most natural way of understanding how *amour-propre* might endow humans with the capacity to assume the perspective of others as reason requires. Clearly, reason as Rousseau conceives it presupposes the ability to anticipate how a proposed action or law will affect the needs and desires of others (since the question reason poses is how a particular policy will affect the fundamental interests of all). But if it is true, as Rousseau appears to maintain, that a being who lacks *amour-propre* 'regards himself as the sole spectator' in the universe—if it is true that for such a being there exists only one perspective on the world (his own)—then it is plausible that *amour-propre* is essential to the cultivation of rational agency. The thought here is that because *amour-propre* seeks the good opinion of others, its satisfaction depends on an ability to anticipate others' desires and needs and to tailor one's own actions in conformity with them. Emile's 'natural' (non-inflamed) desire to be loved by his fellow human beings carries with it, we are told, a desire to please them (*E* IV, 337/*OC* 4, 668), but succeeding at this requires a developed awareness of what is likely to cause pleasure or pain to those whose opinions he cares about. This suggests, then, that by engendering a pressing desire for the good opinion of others, *amour-propre* impels us to perfect a cognitive capacity essential to reason that would otherwise remain dormant in the human spirit, namely, the ability to view the world from a standpoint other than one's own particular perspective.

---

[3] Rousseau seems to be making a similar point when he emphasizes that as long as Emile's *amour-propre* has not been awakened, he is not yet a moral being: 'So long as his sensibility remains limited to his own individual being, there is nothing moral in his actions. It is only when his sensibility begins to extend outside of himself that it takes on, first, the sentiments and, then, the ideas of good and evil' (*E* IV, 219–20/*OC* 4, 501).

There is no doubt some merit to the suggestion that *amour-propre* helps to cultivate rational subjects by providing them with an incentive to develop their ability to imagine, and to be moved by, how the world appears to others. Yet this cannot be Rousseau's main claim concerning the relation between reason and *amour-propre*. This is because *amour-propre* is not *necessary* for fostering the capacity to anticipate others' needs and desires, since *amour de soi* is also capable of producing this result.[4] Given the thoroughgoing interdependence that even the 'non-relative' needs for food, clothing, and shelter soon give rise to,[5] humans have a powerful incentive to develop their ability to perceive others' needs and desires apart from any wish to win their approval or esteem. Since *amour de soi* itself makes us need the cooperation of others—and since my receiving help from you depends on my ability to offer something of use to you in return—it by itself suffices to teach us the benefit of being able to anticipate others' needs and to shape our social activity accordingly. (This is precisely Hegel's point when he ascribes a formative significance to the market-governed 'system of needs' on which modern civil society is based.[6])

If it is true that both forms of self-love can develop the capacity to anticipate others' needs and desires, then we have not yet found any distinctive contribution *amour-propre* makes to the cultivation of rational agency. To make progress here, it will help to focus our attention on

[4] It might be thought that natural pity already presupposes a sensitivity to the pains of others and that therefore neither *amour-propre* nor *amour de soi* is required to account for this aspect of rationality. At issue here, however, is not the mere capacity to be moved by the actual suffering of other sentient beings but the ability to *anticipate* their needs and desires and to let one's own actions be influenced by their anticipated responses. To this one might in turn respond that pity itself is impossible without *amour-propre*. This view is hinted at in *Emile* (though not in the Second Discourse), when Rousseau suggests that part of pity's 'sweetness' is due to the feeling that those whom we pity need us and then explicitly attributes the pleasantness of that feeling to *amour-propre* (*E* IV, 221/*OC* 4, 503–4). For more on the differences between Rousseau's accounts of pity in these two texts, see Chitty, 26, 33–4, 63–5.

[5] Rousseau's position in the Second Discourse is that *amour de soi* does not by itself generate enduring dependence, since in the 'original' state of nature, where *amour de soi* is active but *amour-propre* is not, no such dependence exists. Rather, dependence becomes a necessary part of human existence only when *amour-propre* is awakened and has impressed its character on the greatest part of human desires. This view seems to contradict the obvious and fundamental fact that infants, from the first moment of their existence, are thoroughly dependent on others for the satisfaction of their physical needs. In *Emile* Rousseau explicitly acknowledges this fact (*E* I, 65/*OC* 4, 286), implicitly recognizing that *amour-propre* is not the sole source of human dependence. Perhaps the Second Discourse is best understood as making an analytic (rather than genetic) claim about the source of dependence among *adult* human beings.

[6] *Philosophy of Right*, §§187, 197; for a discussion of these claims, see Neuhouser, *Foundations*, 157–60.

the features of *amour-propre* that distinguish it from *amour de soi*, especially on the two respects in which the former is a 'relative' passion: first, the standing *amour-propre* strives for is always measured comparatively (relative to the standing of others); second, the end it seeks—the good opinion of others—depends on, or resides in, the judgments of other subjects.

Reason and comparative standing

In order to see how the first of these features might serve reason's ends, it will be useful to consider why another component of human nature—pity, the ability to feel the pains of others and to be motivated to alleviate them—is not sufficient to give rise to rational (or moral) agency. The brief answer is that pity is a sentiment (or, as Rousseau sometimes says, a 'passion' (*E* IV, 220/*OC* 4, 502)), and sentiments must be guided by reason if they are to be reliable producers of right actions. Once it has been awakened, Emile's pity naturally extends to those he lives among and to those who share his experiences and ways of thinking (*E* IV, 233/*OC* 4, 520). Rather than serving the ends of justice, though, pity in this form tends to make Emile give undue preference to his intimate circle of friends and associates. But the problem with sentiment from reason's point of view is not merely that it tends to be specific and exclusionary in its choice of objects. For even if Emile's pity were extended to encompass every member of the human species, his sentiment alone could not serve as a morally reliable guide to action. Rather, in order to be the tool of justice, pity must be ordered by reason, or 'generalize[d] ... under the abstract idea of humanity' (*E* IV, 233/*OC* 4, 520). This is because pity, unconstrained by reason, can prompt us to distribute our beneficence arbitrarily—to the wrong objects perhaps, or to the right objects but in the wrong amounts. Although pity can be useful to morality by motivating us to care about the good of distant and unknown others, unless it is subordinated to abstract ideas, which only reason can supply, it remains 'a blind preference' (*E* IV, 252/*OC* 4, 548) and only contingently results in precisely the actions justice calls for. So, even though reason relies on pity to inspire in us a concern for the good of others, it also demands that we hold our pity in check—that we 'yield to it only to the extent that it accords with justice' (*E* IV, 253/*OC* 4, 548). This means that only when pity is 'enlightened by reason' (*E* IV, 235/*OC* 4, 523)—only when its promptings are ordered by the idea of the fundamental interests of each—can it shed its character as blind sentiment and find its way to its proper objects.[7]

Even if we grant, however, that pity must find its measure in reason, it remains unclear what role *amour-propre* could play in this. Implicit in Rousseau's account of Emile's education, I shall argue, is the suggestion that *amour-propre* is the only possible source in humans for one crucial element of the measure reason must provide for pity. More specifically, what *amour-propre* contributes to the proper ordering of pity is an idea that originates in *amour-propre*'s 'relative' character in the first of the two senses articulated above: the idea of the *comparative worth* of human individuals. As we have seen, in directing pity to its proper objects reason makes use of the idea of the equal moral worth of all individuals (where this means that in framing laws no one's fundamental interests count for more than anyone else's). Rousseau's claim is clearly not that a commitment to the equal moral worth of all is a natural or necessary consequence of the mere possession of *amour-propre*. On the contrary, his vivid depictions of the dangers inherent in human sociality and of the pitfalls that threaten the success of Emile's education imply that, without appropriate intervention, an inflamed desire to be recognized as superior to others is the most likely outcome of human *amour-propre*. Rousseau's claim, rather, is that in the absence of *amour-propre* the very idea of comparative worth—and hence the more specific idea of *equal* worth—would have no foothold in the dispositions of humans and hence no power to direct their behavior as reason requires. In short, *amour-propre* makes comparisons and pity does not, and without comparisons (of the appropriate type) there can be no reason.[8]

Of course, in order to be serviceable to reason in this manner, *amour-propre* must be cultivated—that is, its general propensity to make comparisons of individual worth must be directed towards the specific end of fostering a sense of the moral equality of all human beings.[9] It is no coincidence

---

[7] These points are nicely formulated by Chitty, 63–8.

[8] The suggestion that comparison is essential to reason, perhaps even its central operation, is prominent at *DI*, 162/*OC* 3 165–6; see also *DI*, 165/*OC* 3, 169. A similar suggestion is found in Kant's 'Conjectures on the Beginning of Human History' in Hans Reiss (ed.), *Kant: Political Writings* (Cambridge: Cambridge University Press, 1991), 223.

[9] In the Second Discourse Rousseau suggests, without arguing for the claim, that something like this process may be natural to *amour-propre*'s development. For, as he depicts the awakening of *amour-propre*, the first desire to be recognized as the handsomest or strongest quickly leads to concern for the 'duties of civility', which tacitly recognize a right to be accorded certain forms of respect that one is entitled to qua human being (*DI*, 166/*OC* 3, 169–70).

that, as we shall see in more detail below, this is precisely what Emile's tutor takes his central challenge to be once his pupil's *amour-propre* has been aroused. After taking measures to enlarge the scope of Emile's pity beyond its 'natural' limits, his tutor undertakes the more important task of instilling in Emile a sense of his essential equality with all members of his species. Again and again Rousseau insists that whether Emile's character will turn out to be good or evil depends first and foremost on 'what position he will feel he has among men' (*E* IV, 235/*OC* 4, 523).[10] And, not surprisingly (if the interpretation I offer here is correct), the key to achieving this is said to lie in a certain re-formation of Emile's *amour-propre*, one that 'extends [his] *amour-propre* to other beings' so as to 'transform it into virtue' (*E* IV, 252/*OC* 4, 547).[11]

Reason and concern for the opinion of others

Let us turn now to the second sense in which *amour-propre* is a relative passion, namely, that the good it seeks consists in opinions held by other subjects concerning one's own merit or worthiness. How might this feature of *amour-propre* serve to cultivate rationality? As we saw above, Rousseau alludes to the idea that *amour-propre* compels us to abandon our 'natural' solipsism and to acquire a perspective on the world that takes into account, or acknowledges, the subjectivity of others. We also saw that if *amour-propre* is to make a distinctive contribution to the cultivation of rational agency, this recognition of the subjectivity of others must involve more than simply feeling, or even anticipating, their pleasures

---

[10] The same point is expressed in Rousseau's statement that knowing 'the true relations of man with respect to the species' (and ordering the passions in accordance with them) constitutes 'the whole of human wisdom in the use of the passions' (*E* IV, 219/*OC* 4, 501).

[11] From this passage alone it is unclear what 'extending *amour-propre* to other beings' means. (See Dent, 143–5, for a detailed discussion of this passage.) A natural response, endorsed by many commentators, is to think that Rousseau's reference to *amour-propre* is a mistake and that he means to call instead for the extension of Emile's *amour de soi* to others so as to make him able to feel their sufferings as his own. (This is indeed how Rousseau characterizes the expansion of pity (*E* IV, 223, 235n/*OC* 4, 505–6, 523n).) But at this point in the text the cultivation of Emile's pity has already been completed, and attention has shifted to how his *amour-propre* must be transformed so as to complement his newly expanded pity. Moreover, as the immediate context makes clear, Rousseau's concern here is not how to instill 'the love of mankind' in Emile but how to make it equitable, or just. This, I argue, can be accomplished only through the idea of the moral equality of all humans. Thus, my suggestion is that 'extending *amour-propre* to other beings' consists in according to them a kind of dignity that one's own *amour-propre* makes one seek for oneself, the dignity of a 'human being' as expressed in the idea of moral equality. For an alternate reading that does not dismiss the reference to *amour-propre* as a mistake, see Chitty, 73–5.

and pains. One respect in which *amour-propre* differs from both *amour de soi* and pity is that it makes one care about, and aspire to occupy, the points of view others take, not just on the world in general, but on a specific (and highly cathected) 'object', oneself. Thus, someone who seeks the good opinion of others is motivated to imagine how certain aspects of herself (her publicly visible actions and qualities) will appear to other, differently situated subjects and whether what they see of her public self will elicit their esteem. This suggests that one way *amour-propre* helps to foster rational agency is by providing individuals with an incentive to learn to view and judge *themselves*—their own actions and qualities—from an external perspective. The importance of this point must not be underestimated: *amour-propre* impels us to recognize others not merely as sentient, passive beings—sufferers of pleasure and pain—but as active, judging subjects who adopt an evaluative stance to their world, including to other subjects.

The importance of such a capacity for rational agency is evident. For, as we have seen, adopting the standpoint of reason requires an individual to distance himself from his own particular point of view, where only his desires and interests count, in order to regard himself—his desires, intentions, and character traits—from an external perspective that considers only fundamental human interests and accords equal importance to the interests of everyone. In other words, reason demands that we make ourselves into a kind of *object* for our own consciousness—that we view our own actions and qualities as we would those of others, and that we do so through the impartial eyes of a generalized other.[12] *Amour-propre*, then, with its inherent concern for how one appears to other subjects, seems especially well-suited to foster in humans the capacity for self-objectification that rational self-assessment requires. Again, Rousseau is not claiming that simply possessing *amour-propre* is enough to train individuals to take an objective view of their desires and intentions. Clearly, there is plenty of work for education to accomplish if individuals who at first care

---

[12] The position I attribute to Rousseau here overlaps considerably with George Herbert Mead's account of rationality in Part III of *Mind, Self, and Society* (Chicago: University of Chicago Press, 1934). Moreover, Mead argues that it is the very ability to take oneself as an object—to view oneself from the perspective of others—that is the hallmark of selfhood. This suggests one potentially fruitful strategy for making out Rousseau's claim that *amour-propre* is a necessary condition not only of rationality but of subjectivity more generally.

only about the opinions of actual others are to be transformed into subjects who judge themselves from an abstract, impartial point of view. Rousseau's claim, rather, is that the ability to make oneself the object of reason's gaze has its beginnings in, and is but a refinement of, human beings' original impulse, derived from *amour-propre*, to step outside their own subjective vantage point and view themselves through the eyes of the particular others whose good opinion they urgently seek.

Here again it might be objected that, given the thoroughgoing inter-dependence that defines the human condition, *amour de soi* itself provides a sufficient incentive for individuals to learn to assess their behavior from an impartial, third-person perspective. For individuals who rely on others' cooperation to satisfy their needs normally have no trouble learning to discern and conform to the market's demands in deciding what and how to produce, simply because the consequences of failing to do so are so weighty. Yet even if this leaves room for *amour-propre* to work in tandem with *amour de soi* in fostering the capacity to take an objective point of view on oneself, it should lead us to ask whether *amour-propre* has anything distinctive to contribute to this process. In fact, *amour-propre* makes two such contributions. Each is bound up with the distinctive sense in which the *self* is the object of the judgments (of others) that *amour-propre* cares about, and each plays a crucial role in cultivating rational agency.

One salient feature of *amour-propre* is that, in contrast to *amour de soi*, it leads us to care about others' opinions of our deeds and qualities not for instrumental reasons (because meeting others' expectations is necessary if my labor or product is to command a price in the marketplace) but because we value those opinions themselves, as indicators of our worth. Thus, a being with *amour-propre* cares about how she appears to others because she takes her actions and traits to reflect, in a publicly visible manner, something that stands behind those appearances and is the ultimate object of her concern, her 'self' as a possible object of esteem. Insofar as she is motivated by *amour-propre*, the skillful craftsman desires praise for her work not because a good reputation will increase her power in the marketplace but because her work is a reflection of herself, and the recognition of *its* excellence is a public confirmation of *her* worth (as a craftsman). For this reason a being with *amour-propre* is motivated to consider how her own actions and qualities will appear to the other subjects who count for her[13] as the spectators of her self and who are thereby endowed with a power to confirm or deny her worth (including in her own eyes) through their opinions of her. Such a being will be inclined to make herself—or those aspects of herself visible to others—into the object of her own gaze, while asking of herself, Are my actions and qualities likely to be judged by my spectators as befitting a person of merit (of whatever sort she aspires to achieve)? Because it leads them to judge themselves according to non-instrumental standards of worth, the self-examination that *amour-propre* impels individuals to undertake is much closer to moral self-assessment than anything *amour de soi* (or pity) can engender. For one feature of the moral stance is that it judges an intended action with a view not to how instrumentally valuable it is likely to be but to how, in the eyes of an impartial spectator, it would reflect on one's 'inner worth'. In short, *amour-propre* is the affective prototype of the standpoint of reason because it leads individuals to adopt a kind of normative perspective on themselves—it leads them to assess their own actions and qualities according to non-instrumental standards of excellence that transcend the self-interestedness of *amour de soi*, with its exclusive concern for what is useful to securing one's non-relative good.

There is a further feature of the normative perspective implicit in *amour-propre* that points to a second way this passion helps form the capacity to judge oneself 'objectively', from the standpoint of reason. This feature concerns the nature of the authority of the norms that *amour-propre* acknowledges, and, not surprisingly, it is bound up with the fact that the good sought by *amour-propre* resides in the opinions of others. Beyond providing non-instrumental standards of individual merit, the evaluative criteria invoked by *amour-propre* differ from those of *amour de soi* in that they have their source in something external to the person to whom they apply, namely, the judgments of other subjects. By locating the measure of my worth in what others think of me, I in effect make their opinions normative for me—that is, I take their judgments to be valid criteria for my worth, and, by remaking myself in conformity with those judgments, I recognize them as 'laws' for my will. Thus, by the very nature of the needs

---

[13] This qualification indicates the element of reciprocity inherent in the quest for recognition: my desire for your recognition implicitly presupposes that I ascribe value to you (as a judge of me). Hegel's attention to this point marks the most important respect in which his account of recognition goes beyond Rousseau's.

it engenders, *amour-propre* compels human beings to submit their wills to the judgments of their fellow beings and, so, teaches them to accord a kind of normative authority to points of view other than their own.[14]

One way of expressing this point is to say that *amour-propre* is the affective source of the human impulse to objectivity, or rationality, and that, as I suggested in Chapter 6, what Rousseau so forcefully decries throughout his work as the 'reign of opinion' is at the same time a precursor to the reign of reason. This is because the desire to make one's actions and traits conform to the opinions of others—the urge to measure up to *their* perceptions of the good—is merely one (admittedly still primitive) form of taking oneself to be subject to norms whose validity depends on something more than one's own desires or beliefs.[15] This is to say that, although it is the source of many dangers, the pursuit of public esteem is also reason's training ground, where each human being receives his first lesson in the hard truth that his taking something to be good is not sufficient to make it so and that his will is beholden to something beyond his own subjective preferences and beliefs.

Beyond this, though, *amour-propre* prefigures the standpoint of reason even more precisely by locating the source of the constraints on an individual's will not in the world of things but in the judgments of other subjects. *Amour-propre* does more than simply teach humans to judge themselves from a perspective that transcends their own particular desires; it also makes the opinions of other subjects the source of the authority of that perspective. This can be understood as the passions' way of anticipating reason's claim that objectivity in the ethical realm derives from the agreement of rational agents (subject, of course, to the appropriate constraints)—that, in other words, the standard for what is right resides outside the consciousness of each individual in a kind of (ideal) consensus among rational subjects. How else, Rousseau suggests, could humans come to ascribe authority to the dictates of the general will—constituted in part by the opinions of their associates—if not through

[14] Barbara Herman finds a similar point in Kant's treatment of self-love. According to her, Kant thinks that the fact that others' judgments of our worth matter to us gives us a reason to accept their values as our own; see 'Rethinking Kant's Hedonism,' in Alex Byrne, Robert Stalnaker, Ralph Wedgwood (eds.), *Fact and Value* (Cambridge, Mass.: MIT Press, 2001), 137. Herman goes on to note: 'since ... we care about how we stand in the regard of others, we must live in ways that are mutually intelligible. (This is a condition of having a culture.)' (151, n.15).

[15] Another version of this claim can be found at Chitty, 42–3.

the modification of an earlier inclination, furnished by *amour-propre*, to seek confirmation of their value in subjecting themselves to the judgments of others?

Motivational resources

Thus far my discussion of *amour-propre*'s role in forming rational subjects has focused on the ways in which it indirectly furnishes human beings with cognitive resources necessary for assuming the standpoint of reason, namely, the idea of the comparative worth of individuals; the capacity to assess one's 'worth' from an external perspective; and experience in according a kind of normative authority to the judgments of other subjects. The topic of the remainder of this chapter is the conative role *amour-propre* plays in constituting rational agency—that is, how it helps to account for the ability not merely to grasp intellectually what reason demands but to be motivated to comply with those demands even though doing so sometimes requires overriding one's own particular desires and interests. In other words: how is rational (or moral) motivation parasitic on the strivings of *amour-propre*? How does the ability to be moved practically by reason depend on a kind of transfiguration—or sublimation[16]—of *amour-propre*? This is in fact the very issue raised in the celebrated passage in which Rousseau highlights the 'remarkable change in man' that must occur if justice is to take the place of instinct in determining human conduct—if, that is, right and duty are to replace the motives of appetite and physical impulse, thereby endowing our actions with moral significance they would otherwise lack (*SC*, I.8.i). Another way of formulating the present question, then, would be: what precisely is involved in a rational agent's propensity 'to consult his reason before heeding his inclination', and how does *amour-propre* help to make it possible?

Motivation by reason vs. motivation by passion

It is important to see that the motivational role being sought for *amour-propre* here is distinct from the one mentioned at the beginning of the previous

---

[16] I am indebted to Joel Whitebook for the insight that this aspect of Rousseau's position can be viewed as anticipating Freud's (and Nietzsche's) doctrine of sublimation.

chapter in conjunction with what I called the second part of Rousseau's justification of *amour-propre*. There *amour-propre* was said to have the potential to encourage virtuous acts insofar as it can be cultivated (and the social world organized) in such a way that individuals learn to pursue social recognition—honor from their fellow citizens—by dedicating themselves to serving the public good. In this case, the desire to count in the eyes of others is merely harnessed, as it were, to serve rational (collectively good) ends, and in this way the 'desire for reputation' is able to beget 'what is best...among men', including our virtue (*DI*, 184/*OC* 3, 189). Here, in contrast, the question is not whether *amour-propre* can motivate virtuous deeds because they are, in the best social arrangements, a means to gaining public esteem but, rather, whether genuinely *rational* conduct—action determined by non-instrumental allegiance to the ideals of reason as such—might not also draw on *amour-propre* for its motivating power.[17]

This question relies on a distinction between moral and purely prudential action that is similar, though not identical, to the familiar contrast Kant draws between acts done out of duty and those that are merely in accordance with duty. One difference between the two positions is that, although some version of this distinction is relevant to Rousseau, he does not share Kant's stark view on its role in determining the *moral worth* of action.[18] For Rousseau seems to regard externally correct behavior that is motivated simply by passion—whether a desire for public esteem or love for the fatherland—as virtuous (*DI*, 184/*OC* 3, 189; *PE*, 16/*OC* 3, 255). At the same time, the passage referred to above suggests that Rousseau believes that *in its highest form* rational (or moral) agency is in some way motivated by 'the voice of duty', or by ideas of right and justice (*SC*, I.8.i), and not merely by appetite or instinct. The implication seems to be that Rousseau recognizes an ethical hierarchy among the various motivations that can lead to morally worthy action. In this regard his position is closer to Adam Smith's than to Kant's. For Smith, in

[17] Chitty (77–82) gives an interesting, somewhat different account of *amour-propre*'s role in 'moralizing' human beings.

[18] Cohen seems to acknowledge this point implicitly in emphasizing the importance to Rousseau's project of finding 'motivational complements to the sense of duty—motives that are distinct from the sense of duty but that...support our efforts to comply with our duties' (126–7). Although Cohen provides an interesting account of these complements, he says little about how the sense of duty itself acquires motivating power. For more on the relation between Kant's and Rousseau's moral theories, see O'Hagan, 12, 25–7, 29–32, 243–4.

appropriating Rousseau's moral thought,[19] makes a point of distinguishing the *love of true glory*—the desire to acquire esteem through meritorious conduct—from the *love of virtue*, the desire to 'becom[e] what is honorable and estimable'. Smith is in agreement with Rousseau in thinking that, though the second is superior to the first, both are deserving of some degree of moral praise, whereas (for Smith at least) *vanity*—'the frivolous desire of praise at any rate'—deserves to be despised in all its forms.[20]

A second, closely related difference between Rousseau and Kant concerns, as the latter would put it, how 'pure' an agent's motives must be if her actions are to count, not merely as having moral worth, but as *determined by reason* (or by duty or justice). In other words, like Kant, Rousseau distinguishes between externally correct behavior that is motivated only by passion, on the one hand, and rational (rationally determined) behavior, on the other (although, as we have seen, he, unlike Kant, takes merely externally correct actions to have a degree of moral worth). For Rousseau, however, as for Hegel after him, being motivated by what is right—acting according to an ideal of duty or justice—does not require acting on a maxim that abstracts completely from one's own interests or happiness. One way of putting this point would be to say that Rousseau rejects the strict dichotomy Kant sets up in the *Critique of Practical Reason* between the principle of self-love, on the one hand, and the principle of morality, on the other (*KPV*, 5:22, 31–6).

Here, too, Rousseau's position can be illuminated by referring to Smith's. In regarding the lover of true glory as morally superior to the vain individual, Smith commends a mode of acting that relies on what Kant would consider an impure motive, winning public esteem through meritorious deeds. Presumably, what makes the love of true glory praiseworthy for Smith is located in precisely what distinguishes it from the vice of vanity: while the lover of true glory makes social esteem the final end of his action, he—in contrast to the vain individual—pursues that end, not by any

---

[19] Although most interpreters treat Smith as a critic of Rousseau, I see the former's account of moral agency as heavily indebted to—indeed, an extension of—the latter's. Force also reads Smith as more an appropriator than a critic of Rousseau, though he is most concerned with their views on different issues: the nature and significance of *amour de soi* and pity.

[20] *TMS*, VII.ii.4.9–10; III.2.8. I am indebted to Samuel Fleischacker for bringing these passages to my attention.

means whatever, but only through what he takes to be virtuous action. By imposing the latter condition on his search for social esteem, the lover of true glory acknowledges the authority of moral ideals to impose constraints on his self-interested incentives. Such a person falls short of the Kantian ideal of rational determination, however, since for him, presumably—in contrast to the lover of virtue—the ideals of right and justice on their own, without the reward of esteem, are generally insufficient to motivate right conduct. For Rousseau, then—in distinction to Kant—even Smith's lover of true glory counts as rationally determined (to a degree) since in constraining his quest for esteem by standards of right or justice, he accords to ideals of reason an independent authority to determine his behavior.

Distinguishing amour de soi and amour-propre in rational motivation

How, then, might *amour-propre* play a part in making rational motivation possible? How might it work to produce in human beings an efficacious, non-instrumental allegiance to ideals of right (or duty or justice) that sometimes require the subordination of their own particular desires and interests? Or, to reformulate the question yet again: how does the presence of *amour-propre* help to explain how creatures who possess no natural impulse to consult and follow reason can be transformed into beings who regularly do so? One possibility is hinted at in a series of passages in the *Discourse on Political Economy* that emphasize the role of patriotism, or love for the fatherland (*amour de la patrie*), in motivating citizens to obey the general will and to identify the good of the republic with their own.[21] According to these passages, the form of love for the fatherland that conduces to virtue is one in which 'this sweet and lively sentiment combines the force of *amour-propre* with all the beauty of virtue' and thereby 'endows virtue with an energy that, without disfiguring [virtue], makes [love for the fatherland] into the most heroic of all passions' (*PE*, 16/*OC* 3, 255).

It is possible to understand Rousseau's claim here in the following way: love for the fatherland can be made to serve virtue by attaching the affection and concern that individuals naturally have for themselves to the republic as a whole. If individuals can be taught to love the fatherland as they

---

[21] Christopher Bertram helpfully discusses Rousseau's views on patriotism in *Rousseau and 'The Social Contract'* (London: Routledge, 2004), 9, 29–30, 140, 144–6, 178. See also Zev M. Trachtenberg's discussion of *amour-propre*'s involvement in patriotism in *Making Citizens* (London: Routledge, 1993), 131–43, 197–210.

love themselves—'to identify themselves with this larger whole, to feel themselves members of the fatherland' (*PE*, 20/*OC* 3, 259)—then they will desire the good of the republic (the object of the general will) just as they do their own and, so, be motivated to do what they can to realize it. In other words, love for the fatherland can be made the tool of virtue by taking advantage of a basic feature of human nature associated with *amour de soi*, namely, that 'we readily want what the people we love want' (*PE*, 15/*OC* 3, 254)—or, as Rousseau says in the statement quoted above: we readily want the good of those with whom we 'identify' through love. This reading, it should be noted, ascribes to those who love the fatherland a non-instrumental attachment to the collective good that, from the moral point of view, is superior to regarding public service merely as a means to winning social esteem. (At the same time, in grounding this attachment solely in a passion—in a species of love—it explains the possibility of what Rousseau would consider morally worthy, but not *rational*, conduct.)

This interpretation of Rousseau's position recalls the passage encountered in Chapter 6 in which the citizen's ability to 'will the happiness of each' is said to depend on his 'applying th[e] word *each* to himself' and then 'thinking of himself as he votes for all' (*SC*, II.4.v).[22] Especially when read in conjunction with Rousseau's remarks on love for the fatherland, that passage seems to be claiming that citizens' thinking of themselves as 'each' makes it psychologically possible for them to have a general will because doing so turns willing the good of each into an expression of *amour de soi*. For while *amour de soi* leads an individual to seek his own good, the latter is always the good of the individual as conceived under a certain description. What an individual takes his good to consist in—and, so, what his *amour de soi* will lead him to pursue—depends on how he conceives of what he is and of what is central to his being it.

This thought is articulated most explicitly in *Emile*:

When the strength of an expansive soul makes me identify myself with my fellow, and I feel myself, so to speak, in him, it is in order not to suffer that I do not want him to suffer. I am interested in him for love of myself (*amour de moi*), and

---

[22] In interpreting this passage from the *Social Contract* one should bear in mind Rousseau's suggestive remark in his letter to d'Alembert that unity in the state (the presence and vitality of the general will) depends on the citizens participating in forms of entertainment in which, unlike the theater, spectators and performers are identical and each is therefore encouraged to 'see and love himself in the others' (*LMA*, 126/*OC* 5, 115).

the reason for the precept is in nature itself, which inspires in me the desire of my well-being in whatever place I feel my existence.

(*E* IV, 235n/*OC* 4, 523n)

This suggests that Rousseau means to locate the capacity to be motivated by reason in an agent's *amour de soi*[23] joined to an *expanded* self-conception, in which the sphere of what one takes one's own self to comprise is extended to include the entire species[24] (or, as Rousseau tends to speak in the *Social Contract*, all the members of one's political community). And, indeed, in Book IV of *Emile* Rousseau spends a good deal of time thinking about how an adolescent can be taught to enlarge his self-conception so as to be able to feel his own existence in others and, so, to respond to their pains and pleasures out of love for himself.[25]

Several considerations, however, suggest that there is more to Rousseau's account of rational motivation than this. One is that, although some of Rousseau's remarks about love for the fatherland seem to warrant this interpretation, it does not capture everything those passages suggest. For on this way of understanding the connection between patriotism and virtue, it is *amour de soi*, not *amour-propre*, that animates virtue. Insofar as individuals love their republic and its members, their understanding of their own good expands to include that of the whole. Since they take working for the whole to be working for themselves, their allegiance to the collective good relies on nothing more than *amour de soi*, coupled with an enlarged conception, grounded in love, of who they are and what their good consists in. Yet more than once in these passages Rousseau identifies *amour-propre*, not *amour de soi*, as the passion from which virtuous love for the fatherland draws its energy. In addition to claiming that love for the fatherland 'combines the force of *amour-propre* with all the beauty of virtue' (*PE*, 16/*OC* 3, 255), he says that it is *amour-propre*, when properly habituated, that is able to 'draw us out of ourselves', expand the human self (*le moi humain*), and bring us to care about the larger good (*PE*, 21/*OC* 3, 260). And, if more proof than this is needed, it is precisely here that

---

[23] In the Second Discourse, too, it is *amour de soi* that is said 'to produce humanity and virtue' when 'guided ... by reason and modified by pity' (*DI*, 218/*OC* 3, 219).

[24] Rousseau expresses this point by saying that Emile's 'particular affections' must be engaged in a way that enables him to 'identify with his species' (*E* IV, 233/*OC* 4, 520).

[25] This claim points out just how unclear the dividing line between pity and *amour de soi* is in Rousseau's thought.

Rousseau expresses his intention—the central theme of this chapter—to discover how it is possible to 'transform into a sublime virtue the dangerous disposition out of which all our vices are born' (*PE*, 20/*OC* 3, 260). That dangerous disposition, if I am at all on track in this inquiry, can only be *amour-propre*.[26]

A more substantial reason for not locating the source of rational motivation in an expanded *amour de soi* is that, first impressions notwithstanding, such a view does not cohere well with Rousseau's description of the legislating citizen as applying 'each' to himself and then thinking of himself as he votes for all. This is because there is an important difference between identifying with a specific people—with Rome and its inhabitants, for example—and identifying with 'each' (or, alternatively, identifying oneself *as* 'each') as the rational citizen is said to do. It is plausible to imagine the former as involving an expanded self-conception, grounded in love, that makes it possible for individual Romans to act virtuously out of a concern for their own good (in the expanded sense). It is much less plausible that the deliberating citizen's identifying with 'each' can be understood in the same way. Because it is an abstraction in a way that Rome is not, 'each' is an unlikely object of the sort of affective identification that is required by a view that reduces rational motivation to an expanded *amour de soi*.

This becomes easier to see if one thinks more carefully about what the citizen does when she applies 'each' to herself while deciding on which laws ought to govern her republic. As the previous chapter's account of the standpoint of reason makes clear, the idea of 'each' employed by the citizen to guide her deliberations is less an expansion of her self-conception than a contraction of it. Expanding my self-conception so as to identify my good with that of my community gives me a reason, grounded in *amour de soi*, to care about the good of my fellow members generally, but it does not—at least by itself—give me reason to narrow my concern to the specific subset of my associates'—*and my own*—interests that the general will seeks to promote. As we have seen, adopting the standpoint of

---

[26] Further evidence that *amour-propre* is the passion at issue here is Rousseau's talk of teaching citizens 'from sufficiently early on never to look upon their individual [self] except in its relations with the body of the state and to perceive their own existence as ... only a part of the state's' (*PE*, 20/*OC* 3, 259). This language recalls his frequent claims about the relative nature of *amour-propre*. This view is shared by Cooper (25–6, 122, 125–30), who emphasizes that it is the virtuous citizen's *amour-propre* that is extended to the republic at large.

reason means focusing only on the fundamental interests of all citizens. This involves not a straightforward expansion of my self-conception but instead a contraction of it—to what is essentially human in me—together with a commitment to extend the same identity to every one of my associates. This structure of the legislating citizen's point of view—more complex than that of the Romans described above—makes it unlikely that the former can be understood simply as a straightforward extension of *amour de soi* to others.[27] Since the standpoint of reason is best understood not as a general concern for the good of one's associates but as a recognition of their equal—and, so, relative—worth (under the abstract description 'human being'), it is best to take Rousseau at his word when he names *amour-propre* as the passion that has the power to 'draw us out of ourselves' (*PE*, 21/*OC* 3, 260) and enable us to be moved by considerations of justice and duty.

The motivational role of amour-propre in ancient citizenship

How, then, might we conceive of *amour-propre*, rather than *amour de soi*, as the passionate basis of rational motivation? One way of imagining how love for the fatherland joins *amour-propre* with virtue is, of course, the possibility referred to earlier, where individuals dedicate themselves to serving the public good as a means for winning their fellow citizens' esteem.[28] But the question here is whether *amour-propre* is also the source of a less instrumental attachment to moral ideals in which the promise of social esteem is not the only motivation for serving the collective good. Indeed, a careful reading of the passages just considered provides the resources for constructing such a view. Seeing this, however, requires thinking further about the kind of identification with the republic—or with 'each'—that must be at issue if *amour-propre* rather than *amour de soi* is to be its source.

An alternative to the possibility sketched above (where an extended *amour de soi* makes one desire the republic's good because of one's affective attachment to it and its members) is suggested in Rousseau's statement of how, in

[27] Similarly, it is a mistake to think of the deliberator in Rawls's original position as an exclusively self-interested agent who strives only to promote his own interests as defined by the reduced self-conception that the veil of ignorance demands.

[28] This appears to be Cooper's understanding of the relevance of *amour-propre* to classical virtue: though the classical citizen 'wished to distinguish himself individually, his personal ambition was still civic in its substance: he wished to be recognized for excellent service to the nation' (25).

classical Rome, individuals' *amour-propre* was extended to the republic:[29] for the citizens of Rome, 'esteem[30] for the name Roman ... roused the courage and animated the virtue of anyone who had the honor to bear it' (*PE*, 18/*OC* 3, 257). The talk of esteem and honor that accrue both to citizens and to the republic with which they identify suggests a picture of how *amour-propre* can animate virtue different from any we have considered thus far. On this picture, individuals do not win honor by impressing fellow citizens with their extraordinary public service but simply by belonging to a particular people and participating in its civic life. As described here, citizens of Rome found their honor in civic life not by distinguishing themselves individually through supererogatory deeds but by identifying themselves as members of a social group that itself commanded their highest esteem. To bear the name 'Roman' was an honor for them because of the esteem they had for Rome.

In linking Roman patriotism with *amour-propre* and virtue, Rousseau makes clear that 'Roman' was not primarily a descriptive title but a normative one: to be a Roman was to have a specific *practical* identity,[31] since identifying oneself as Roman animated one to perform acts of courage and virtue. The type of identification at issue here is grounded not primarily in affection—where citizens desire the collective good because they love their fellow Romans—but in a *normative* stance, an allegiance to the civic values that informed Roman life.[32] The honor of being called Roman was something citizens won by demonstrating, in their daily lives, their faithfulness to the civic norms they recognized as their highest values. Through such conduct they proved themselves to *be* Romans, and in establishing their identities as such in reality, they experienced Rome's

---

[29] Compare Rousseau's remark that by 'extending [Emile's] *amour-propre* to other beings. ... we shall transform it into virtue' (*E* IV, 252/*OC* 4, 548).

[30] Rousseau's word here is *respect*; I use 'esteem' to preserve consistency with my usage of the two terms as explained in Ch. 2.

[31] Both the term and the concept come from Christine M. Korsgaard, *The Sources of Normativity* (Cambridge: Cambridge University Press, 1996), 100-2.

[32] This interpretation is supported by the fact that the civic education Rousseau prescribes in order to foster this sort of identification is said to require teaching children 'to love what is truly fine (*beau*) rather than what is malformed' (*PE*, 20/*OC* 3, 259). In other words, love for the fatherland in its proper form is a love of—a commitment to—normative ideals that distinguish the fine from the base. The use of *beau* here (rather than *bon* or *juste*) suggests that an appreciation for beauty plays some important role in the education Rousseau has in mind. This coheres nicely with the fact that the last phase of Emile's education—just before, in Book V, he is released into the social world—is devoted to forming his aesthetic judgment (*E* IV, 340-8/*OC* 4, 671-83).

greatness as their own. Individuals of this sort can be said to be 'drawn out of themselves' in that they satisfy their need to have a standing for others (they win their honor) by embracing and expressing practical identities as members of a larger social group—identities that depend on, even consist in, an allegiance to certain normative ideals. This results in those 'expanded selves' described by Rousseau whose *amour-propre* has been trained to seek honor in genuine merit rather than in 'greed, a mistress, and vanity'—in 'the contemptible concerns that leave no room for virtue and make up the life of petty souls' (*PE*, 21/*OC* 3, 260).

A similar line of thought could be pursued to make sense of how *amour-propre* rather than *amour de soi* could motivate a member of Rousseau's ideal republic to identify with 'each' as he assumes the standpoint of reason. Rather than explaining the rational agent's concern for the good of others as due to an expanded *amour de soi* that enables him to 'feel himself' in others and, so, to 'desire his well-being in whatever place he feels his existence' (*E* IV, 235n/*OC* 4, 523n), identifying with 'each' might be understood as offering a certain satisfaction to the drive for standing in the eyes of others. As we have seen, the 'each' at issue in rational legislation refers not to real individuals but to an ideal, abstract *status* that a legislator accords to his (real) associates. To assume the identity of 'each' is, in effect, to affirm the equal moral status of all associates. *Amour-propre* would be able to take an interest in assuming the standpoint of reason, then, if applying 'each' to oneself in rational deliberation were simultaneously bound up with publicly establishing oneself as an 'each', which is to say: with winning recognition from one's associates of one's (equal) moral worth. In other words, if willing from the standpoint of 'each' were to be conjoined with others doing the same—with being recognized by *them* as 'each'—then it is not difficult to see how *amour-propre* might be educated to take an interest in the self-conception that for Rousseau lies at reason's core.[33]

Other texts support the idea that for Rousseau something akin to the honor that Roman citizens won in their civic life, or to the honor to be found in identifying as 'each', is an essential component of rational motivation. The adolescent Emile, for example, who is about to enter 'the age of reason' and whose newly awakened *amour-propre* has for most of

[33] Such a view is suggested even by Nietzsche, a philosopher not usually counted among theorists of recognition; see *Beyond Good and Evil*, trans. Walter Kaufmann (New York: Vintage Books, 1989), §265.

Book IV been the principal object of his tutor's concern, is described as someone who 'honors himself (*s'honore*) ... in subjecting himself to the yoke of nascent reason' (*E* IV, 315/*OC* 4, 637). At least part of what motivates a rational agent, then, seems to be a sense that in subjecting himself to reason's demands he does honor to himself, or wins esteem of some kind in his own eyes.

The problem with this interpretive suggestion, however, is that if Emile's education converges with the example of Rome on this crucial point—that the winning of honor plays some important role in rational motivation—they appear far apart on many others. Using Rousseau's depiction of ancient Rome to help reconstruct his account of moral agency in *Emile* raises at least as many questions as it answers. Two sets of issues are especially relevant. First, the radically individualized education to which Emile is subjected—the fact that he is raised as an Everyman, free of every possible identity-conferring social bond—contrasts starkly with the communitarian character of civic virtue in Rome. This point raises a pair of related questions: is membership in some actual community a prerequisite for rational agency? and, conversely, to what extent do practical identities tied to a particular society—to the specific ideals of ancient Rome, for example—constitute for Rousseau a standpoint of *reason*? The second set of issues is bound up with the fact that Emile is said to honor *himself*, whereas the Romans, presumably, honor each other. This difference should make us wonder whether the two cases are as closely related as I have been assuming. More precisely, it should lead us to ask in what sense the honor Emile wins in following reason could qualify as an outgrowth of *amour-propre*, given the latter's essential relativity to others: is Emile's honoring himself also in some way a winning of standing both *among* and *for* his fellow human beings? The remainder of this chapter will be devoted to answering these questions in a way that reconciles Rousseau's accounts of Emile and ancient Rome so as to yield a unitary picture of rational motivation.

The motivational role of amour-propre in Emile's 'man of reason'

Let us begin with the second of these issues. As noted earlier, Emile is said to 'honor himself' when he subjects his will to the demands of reason. So, even though winning esteem is involved in his subjection to reason, it appears to be an esteem that Emile confers on himself rather than one that depends on the judgments of others. Hence the honor that comes from obeying reason seems to lack one of the two kinds of relativity that define *amour-propre*, its quest for standing *in the eyes of others*. What is more, the second kind of relativity seems to be missing as well. For, presumably, the honor Emile feels in following reason comes not from comparing himself with other subjects—not from looking to see how much better or worse others do in complying with reason's demands—but instead from measuring himself against some absolute (non-comparative) standard of right. These observations pose significant problems for the project of this chapter, for if both moments of relativity are lacking in the honor won through obeying reason, then rational motivation appears to be unrelated to the strivings of *amour-propre*. Perhaps it is more prudent to conclude for now only that, at best, the two must be quite remote from one another, in order to leave open the possibility that further investigation might show the capacity to be moved by reason to be a distant descendant of *amour-propre*—a sort of reconfiguration or sublimation of the original human drive to achieve comparative standing in the eyes of others.

If we return to the example of ancient Rome with these questions in mind, we find that it occupies an intermediate position between public service undertaken merely for the sake of social esteem, on the one hand, and Emile's self-honoring obedience to reason, on the other. For while the Roman citizen does win honor in his own eyes—he acts on values he himself endorses, and he achieves, for himself, a kind of satisfaction in doing so—he also expresses his identity as a Roman publicly, in full view of his like-minded fellow citizens, who approve of his actions and esteem him because of them. In the case of Rome there seems to be a convergence of self-bestowed honor and honor conferred by others. This convergence is possible only because Rome, as Rousseau imagines it, is a community defined and governed by publicly shared norms; (as Hegel would put the point later: Rome is a 'spiritual' entity[34]). This means that, typically, the reward of recognition from others is an expected accompaniment of the virtuous action that Rousseau associates with the classical republic.

---

[34] Hegel's conception of *Geist* is heavily indebted to Rousseau's account of the 'public person', or *moi commun*, that issues from the social contract: a 'moral and collective body made up of as many members as the assembly has voices that receives by [the act of association] its unity, ... its life, and its will' (*SC*, I.6.x).

The Roman's civic participation is not purely instrumental in character because his actions are expressive of moral ideals he himself endorses, but at the same time his actions win him the esteem of his compatriots, who share his ideals and therefore think highly of him when he acts in accordance with them. In such a community the desire for social esteem reinforces the voice of duty but does not completely replace it. Although the Roman citizen genuinely 'honors himself' in enacting the ideals of his society, his satisfaction is not entirely independent of the judgments of his fellow citizens that his conduct—along with the 'self' reflected in that conduct—is good.

Something like this vision of how a virtuous character depends on esteem from both internal and external sources can be found in the views of other moral philosophers close to Rousseau in spirit. Thus, Smith, while admitting the possibility of an agent motivated by duty alone (the lover of virtue), recognizes that in ordinary virtuous behavior the desire for praise and the desire for praiseworthiness are 'blended together' to such an extent that it is hard to tell how much of each motivates any particular act:[35] what moves virtuous agents in the typical case is 'the desire of... deserving *and* obtaining this credit and rank among our equals' (*TMS*, VI.i.3; emphasis added). Aristotle, too, comes close to Rousseau's view when he allows for the pleasure that is a 'consequent end' of virtue—a pleasure that 'completes' virtuous activity—to count also as that activity's *aim* (*NE*, 1174b–1175a). More to the point, the picture I have extracted from the example of Rome and found echoes of in Smith and Aristotle exhibits striking similarities to Rousseau's own characterization of the like-mindedness that Emile, after his *amour-propre* has been properly molded, finds in some of his fellows, as well as the convergence between honor from himself and honor from others that accompanies this like-mindedness:

[Emile] loves men because they are like him (*ses semblables*), but he will love above all those who resemble him most, because he will feel that he is good (*se sentira bon*); and since he judges this resemblance by agreement in moral taste, he will be quite gratified to be approved in everything connected with good character. He will not precisely say to himself, 'I rejoice because they approve of me,' but rather,

[35] *TMS*, III.2.26. Here Smith explicitly describes the desire for praise as *motivating* (in part) the virtuous act; see also *TMS*, III.2.29.

'I rejoice because they approve of what I have done that is good. I rejoice that the people who honor me do themselves honor. So long as they judge so soundly, it will be a fine thing to obtain their esteem.'

$(E \text{ IV}, 339/OC 4, 671)^{36}$

Beyond its similarities to the views of Smith and Aristotle, though, this passage points to three additional features of the approval Emile finds in following reason that need to be taken account of in refining our understanding of Rousseau's ideal of rational agency. The first is bound up with the claim that, although Emile is not insensitive to the approval of his fellow beings, he—like the lover of true glory, as well as, presumably, the Roman citizen—values it only conditionally. That is, Emile rejoices in esteem from others only so long as he merits it, both because he truly possesses the qualities he is being esteemed for and because those qualities are in his own view genuinely worthy of esteem. Yet this description of Emile brings out something missing (or not explicit) in Smith's characterization of the lover of true glory. While the latter is described as wanting the esteem she wins from others to be commensurate with actual merit, Emile is said to want something more: for him it is not enough that the esteem he receives be genuinely deserved; he also wants those who confer it on him to do so for the right reasons. Thus, Emile takes the following attitude to the recognition he desires from others: even if I am deserving of the esteem I win from my fellows, what is it worth to me if they esteem me for the wrong reasons? Of what value is their good opinion if that opinion is grounded in error, if it is mistaken as to the true basis of my honor? For Emile, in other words, finding satisfaction in the good opinion of others requires as one of its conditions that he, in turn, have a certain good opinion of them. More precisely, Emile is able to find gratification in the esteem of those around him only to the extent that he takes them, too, to be competent judges of human goodness. But since that is itself a virtue—it is a sign of good character, of valuing what is truly fine—Emile's seeking or delighting in their esteem is always implicitly also a mark of his esteem for them. It would not be an exaggeration to say that this moment of esteeming

---

[36] Something similar is true of Sophie as well: 'She has that noble pride (*orgueil*) based on merit that feels itself, esteems itself, and wants to be honored as it honors itself. She would disdain a heart that...did not love her for her virtues...more than for her charms and did not prefer its own duty to her' (*E* V, 439/*OC* 4, 809).

those whose judgments of ourselves matter to us is a constitutive part of the 'spiritual' community exemplified above by ancient Rome, an association whose publicly shared norms give it the character of a *moi commun*. Another way of formulating this point would be to say that in the case of rational agents, satisfying recognition can never be merely one-directional. When educated so as to accord with reason, the desire for standing in the eyes of others always includes a corresponding need to accord a certain standing to them. For well-formed human subjects, the satisfaction of *amour-propre* is possible only through *reciprocal* recognition (of a certain kind).[37]

The second point to be made about the community of *semblables* that Emile belongs to as a man of reason is that, unlike ancient Rome, this community is not tied to a particular time or place, nor does membership in it depend on being born into a specific nation or class. What unifies Emile's community of fellows is merely their like-mindedness—their 'agreement in moral taste', or shared allegiance to certain ethical ideals. And while similarities in circumstances of birth might facilitate community of this sort, they are not the essential criteria of membership. This suggests that part of what rational agency involves for Rousseau is a commitment not just to 'our' practices and values (the ones we Romans, or we Genevans, happen to have) but to norms that *human beings* can recognize as valid, even while inhabiting different places and times. It involves, in other words, the conviction that if norms are to possess genuine authority, they must reflect not merely contingent or parochial beliefs and practices but, as Rousseau puts it, 'a universal justice that emanates from reason alone' (*SC*, II.6.ii). For rational beings, then, local norms are authoritative—they are the source of real obligation—only to the extent that they express (or are at least consistent with) universal ideals of reason. Even if we were to conclude that Rousseau ultimately overestimates the capacity of 'reason alone' to yield contentful ethical principles valid for humans at all times and places, there is a core idea in his picture of rational agency that remains compelling: a normative principle merits our allegiance only if it can be

---

[37] Although Rousseau's position anticipates Hegel's account of recognition in the 'Self-Consciousness' chapter of *Phenomenology of Spirit*, the two are not identical. For Rousseau reason has independent content that places constraints on the proper satisfaction of *amour-propre*, whereas for Hegel the principles of reason derive their content from a dialectical argument that uncovers the conditions under which the drive for recognition can be systematically satisfied, i.e. fully and for all subjects.

justified to everyone it purports to obligate, regardless of the particular position or perspective of each.

Clearly, this point is relevant to the first set of issues raised above concerning the relation between rational agency and membership in a community of *semblables*. It is significant, first, that Rousseau speaks of Emile's obedience to reason as though it, too, were located within a specific human community, even if that community is defined not geographically, like ancient Rome, but simply by the like-mindedness of its members. This suggests, though it does not yet prove, that for Rousseau membership in some actual human community is essential to rational agency.

Moreover, this point furnishes an answer to our earlier question about the extent to which practical identities that attach themselves to the values of a particular society can be the source of *rational* agency, where what motivates action is reason—that is, principles of justice or duty or right, as opposed to instinct, appetite, or physical impulse. Rousseau's position appears to be—and this marks a further difference between him and Kant—that practical reason of a sort is at work whenever individuals act in accordance with a conception of the good that transcends merely utilitarian considerations[38] to include ideas of what is honorable or fine, in contrast to what is base or contemptible, or merely advantageous. In this broad sense the citizens of Rome described above qualify as rationally motivated. But, as evidenced by his remarks in the *Social Contract* (*SC*, I.8.i), Rousseau seems also to hold that reason—in a more robust sense of the term—includes an allegiance to *principles*, which, because they are grounded in abstract concepts, claim a more general validity than merely local practices and mores.[39] In Rousseau's case, as we have seen, the basic principle of justice abstracts from a multitude of human particularities in order to locate, and then accord priority to, the essential, or fundamental, interests of every individual qua human being. Since a universal principle of this sort is missing (or, at best, present only obscurely) in the case of the ancient Romans, perhaps they can be thought of as occupying in

[38] This is a feature shared by moral and aesthetic ideals since, like the morally good, the beautiful is defined not by 'what we love because it is useful to us nor [by] what we hate because it harms us' (*E* IV, 340/*OC* 4, 671).

[39] The same view is implicit in Rousseau's distinction between natural religion, the doctrines of which are universally valid and knowable by reason alone, and religions that depend on 'the authority of men or the prejudices of the country in which one was born' (*E* IV, 313/*OC* 4, 635–6).

this respect an intermediate stage between the primitive human condition, where instinct rather than reason determines behavior, and the fullest expression of rational agency that humans are capable of achieving.

The third feature of Emile's relations to his fellows brought out by the passage cited above (E IV, 339/OC 4, 671) distinguishes him more fundamentally from Smith's lover of true glory, as well as from the Roman citizen. When Emile follows his reason, he is described not as seeking the approval of others but as taking delight in it; he is said to rejoice in their good opinion of him but not to act for the purpose of attaining it. The implication is that Emile, *as depicted towards the end of Book IV*, does not to any degree make esteem from others the *aim* of his virtuous action, though he is pleased when he is fortunate enough to find it, accepting their approval of him as a bonus, as it were, that acting rightly sometimes brings with it. In this respect Rousseau's well-educated man seems to approximate Smith's lover of virtue: if Emile appreciates his fellows' esteem but regards it merely as a bonus, then for him the satisfaction that comes simply from knowing that he has acted well must by itself be sufficient to motivate his virtuous conduct. And since for Rousseau some kind of finding of honor seems to be essential to rational motivation, this only reinforces the idea that Emile does honor to *himself* —that it is his *self*-regard that motivates him—when he subjects himself to reason's yoke.

Emile's moral self-sufficiency vs. citizens' dependence on the recognition of others

There is, then, an important difference between the Roman citizen and lover of true glory, on the one hand, and Emile as portrayed at the end of Book IV, on the other: the latter, unlike the former, is wholly self-sufficient with respect to the motivational resources needed for rational agency. The honor Emile bestows on himself when he obeys reason is by itself sufficient to motivate that obedience and to make it satisfying. But since, as we already know, Rousseau also regards Smith's lover of true glory as motivated by reason (since, though seeking social esteem, he constrains his quest for it by standards of right to which he accords independent authority), we are left wondering which picture of rational motivation Rousseau ultimately endorses. It is tempting to reconcile these two views by following a strategy I have relied on before: regard them as depicting *different degrees* of rationality, where the Emile of Book IV counts as the more perfect embodiment of 'the man of reason'. Later I shall argue that this is not the best way to interpret Rousseau's position and offer an alternative account of the role that the figure of Emile (in Book IV) plays in Rousseau's more general conception of rational agency. Before doing that, however, it will be helpful to examine in more depth the form of rational motivation ascribed here to Emile. Since Emile's self-sufficient honoring of himself for following reason seems to be presented in Book IV as at least a possibility for human beings, it is worth asking how Rousseau thinks that phenomenon can come about and whether *amour-propre* plays a role in its emergence.

Rousseau's more or less offhand remark that Emile honors himself in following reason is bound to remind readers of more famous statements Kant makes when undertaking to explain how pure practical reason can motivate human agents. Although Kant famously locates our capacity to determine our wills by pure reason in a respect we feel for the moral law, he does not regard this respect as only externally directed. Rather, respect for the moral law is inseparably bound up with a respect the rational agent feels for herself (under a certain description) (*KPV*, 5:80). In Kant's view, being moved by reason involves not only the experience of pain or humiliation in the face of something we acknowledge as higher than ourselves but also an 'elevating' feeling of self-approbation that comes from recognizing ourselves—our law-giving reason—as the moral law's source (*KPV*, 5:81). Not unlike the Roman citizen, whose ability to find honor in acting virtuously depends on his identifying with something greater than himself (Rome and its values), the Kantian moral subject is able to experience her subjection to morality's demands as self-elevating because she identifies with something 'sublime and great' (*KPV*, 5: 86), the nature-transcending law of reason: it is 'by setting before our eyes the sublimity of our nature' (*KPV*, 5: 87) that a practically efficacious respect for the moral law is awakened in us. This connection between moral obligation and self-approbation means that obeying the moral law produces a feeling of self-satisfaction that is crucial to our ability, as beings with sensuously affected wills, to take a practical interest in morality. And in case we are tempted to respond that Kant understood this feeling of self-approbation only as a satisfying consequence of moral action, not as part of its motivation, it is worth recalling his own remarks on the role self-honoring plays in moral practice:

Has not every ... honorable man sometimes ... abstained from an otherwise harmless lie ... solely in order not to have to despise himself secretly in his own eyes? ... Is [an upright man] not sustained by the consciousness that he has maintained humanity in its proper dignity in his own person and honored it, that he has no cause to shame himself in his own eyes?

(KPV, 5: 87–8)[40]

The position articulated by Kant surely comes close to what Rousseau has in mind, if less explicitly, when describing Emile as one who finds honor in subjecting himself to reason. Moreover, Kant's view can be seen as an elaboration of Rousseau's, insofar as it offers an explanation of how beings who cannot avoid a certain concern with the question of their own worth are able to find satisfaction in obeying reason. But however helpful it may be in filling in some of the details of Rousseau's view of rational agency, Kant's account of moral respect does little to clarify how this aspect of rational motivation could depend on a relative passion like *amour-propre*, with its characteristic concern for how one appears not to oneself but to others.

Amour-propre *and the formation of conscience*

Unfortunately, Rousseau's texts furnish little guidance on this question beyond the few scattered remarks we have already surveyed. However, one possibility that is broadly compatible with Rousseau's project is suggested by the position taken several years later by Smith, who recognized in Rousseau (as did Kant) a moral theorist of the first rank.[41] Like Kant, Smith believes that a moral agent of the highest type, the lover of virtue, is moved to act rightly by an internal sense of duty that motivates him even when the agent expects to receive no approbation—or, in the case of vicious action, no condemnation—from his fellows. What keeps such an agent from acting wrongly, then, is not the prospect of incurring the actual condemnation of

[40] See also *KPV*, 5:37–8.

[41] Smith published a largely positive review of the Second Discourse in 1759, four years after its publication: Letter to the *Edinburgh Review*, in *Essays on Philosophical Subjects*, eds. W. P. D. Wightman and J. C. Bryce, *The Glasgow Edition of the Works and Correspondence of Adam Smith* (Oxford: Oxford University Press, 1980), vol. 3, 242–54.

others but the thought that if one acted wrongly, one would *deserve* their condemnation—one would make oneself 'the just and proper object of the hatred and contempt of [one's] fellow creatures' (*TMS*, III.2.9). For Smith, this capacity to be motivated by wholly internal standards of virtue requires becoming the observer and judge of one's actions, as well as the source of a 'self-approbation [that] stands in need of no confirmation from the approbation of other men' (*TMS*, III.2.8). In explaining how behavior can be regulated by self-approbation (or self-condemnation), Smith conceives of the moral agent as taking up a certain idealized perspective—that of an impartial spectator—from which he observes and appraises the worthiness of his own actions. In the case of an evil deed, this involves anticipating in imagination 'the contempt and…shame which he would be exposed to, if his actions should ever come to be generally known' (*TMS*, III.2.9). Thus, even though he may not be exposed to the actual judgments of his fellow beings, it is still a form of approval (or condemnation) from others—in this case, from an imagined impartial spectator—that moves the lover of virtue to act. Put differently, the satisfaction that even the lover of virtue finds in acting rightly, however refined and internalized, always retains some of the character of being observed and esteemed by another subject—or, as Smith puts it, of being the object of a *spectator*'s evaluative gaze.

Insofar as he holds that moral motivation is possible for human beings only as a reconfiguration—an education and refinement—of the desire for the approbation of others that nature has implanted in us (*TMS*, III.2.7), Smith's position is consonant with Rousseau's intent to find in *amour-propre* the psychological basis of moral agency. Indeed, it is only a short step from Smith's conception of moral agency, with its emphasis on the perspective of the impartial spectator, to the view—articulated much later by Freud but still Rousseauvian in spirit—that, in effect, accords to *amour-propre* an essential developmental role in the formation of moral conscience.[42] On one version of Freud's claim,[43] the development of

---

[42] Smith hints at a similar view when he underscores the role played by the child's desire to gain the favor of parents and schoolmates in acquiring the capacity to internalize the viewpoint of the impartial spectator; *TMS*, III.3.21–2.

[43] For a helpful account of the changes Freud's view underwent, see Joseph Sandler, Alex Holder, and Dale Meers, 'The Ego Ideal and the Ideal Self', *The Psychoanalytic Study of the Child* 18 (1963), 139–58; and David Velleman, 'A Rational Superego', *The Philosophical Review* 108 (1999), 529–58.

conscience depends on the young child first imagining himself the object of the disapproving gaze of the powerful, loved parental authority and then transforming that gaze into the punishing superego, an internalized spectator that 'constantly observes the actual self' and 'discovers and criticizes all [its] intentions'.[44] That something like *amour-propre* must be at work in Freud's account is implied by the nature of the emotional attachment that binds the young child to his parental caregiver. As Rousseau makes clear (despite his persistent but unconvincing denials that *amour-propre* plays any significant role in the pre-adolescent's character), the love a young child feels for his powerful caregiver, like any love, demands reciprocation (*E* IV, 213–14/*OC* 4, 492–4), and this desire to be loved in return includes the desire to appear a certain way—estimable, worthy, admirable—in the eyes of his beloved. Without the presumption that the young child cares deeply about how he is judged by those whose love and protection he needs, Freud would be unable to explain how parental ideals gain a foothold in the child's psyche. If the criticism of his caregivers is to disrupt his original narcissism and lead to the internalization of their ideals, the young child must not only be able to view himself through their eyes; he must also be motivated to secure their good opinion by conforming to their demands.

Even though Rousseau never envisages a stage in childhood development analogous to the birth of the superego in Freud's theory, it is striking that he senses the need for some such event at the very point in Emile's education at which, because adolescent sexual desire no longer permits *amour-propre* to remain dormant, he is about to assume full membership in the social and moral world, free for the first time of the supervision and control of his tutor. The strategy Rousseau recommends for securing Emile's faithfulness to his duties once his tutor is no longer present to guide him is but a version of the Freudian idea that conscience depends on internalizing the viewpoint of a loved external authority. This strategy, as related by Emile's tutor, consists in the following:

If I have been able ... to take all the necessary precautions ... suitable for the juncture of life that [Emile] has reached, I do not doubt for an instant that he will come

[44] Sigmund Freud, 'On Narcissism', in *The Standard Edition of the Complete Psychological Works of Sigmund Freud*, trans. James Strachey (London: Hogarth Press, 1953–1974), vol. 14, 95. It is fascinating that, at least here, Freud follows Rousseau in locating the psychic source of conscience in narcissism, a species of self-love that, though not identical to *amour-propre*, bears many similarities to it.

by himself to the point where I want to lead him, that he will eagerly put himself in my safekeeping, ... and will say to me with all the warmth of his age, 'O my friend, my protector, my master! Take back the authority you want to give up at the very moment it is most important for me that you retain it. Until now you had this authority only due to my weakness; now you shall have it due to my will. ... *Watch over your work in order that it remain worthy of you. I want to obey your laws*; I want to do so always.'

(*E* IV, 325/*OC* 4, 651; emphasis added)

Although Emile's internalization of authority is characterized here as a conscious, voluntary act of submission—reminiscent of a similar moment in the *Social Contract*[45]—his transformation into a self-regulating moral being exhibits some important similarities with the birth of conscience as Freud understands it. Most significantly, what motivates the adolescent Emile to be faithful to his duty—to obey his tutor's laws even when unobserved—is a desire to prove himself worthy in the (imagined, internalized) eyes of his childhood protector and master. As it is depicted here, then, Emile's capacity to transform the demands of an external authority into the internal demands of conscience depends on motives that have their origin in *amour-propre*. The basis of Emile's later disposition to virtue—his finding *honor* in subjecting himself to reason—is, it seems, merely a refinement of an earlier longing to be found good and lovable by another subject, his powerful protector and the first object of his love.

It is not unreasonable, then, to conclude that Rousseau's account of Emile's moral development provides the resources for ascribing at least one essential role to *amour-propre* in the formation of agents who can be motivated by reason: to the extent that such agents rely on internal sources of approbation or esteem in order to act as reason demands, their rational agency depends (genetically) on *amour-propre*. For they acquire the capacity to 'honor themselves' for their rational conduct only by internalizing the point of view of an originally external authority in whose eyes they long to appear as worthy. Yet, I shall argue, this is not the only, nor the most important, role the desire for recognition plays in Rousseau's conception of rational motivation.

---

[45] Emile's submission to reason recalls the original consent to obey the general will that in the *Social Contract* marks the beginning of rational self-governance.

Amour-propre *in the exercise of conscience*

It is tempting, especially since Kant, to read Rousseau as holding that an action is rationally determined only when all traces of being motivated by honor from others have given way to the prospect of winning honor in one's own eyes—only, in other words, when a concern for self-esteem has completely replaced *amour-propre* as the action's passionate basis.[46] Indeed, as we have seen, something like this ideal seems to underlie Rousseau's description of Emile (in Book IV) as honoring himself when he obeys reason and as delighting in, but not seeking, the approbation of others for his virtuous conduct. I shall argue, however, that Rousseau's conception of rational motivation is more complicated than this description of Emile implies. Moreover, the main respect in which Rousseau's conception diverges from this picture goes hand in hand with ascribing to *amour-propre* a greater role in rational motivation than the Kantian view permits. On my reading, Rousseau's position incorporates the views of Smith and Freud on the nature and origin of conscience examined above but takes a more moderate view than Kant's on the source of the honor that an adult, socially immersed rational agent (typically) finds in obeying reason. By allowing for the quest for social esteem to play a significant role in rational motivation, Rousseau, on my reading, appears more the forerunner of Hegel than of Kant.

There are three considerations that count against ascribing to Rousseau the Kantian view of rational motivation implicit in his description of Emile at the end of Book IV (that the rational agent must rely only on internal standards and sanctions in following reason). The first is that the Kantian position seems to conflict with the general picture of human psychology—especially its view of the nature and centrality of *amour-propre*—that is articulated in both *Emile* and the Second Discourse. The relativity of *amour-propre*, its ineliminability as a psychological force, the power with which it moves us, its ability to pervade every sphere of human endeavor—all of these claims diminish the plausibility of positing one significant sphere of human action—rational agency—where every manifestation of the longing for standing in the eyes of others must be eliminated, overcome, or sublimated into a desire to be worthy merely in one's own eyes.

---

[46] This would not require that the rational agent be free of all desire for recognition from others—which would contradict Rousseau's thesis regarding the ineliminability of *amour-propre*—but only that he be sufficiently motivated to obey reason independently of the social esteem it promises.

The second consideration is that the Kantian view of rational motivation is hard to reconcile with Rousseau's laudatory description of Roman citizens and of what moves them to (a form of) rational action. As noted above, Rousseau appeals to classical Rome as a model for how an expanded *amour-propre*—winning standing as a self by identifying with one's community and the shared values that define it—can transform creatures of self-love into moral beings by making the self-approbation won through virtuous conduct converge with the reward of honor in the eyes of one's compatriots. In the case of the Romans, establishing a recognized identity before others is always (or normally) part of what motivates virtuous action and makes it satisfying. Thus, for the citizens of Rome, in contrast to Kant's rational subject, the motivation for rational action appears to incorporate, even depend on, the desire to be regarded by one's compatriots as good. If, however, we take Rousseau to espouse a Kantian picture of rational motivation, it is difficult to see what positive role the example of Rome could play in his account.

The third, most important reason for rejecting the Kantian interpretation is that it sits uneasily with the account of reason developed in the previous chapter. According to this account, subjection to rational authority is an inherently intersubjective phenomenon, requiring the acknowledgment that no single person's opinion as to what is right is capable by itself—without the concurrence of others—of constituting legitimate laws and imposing obligations on rational beings. But if an individual's subjection to reason requires recognizing the authority of other wills—if only public reason can ultimately determine what reason demands—how could satisfaction as a rational agent depend on an individual's judgments alone? Or, to direct this question to Rousseau's own pedagogical theory: how is this view of rational obligation consistent with the thoroughgoing self-containedness that appears to be the goal of Emile's education, including the self-sufficiency he achieves (at the end of Book IV) as the source of the honor he finds in following reason?

Since Rousseau himself appears to endorse the Kantian picture of rational motivation in his portrayal of Emile, the conflicts I have been describing could easily be seen as internal to Rousseau's thought. It is possible even to view them, not as a problem in need of resolution, but as evidence that Rousseau means to present two *competing* accounts of rational motivation corresponding to the different—and likewise competing—projects carried out in the *Social Contract* and *Emile*. As I have already indicated, Rousseau himself seems to invite this reading in his well-known remarks on the necessity of choosing between educating Emile to be a man and educating him to be a citizen (*E* I, 39–41/*OC* 4, 248–51). But, as I have suggested, setting Rousseau's political philosophy in opposition to his moral pedagogy gravely misrepresents those projects. For despite the apparently unambiguous opposition between man and citizen set out in Book I of *Emile*, Rousseau expressly revokes this dichotomy towards the end of Book IV,[47] when he announces—clearly and more than once—the need for Emile, now that his *amour-propre* and pity have been properly educated, to enter society and become a citizen. That the completion of Emile's education requires his entry into the civil order could hardly be more plain: 'If I keep him away from society to the end, what will he have learned from me? Everything perhaps, except the most necessary art for *a man and a citizen*, which is knowing how to live with his fellows' (*E* IV, 328/*OC* 4, 655).[48] And much later, as if to dissolve any lingering doubts as to his intent to make moral pedagogy consistent with political philosophy, Rousseau presents what Emile must know in order to take his place in the state by repeating in more or less the same order—sometimes summarizing, sometimes quoting—the contents of the *Social Contract* (*E* V, 458–69/*OC* 4, 836–52). Evidence such as this makes it hard to avoid concluding that Rousseau intends for his readers to find a way of reconciling the two works, including their apparently conflicting views on the nature of reason. The difficult issue is how, precisely, this is to be done.

It might seem that this conflict could be resolved simply by distinguishing two issues that appear to be conflated in my statement of it, namely, whether the rational agent is self-sufficient with regard to *motivation* (whether she alone is the source of the honor she finds in submitting to reason) and whether the rational agent is self-sufficient in determining reason's *content*

[47] Indeed, the dichotomy is revoked much earlier, already in Book I just several pages after Rousseau first mentions the opposition between man and citizen: 'Swept along in contrary routes by nature and by men, ... we follow a composite force that leads us to neither one goal nor the other. ... If perhaps the double object we set for ourselves could be joined in a single one, then by removing the contradictions of man a great obstacle to his happiness would be removed. ... I believe one will have made a few steps in this quest when one has read this book' (*E* I, 41/*OC* 4, 251). See also Ch. 5, nn. 5 and 28.

[48] Emphasis added. And just before this: 'Emile is not made to remain always solitary. As a member of society he ought to fulfill its duties. Since he is made to live with men, he ought to know them' (*E* IV, 327/*OC* 4, 654); see also *E* V, 448, 455/*OC* 4, 823, 833.

(whether by herself she can determine what precisely reason obligates her to do). This distinction, it might seem, would allow us to reconcile the type of rational self-sufficiency that Rousseau ascribes to Emile with the *Social Contract*'s view of the intersubjective character of rational authority: while the individual cannot by herself determine her specific duties and rights—while she lacks the authority to decree what the general will wills in particular circumstances—the incentive for complying with reason's (publicly determined) demands is an honor whose source is wholly internal to the rational agent.

Though separating the two types of rational self-sufficiency in this way is logically possible, it produces an odd incongruence in the resulting picture of rational agency. It would be strange, at the very least, to suppose that the authority to say what reason demands and the authority to honor one who does it should have such disparate sources. On this view, a rational agent would depend on the judgments of others to determine what he ought to do and then, relying solely on his own internal resources, would approve (or honor) himself for complying with their collective determination.

The real difficulty with this position, though, lies elsewhere. It comes into view when one considers that the problem that motivated Rousseau's appeal to the authority of the judgments of others in the first place—the indeterminacy of the abstract principles of justice—arises not only in the sphere of legislation but in the 'judicial' domain as well. The task of judicial authority is not to specify which laws bind the members of a community but to determine whether particular actions undertaken by those members conform to established law. Since a judgment of the latter type logically precedes any 'self-honoring' a rational agent might engage in, the view that the individual alone can be the source of the honor she finds in submitting to reason presupposes that individuals themselves possess the ultimate authority to judge whether what they do accords with valid law. But since the problem of indeterminacy arises not only in deciding which laws follow from the principles of justice but also in deciding whether a particular act accords with those laws, there is no more reason to grant individuals (as such) this judicial authority than there is to accord them the right to make law. Although Rousseau makes no explicit mention of this problem, it must have been familiar to him from his reading of Hobbes, who argues that judicial authority in the state is necessary not only because some individuals will be motivated to circumvent the law for their own gain, or unable to judge impartially in their own cases, but also because, even with the best of intentions, they will sometimes disagree about whether particular actions conform to established law.[49] If we take this thought seriously—even without firm evidence that Rousseau himself did[50]—it is difficult to avoid concluding that Emile's apparent self-sufficiency in supplying the honor he finds in following reason is not only at odds with the larger conception of rational agency to which Rousseau is committed but also a manifestation of moral arrogance, which is to say: a species of inflamed (inflated) *amour-propre*.

This point, Rousseauvian at least in spirit, gives us a philosophical reason for according priority to the picture of rational motivation implicit in the example of ancient Rome—and to the concurring views of Aristotle and Smith—over the one presented in Book IV of *Emile*. It enables us to see why recognition from others might be intrinsic to, not merely an accompanying bonus of, rational agency. For, on this view, knowing that one has followed reason depends on the concurrent judgments of others. This concurrence, though, amounts to a kind of approval in the eyes of others—a recognition from one's associates that one is a competent interpreter and applier of the community's moral ideals.[51] This implies that for human beings, successfully determining one's actions in accordance with reason cannot be separated from winning esteem from others. Knowing oneself as obeying reason and being recognized as rational by one's associates are coincident phenomena.[52] And so, insistence on being the sole source of the honor one finds in following reason reveals itself to be a form of *superbia*, an overestimation of self that reflects a failure to appreciate how one's own rational agency depends on the participation of others.

---

[49] See *L*, xxvi.20–3, where Hobbes grounds judicial authority in the state, in part, in the claim that 'all laws, written and unwritten, have need of interpretation.'

[50] Even if Rousseau failed to see this point, it is congruent with, perhaps entailed by, the problem of legislative indeterminacy that he did recognize. His failure to consider this point is no doubt related to his general silence on the topic of judicial, as opposed to legislative and executive, authority.

[51] Brandom emphasizes this point in his enlightening account of recognition and normativity in Hegel.

[52] This view is endorsed by Smith: 'Very few men can be satisfied with their own private consciousness that they have attained those qualities...which...they think praiseworthy in other people...unless they have actually obtained that praise which they think due [to those qualities]. No man can be completely, or even tolerably satisfied, with having avoided everything blameworthy in his conduct, unless he has likewise avoided the blame or the reproach....[I]n all matters of serious consequence, [a wise man] will most carefully endeavour so to regulate his conduct as to avoid, not only blameworthiness, but, as much as possible, every probable imputation of blame' (*TMS*, III.2.28–9).

Accepting this account of the judicial authority of reason makes it possible to grasp, in outline, the view of rational motivation Rousseau must have been groping towards when he made it his task to 'transform into a sublime virtue the dangerous disposition out of which all our vices are born' (*PE*, 20/*OC* 3, 260). Reason is able to employ for its own ends the very passion responsible for the world's evils—the longing for standing in the eyes of others—because it can be educated to find satisfaction in the type of recognition that rational agency depends on. In the fortunate circumstance in which good education complements a good social environment, *amour-propre* is able to supply a large part[53] of the motivating force that ordinary human beings rely on in order to have, and consistently to act on, a non-instrumental allegiance to what reason demands. Moreover, beyond merely explaining how reason can be efficacious in human action, this view is more consistent than the Kantian reading with Rousseau's general picture of human psychology, especially with the prominent place it accords to *amour-propre* in motivating action. By allowing the desire for recognition to play a part in what moves us to act rationally, Rousseau's view makes it possible for a large sphere of human action—obedience to reason—to be a source of satisfaction of the need for recognition. In doing so, this view does justice to Rousseau's fundamental assumption that *amour-propre* can be neither extinguished nor forced to play a merely subsidiary role in human affairs.

Reconciling Emile *and the* Social Contract *in a unitary account of moral motivation*

What, then, are we to make of the ideal of self-sufficiency that looms so large over Emile's education? It is impossible, after all, to deny the importance Rousseau places on Emile's learning to 'make use of *his* reason, not that of others' (*E* III, 207/*OC* 4, 486; emphasis added) and on his 'honoring himself' when he follows his reason (*E* IV, 315/*OC* 4, 637). Before conceding that Rousseau is inconsistent or that *Emile* and the *Social Contract* articulate mutually exclusive ideals, it should be noted that the rational self-sufficiency alluded to in these passages is presented as a goal of Emile's education in Books III and IV—in the one case, before his *amour-propre* has been fully awakened and, in the other, before he has

---

[53] It is important to remember that *amour-propre* is not the only psychological resource rational agency relies on. Pity and *amour de soi*, properly educated, also play necessary roles, though these are not my topic here.

entered into moral and social relations to others. This is an important detail that interpreters of *Emile* tend to overlook, although doing so has grave consequences for understanding Rousseau's position. In order to grasp the true significance of Emile's self-sufficiency it is necessary to bear in mind that each book of *Emile* corresponds to a distinct stage in a child's development and that the pedagogical aims articulated in each are relative to the specific developmental stage under consideration.[54] Adopting this perspective opens up the possibility that self-sufficiency may be the supreme pedagogical objective at one stage in Emile's life but not the only, or even the highest, ideal that the man of reason will embody at the end of his education. If this interpretive strategy is to be convincing, sense must be made of the idea that self-sufficiency is an appropriate pedagogical aim for Emile the child (and adolescent) but one that must be replaced or tempered when he leaves the secluded domain of domestic education in order to take his place in the world of moral and social relationships, where deep and enduring attachments to others replace carpentry, map-making, and foot races as Emile's dominant concerns.

That self-sufficiency of some sort is essential to rational agency is suggested not only by *Emile* (and good philosophical sense) but also by the very social and political writings of Rousseau that underscore the necessity for rational agents to submit to the authority of others. Indeed, it is no exaggeration to say that the tension found here between *Emile* and the *Social Contract* on the issue of rational self-sufficiency is but a variant of the dilemma we encountered in the previous chapter in reconstructing the view of rational agency implied by Rousseau's claim that public reason, or law, is the citizen's supreme authority. There, too, we found an unresolved tension—'dialectic' may be a more apt description—between the moral authority of the individual and that of her fellow citizens when the former finds herself on the losing side of a majority decision. For the legitimacy of the submissive attitude Rousseau prescribes in such a case—'it proves only that I was mistaken' (*SC*, IV.2.viii)—turned out to depend on a logically prior judgment on the part of the dissenter herself as to the overall moral condition of her community—on her judgment, in other words, that 'all the characteristics of the general will are still in the majority' (*SC*, IV.2.ix).

---

[54] Hence Rousseau's injunction, 'Treat each pupil according to his age' (*E* II, 91/*OC* 4, 320); see also *E* II, 79/*OC* 4, 302.

A similar tension showed itself in this chapter's earlier discussions of both Emile and the Roman citizen. In each case the value of the esteem won from others for obeying reason was seen to be conditional on a reciprocal judgment on the part of the esteemed individual as to the worthiness of his fellows to bestow the esteem in question. In the case of Emile this condition is explicit (*E* IV, 339/*OC* 4, 671); in the case of the Roman citizen it is implied by the fact that the honor sought is normatively constrained, conditional on the citizen's independent judgment that the values of his community are worthy of his allegiance. And, most recently, we encountered this same tension in attempting to sort out Rousseau's view on whether the source of the esteem won through rational agency is internal or external to the agent. By concluding that rational motivation depends on a convergence of the two kinds of esteem, we granted, in effect, that rational authority flows from two potentially conflicting sources, the judgment of the individual as such and the collective judgment of his community.

The recurrence of this tension in various guises suggests that we should view it not as a conflict to be decided in favor of one side or the other but instead as evidence of a fundamental antinomy of rational agency that, unannounced, pervades Rousseau's thinking on the topic. The antinomy, as it were, comprises two opposing claims concerning where the ultimate source of rational authority is to be located: in the individual's judgment, in which case self-sufficiency is essential to rational agency, or in the collective judgment of one's community, in which case obeying reason involves recognizing the judgments of others as having authority over one's own. Thinking through Rousseau's treatment of these issues in *Emile* and the *Social Contract* suggests, I submit, that the antinomy of rational agency can be resolved only by abandoning the assumption that rational obligation must have a single, supreme source and by regarding it instead as flowing from two independent sources, neither of which can be granted a priori the authority to trump the other in cases of conflict. This means that rational agency requires some combination of both independence from and submission to the authority of others. It also implies that conflicts that emerge in the real world between the two sources of reason's authority may be undecidable by theory alone. This is to say that philosophy provides no algorithm, nor any other sure procedure, for settling the kind of dispute over what reason requires that arises when, for example, an individual ceases to regard her community as animated by the spirit of justice—by a genuine concern for the common good and the fundamental interests of each—and, so, no longer recognizes its authority to make laws that obligate her or its other members.

Put differently, Rousseau's attempts to develop an account of what it is 'to consult one's reason before heeding one's inclination'—to act on the basis of rational norms that one regards as authoritative for oneself and other rational beings—end up conceiving of rational agency as an *ideal* that is fully realized only when individual and community stand in a specific and delicate relation, a relation of reciprocal recognition in which creatures of *amour-propre* receive and extend to one another a kind of confirmation of their standing in the eyes of their fellow beings. Rousseau himself was acutely aware of the rarity and fragility of the conditions under which rational agency can be fully realized, and he concluded from this that the most philosophy can demonstrate with respect to this topic is that human nature and the basic features of the world are *compatible with* those conditions. This, for him, was enough to ward off a metaphysical pessimism or despair (though not a more limited despair over the present) that threatens to undermine moral agency entirely by seeing it as impossible, contradictory, or necessarily repressive. It was enough, in other words, to ensure that in the less than perfect conditions in which humans are fated to live, the ideal of rational agency, even if not fully realizable, is able nonetheless to have a real—*practical*—influence on how we choose to act. At the same time, allegiance to the rule of reason can lead in the real world to philosophically irresolvable conflicts between the individual's authority and that of his community. Rousseau takes these conflicts to be genuine problems, though not of the sort that philosophy can be expected to solve. That some such conflicts are, in most times and places, inevitable—that for real human beings, determination by reason involves a never finally resolved tension between two poles of authority—Rousseau seems both to have seen and to have considered fundamental to the human condition.

We are now in a position to place Emile's self-sufficiency in its proper context. If Emile's education in boyhood and adolescence is directed at making him self-sufficient—at teaching him to rely on his own reason, to honor himself for doing right, and to seek esteem only from those he himself esteems—it is not because as a man he is to strive for perfect self-sufficiency. Rather, it is because once Emile has taken up his place in society, he will need certain internal resources—the strengths of a self-reliant character—in order to confront the moral dangers posed by his dependence on others in love, in work, and in citizenship. If as an adult Emile is to avoid enslavement to flattery and approval, if he is to be capable of moral action when the eyes of the crowd are not upon him, if he is to be able to think for himself in political deliberations and evaluate the opinions of others, he will need to rely on the capacities for self-sufficient judgment and self-esteem that he acquired under his tutor's care. Of course, Emile must avoid the converse vices as well. Unless he is also capable of ceding authority to others' opinions and giving weight to their valuations, he is certain to appear—indeed, to be—willful, arrogant, and narcissistically detached from his fellows. Rousseau's view seems to be that because of the extraordinary force and tenacity of *amour-propre*—its power to make humans susceptible to the judgments and valuations of others—the latter capacities come more naturally[55] to humans and, so, pose less of a challenge for education than instilling in them the virtues of self-sufficiency. When Rousseau insists that it is impossible for a single education to make both a man and a citizen, it is essential to hear him out to the end. What he says is that 'one cannot make both *at the same time*' (*E* I, 39/ *OC* 4, 248; emphasis added). That crucial qualification is meant to signal not that, as an adult, Emile must be one or the other but rather that the only possibility of his avoiding the moral pitfalls of social membership is if, prior to becoming a citizen, he is formed as a 'human being'—that is, subjected to an educational regime that shields him for as long as possible from the dangers of *amour-propre* in order to instill in him the capacities for self-sufficiency he will eventually need if his later attachments to others are to be compatible with his freedom and integrity.

Let us return now to the role *amour-propre* plays in rational motivation and summarize Rousseau's position as it has been reconstructed here. According to this view, human beings are able to 'subject themselves to the yoke of reason' only because they can be educated to find a kind of honor or esteem in doing so. The honor at issue in rational agency is of the sort one wins in giving expression to a practical identity—as, say, a man of

---

[55] That is, they flow from human nature in the expanded sense, which includes not only the individualistic components of our 'original' nature but also the basic psychological feature of human social existence, *amour-propre*.

reason, a citizen of Rome, or a sovereign member of the republic—where having such an identity implies a normative commitment, an allegiance to some standard of what is good, or worthy of honor. As we saw, Rousseau follows Aristotle and anticipates Smith in holding that for human beings the honor won by following reason normally comes from two sources. First, rational agents must have some capacity to bestow honor on themselves for virtuous action; they must be able to be motivated, not only by the prospect of actual esteem from others, but also by esteem they accord to themselves when they know that their actions *ought* to elicit their fellows' esteem. Even here, where what is at stake is honor in one's own eyes rather than in others', *amour-propre* plays a crucial developmental role in the constitution of rational agency. For humans acquire the capacity to 'honor themselves' for their rational conduct only by internalizing the evaluative perspective of an originally external authority whose approval or esteem they long to secure.

Secondly, rational motivation normally relies also on actual esteem one receives, or hopes to receive, from one's like-minded associates. In other words, in being moved by reason, the concern to find honor in one's own eyes typically converges with, and is reinforced by, a concern to win it from others. This means that the drive to be recognized by others as worthy is not only developmentally necessary for rational agency; it also plays an ongoing role in motivating fully educated rational agents. There are two sets of reasons—one psychological, the other philosophical—behind Rousseau's claim that the drive for the actual esteem of others is indispensable to rational motivation. *Amour-propre* is psychologically indispensable because the 'higher' (more sublimated) desire to be merely *worthy* of honor is generally too weak, and too difficult to acquire and maintain, to be relied on alone to sustain moral agency over time in the face of powerful, competing motivations.[56] For most human beings, a wholly internally sanctioned sense of what is right is seldom enough to produce virtuous behavior over a long period of time. This psychological point converges with Rousseau's philosophical reasons for believing that winning—if not necessarily *seeking*[57]—the esteem of others is intrinsic to rational action.

[56] See Cohen, 107, 126.
[57] Strictly speaking, the philosophical point that *winning* esteem from others is intrinsic to rational agency does not imply that rational agents must *seek* that esteem for its own sake, or make it (part of) their final aim in following reason. Although a rational agent must care about his associates'

Since no individual by herself possesses the authority to be reason's legislator or judge, a commitment to let reason determine one's will must include a concern for whether others concur with one's opinions as to what reason requires and whether one's own behavior conforms to established law. Because concurrence of this sort implies a kind of approval by others, having no regard for the judgments my associates make of me indicates my contempt not only for them but for reason and its authority as well.

The significance of comparative standing in rational motivation

Having examined the ways in which the desire to achieve standing in the eyes of others enters into rational motivation, it is time to consider briefly whether the other respect in which *amour-propre* is relative to others—that it aims at *comparative* standing—also plays a role. As noted above, it seems strange to think that the honor a rational agent wins in following reason, whether it comes from himself or from others, depends on comparing his behavior with his fellows' in order to see how much better or worse he does in complying with reason's demands. More plausible, it would seem, is the Kantian view that whatever esteem is at stake in obeying reason depends instead on the agent's measuring his deeds against an absolute (non-comparative) standard of right.[58] That it would be a mistake, however, simply to assume the correctness of Kant's position is shown by the fact that at least two of Rousseau's most illustrious contemporaries appear to reject it. As we noted earlier, Hume suggests that esteem of any sort is intrinsically comparative since the quality that elicits it is always an excellence, some respect in which the esteemed individual stands out from his fellows.[59] And, after him, Smith takes this point one step farther. In what is surely an appropriation of Aristotle's account of magnanimity (*NE*, 1123a–1125a), he explicitly characterizes the self-approbation that a 'wise and virtuous'

---

concurrence—and, so, about their recognition of him—he could, in principle, care about their recognition only as a confirmation of his success in obeying reason. In addition to regarding this attitude as psychologically unlikely, Rousseau would probably also view it as reflecting a nearly pathological *oversublimation* of the passions, in which the desire to be rational is excessively asceticized—too far removed from the original passion it derives from—and every trace of the human basis of reason's authority is compulsively denied.

[58] This point is emphasized by Allen W. Wood: moral judgments 'involve a comparison of ourselves only with the moral law, not with others at all;' *Kant's Ethical Thought* (Cambridge: Cambridge University Press, 1999), 136.

[59] See Ch. 3, n. 3.

man finds in his praiseworthy behavior as resting, in part, on a comparison he makes between himself and his peers. According to Smith, one of the standards we 'naturally' use to assess the merit of our own character and conduct is the degree to which the (absolute, or non-comparative) ideal of perfect virtue 'is commonly attained in the world, and which the greater part of our friends and companions, of our rivals and competitors, may have actually arrived at' (*TMS*, VI.ii.3.23). Although the best human beings are *principally* concerned with measuring themselves by the absolute ideal—'the idea of exact propriety and perfection'—part of even their satisfaction in being virtuous derives from a comparative judgment of this sort (*TMS*, VI.iii.25).

The thought behind Smith's claim here must be that the constraints of human nature make it practically impossible for even the best individuals fully to realize the absolute ideal of virtue. Given these constraints, it would be unreasonable to measure ourselves by only the absolute ideal when reflecting on the merit of our character and conduct. Rather, it makes sense for us to be concerned as well with how close others come to realizing virtue's ideal, not, presumably, because we want to prove ourselves superior to them but because their successes and shortcomings, taken collectively, provide an approximate indication of the extent to which forces within human nature itself are at work in our failure to attain that ideal. Judging ourselves in part by this comparative standard—a measure of the degree of virtue human beings can reasonably be expected to achieve—is essential, then, to avoiding excessively severe forms of self-reproach that, by leading to guilt and despair, make humans miserable but do little in the end to improve their conduct.

Even if this claim of Smith's is correct, it does not follow that a comparative standard of virtue is, or ought to be, involved in *motivating* rational behavior. Such a standard might indeed enter into a reflective assessment of how well we have lived up to our ideals without playing a motivational role in our conduct. If Rousseau takes rational motivation to depend on an ability to find honor in the expression of a normatively grounded practical identity, it cannot be an identity based on the less demanding, comparative ideal that he has in mind. It may well be that in looking back on a life that includes both failures and successes, I am entitled to measure the moral approbation I deserve according to the less demanding standard of how well humans in general do in this regard. But it would be a sign of an objectionable half-heartedness—a lack of genuine commitment to the values I supposedly endorse—if I were to use the same standard when deliberating about my future actions. An agent's aspiration to live up to the description 'more virtuous than most' does not qualify as the kind of expression of identity that defines rational (or moral) agency.

A similar conclusion is arrived at by thinking more carefully about the kind of recognition from others that was said earlier to be inseparable from determining oneself by reason, namely, the recognition of the individual agent as a competent interpreter and applier of the community's shared ideals. When my associates recognize my acts as consistent with established law, when they accept my legislative proposals as compelling interpretations of our shared principles, they recognize me not as one who 'stands out' among them as a paragon of virtue but, instead, as a like-minded associate—someone who, by applying our normative concepts in ways that elicit the agreement of others, has shown himself to be 'one of us'. If comparative standing of any sort plays a role in this form of recognition, it is closest to the standing enjoyed by the citizens of a true republic, where equal, mutually recognized subjects constitute the sole authority for their shared normative practices. In such a context, as I have shown, rational agency cannot do without some form of the desire for standing in the eyes of others that is intrinsic to *amour-propre*. At the same time, genuinely rational motivation requires that the drive for relative standing be sublimated—transformed, or educated—into a concern to be recognized as a more or less equal member of a 'spiritual' community that, because of the values that define it, is the object of one's esteem. This is not, of course, to say that all forms of the quest for superior standing can or must be eradicated from human life. (This would contradict a central claim of Chapter 3.) It is to say only that such an aim can have no place in one circumscribed though highly significant sphere, that in which reason—principles of justice and duty—replaces appetite and inclination as the determiner of human conduct.

Conclusion

What, in the end, has Rousseau's theory of *amour-propre* accomplished? In my view, a great deal. As I hope to have shown in the preceding chapters, Rousseau offers a uniquely rich and compelling account of the role the human drive for recognition plays in human affairs. Indeed, I hope my reconstruction of his theory has shown that its most important claims are *correct*, especially concerning the nature and aim of *amour-propre*; its centrality to and ineradicability from human existence; its great and multifarious capacity to wreak havoc in human affairs; the ways in which appropriate social institutions and educational measures can remedy the very ills inflamed *amour-propre* is responsible for; and even—Rousseau's most original claim—how *amour-propre* is an indispensable component of human rationality, freedom, and subjectivity.

There are, however, important respects in which Rousseau's theory of *amour-propre* falls short of its aims, and it is appropriate here to indicate briefly where these shortcomings lie. The respects in which Rousseau's theory does not fully succeed are all connected with its aspiration to deliver a systematic account of the perils and promise of human existence that proceeds from an analysis of a single component of human nature, broadly construed:[1] *amour-propre*. Another way of formulating this point would be to say that the respects in which Rousseau's theory falls short of its own aims are bound up with its ambition to construct a *theodicy* of *amour-propre* that offers a comprehensive explanation of the human tendency to evil while establishing both the essential goodness of nature (especially human nature) and the possibility of a redemption in which human evils are fully eliminated and the beings who created them are 'lifted up', or ennobled. This is not to say that Rousseau's being guided by the aims of traditional

---

[1] See Ch. 1, n. 40.

theodicy is at every point a source of error. Understanding *amour-propre* from the point of view of theodicy helps him to see, for example, not only that passion's negative potential but also its great capacity for enriching and elevating human existence. More specifically, Rousseau's theodicean perspective—his insistence on finding in evil itself a promise of redemption—is what makes possible his most fruitful philosophical insight: that the drive for recognition, properly configured, is a central component of human rationality.

There is one problem that plagues Rousseau's execution of his project to which I have already alluded: the great power and reach of his account of the pernicious potential of *amour-propre*, as reconstructed in Chapters 2 and 3, so greatly multiply the tasks faced by his remedial enterprise that it becomes nearly impossible to determine whether the remedies proposed in *Emile* and the *Social Contract* constitute a comprehensive solution to human evils rather than a series of piecemeal responses that address some of those evils but leave others untouched. If the tendency towards inflamed *amour-propre* is a nearly unavoidable consequence of certain fundamental, nearly universal features of human existence; if so much wisdom and artful intervention—requiring a godlike legislator and a superhumanly wise tutor—are necessary to avoid the evils of *amour-propre*; if the number and variety of those ills are so great, then is a genuinely comprehensive solution to *amour-propre*'s dangers possible? At times, Rousseau seems close to recognizing the magnitude of this problem: 'it is almost impossible for [education] to succeed, since the conjunction of the elements necessary to its success is in no one's control. All one can do…is come more or less close to the goal' (*E* I, 38/*OC* 4, 247). The problem, however, is not merely that, practically speaking, no actual attempts at reform will ever completely succeed in eradicating inflamed *amour-propre* from human existence. As I suggested at the end of Chapter 5, it is unclear even at the purely theoretical level that the scattering of educational measures proposed in *Emile* (especially in Book IV) can counter, even in principle, the full range of psychological obstacles to human well-being that *amour-propre* poses, especially since, as I argued in Chapter 2, *amour-propre* is subject to inflammation in many ways other than those that spring from an inegalitarian self-conception.

There is, however, a more fundamental respect in which Rousseau's theodicean ambitions lead him astray: his wish to clear Nature, and thereby its Creator, of all responsibility for evil leads him to conclude too quickly that the full range of ills he finds in actual societies—enslavement, domination, conflict, vice, misery, and self-estrangement—have a *single* source in human nature (*amour-propre*, in its inflamed forms) and that in itself this source is ethically neutral (not necessarily productive of evil). More precisely, the most problematic element of Rousseau's theodicy is his claim that what appears to many theorists of human nature—to Augustine, for example—as an independent, non-derivative drive to *dominate* others can be understood as merely a particular form of the drive for recognized standing that has been contingently perverted by human intervention (by bad social institutions or a faulty education). Moreover, as I have shown, this diagnostic thesis has a remedial corollary: by providing individuals with both sufficient opportunities to find healthy forms of social recognition and an education that teaches them how and where satisfying recognition is to be sought, it is possible to satisfy *amour-propre*'s urgings through wholly benign measures and thus, in effect, to eliminate from human affairs the (merely derivative) drive to dominate others.

There are in fact two distinguishable theoretical impulses at work in Rousseau's taking this position, though both are related to his theodicean aims. The first is the urge to locate a single *psychological* cause of the ills of human existence. The second is the urge to show that all pernicious manifestations of this single psychological force are in principle avoidable perversions of an original, neutral disposition, thereby demonstrating the 'goodness' of human nature. Though these two impulses are logically independent, they converge in Rousseau's project insofar as locating a single psychological source of human ills greatly simplifies the, for him, more important task of demonstrating that whatever in their psychology leads humans astray could in principle have different, non-malignant consequences. My aim here is not to criticize this 'goodness of human nature' thesis in the relatively weak form it assumes in Rousseau's thought but instead to point out the problems in one of the crucial claims that support this thesis, namely, that the drive to domination so familiar to observers of human affairs is nothing but a (perverted, or inflamed) form of *amour-propre*.

One way to articulate the problem I have in mind is via a critique of the monocausal explanation of human evils presented in the Second Discourse. Recall that part of that text's 'genealogy of vice' (LCB, 28/*OC* 4, 936) consisted in arguing that the drive to dominate others is not a basic urge of human nature but instead a contingent deformation of the more basic human drive to achieve a recognized standing for others: achieving mastery over others' wills is tempting to humans because being obeyed is easily construed as a confirmation by others of one's superior status. In arguing that inflamed *amour-propre* is the principal cause of moral inequality, as well as of the many evils bound up with it, Rousseau commits himself to the view that every desire to win power over others—every desire to subjugate or enslave—is at root a desire to find recognition (in someone else's eyes) of one's superiority in relation to others (to those one has subjugated or enslaved). But despite the overwhelming force of so much of Rousseau's account of the mischief *amour-propre* is capable of unleashing, it is difficult to follow him the entire length of this path to his conclusion that what motivates aggression and cruelty of all kinds—genocide, imperial wars, the rationalized slaughter that characterized the twentieth century—is but a version, however perverted, of the desire to count for something in the eyes of others.

Although the quest to exercise arbitrary power over others can indeed be motivated by recognitive ends—and it is Rousseau's achievement to have made this especially clear—it is not plausible that domination is attractive to humans *only* because it is a particularly dramatic way of winning recognition. To reformulate this objection within the framework of the Second Discourse: what is it that motivates those still relatively primitive humans, once the objective conditions for economic exploitation obtain, to use the surplus their collective labor has produced to amass property, to prevent others from holding on to theirs, and to use their newly created inequality to subjugate and exploit, 'chang[ing] vast forests into smiling fields that had to be watered with the sweat of men' (*DI*, 167/*OC* 3, 171)? Do those beings—do we?—seek domination merely in order to be *recognized* as powerful and not therefore because power for its own sake, independently of how it makes us appear to others, can also motivate human action? If the answer is no—and it is hard to conclude otherwise—then Rousseau has failed in his attempt to trace all human impulses to violence, destruction, and subjugation back to inflamed manifestations of the desire for standing in the eyes of others. Or, to put the point differently, Rousseau has shown that *amour-propre* plays a much greater role in causing a state of war of all against all than Hobbes's listing of glory as one of its three causes implies (*L*, xiii.6),[2] but he has not established that it is the only, or even the primary, psychological source of domination. Later philosophers, among them Nietzsche and Freud, have implicitly denied the plausibility of Rousseau's explanation of the will to dominate others, and even if their accounts have problems of their own—even if the nature of power and what makes it attractive to humans remains a puzzle today—that does not render Rousseau's position any more compelling.

That Rousseau does not fully succeed in explaining the drive to dominate as a perverted form of the drive for recognition can be seen in his account in *Emile* of the infant's 'spirit of domination' or 'desire to command' (*E* I, 67–8/*OC* 4, 289–90). Recall that in order to explain the urge to dominate as a manifestation of (inflamed) *amour-propre* Rousseau found it necessary to introduce a new[3] and unexplained element into his picture of human psychology, the active principle. According to this explanation, the drive to dominate—just like the more general drive for recognition of which it is a subspecies—is nothing but one possible manifestation of the more fundamental longing to 'animate' the surrounding world, by causing it to bear the imprint of, and so to reflect, one's own subjectivity. The problem in this move, viewed from the perspective of Rousseau's own theoretical aims, is that introducing the active principle into human psychology in order to subsume the drive to dominate under *amour-propre* undermines the fundamental status the latter is supposed to have in his theory. By positing a drive more basic than the longing for recognition—a drive more general than *amour-propre* but still independent of *amour de soi*—Rousseau opens up the possibility that there could be forms of the active principle that are distinct from *amour-propre* but still pernicious in their consequences. Indeed, aggression, cruelty, and the desire to subjugate are examples of drives that cry out to be understood in precisely this way since it is difficult to imagine that what such drives aim at is merely comparative standing as confirmed in the opinion of others. Many instances of human aggression, for example, seem not to be directed at winning the esteem or approval of anyone at all, and this is exactly what we would suspect if, as Rousseau implies in *Emile*, the active principle that is supposed

---

[2] Or seems to imply, since it is possible to argue that Hobbes, too, thinks of glory as the primary, though not the exclusive, cause of the state of war. I am indebted to David Johnston for drawing my attention to this possibility.

[3] New in relation to the Second Discourse's account of human nature.

to account for aggression is even more basic than *amour-propre*. Of course, even if this criticism is correct, it does not yet follow that the 'goodness of human nature' thesis is wrong, for the will to dominate might itself be understandable as a *non-necessary*, perverted form of whatever drive is posited as more basic than *amour-propre*. What this criticism does imply, however, is that Rousseau's theodicy of *amour-propre* has failed to show both that a satisfying and harmonious system of recognition is in principle achievable for human subjects and that the remedy for human evils in general depends alone on bringing such a system into being.

Bibliography

Abbadie, Jacques, *L'art de se connâitre soi-même* (Paris: Librairie Arthème Fayard, 2003).

Abizadeh, Arash, 'Banishing the Particular: Rousseau on Rhetoric, *Patrie*, and the Passions', *Political Theory* 29 (2001), 556–82.

Ainslee, Donald C., 'Scepticism About Persons in Book II of Hume's *Treatise*', *Journal of the History of Philosophy* 37 (1999), 469–92.

Aristotle, *Nicomachean Ethics*, trans. Terence Irwin (Indianapolis: Hackett, 1999).

Augustine, *Confessions*, trans. R. S. Pine-Coffin (New York: Penguin, 1961).

Bertram, Christopher, *Rousseau and 'The Social Contract'* (London: Routledge, 2004).

Brandom, Robert, 'Some Pragmatist Themes in Hegel's Idealism', *European Journal of Philosophy* 7 (1999), 164–89.

Cassirer, Ernst, *The Question of Jean-Jacques Rousseau*, trans. Peter Gay (New Haven, Conn.: Yale University Press, 1989).

Charvet, John, *The Social Problem in the Philosophy of Rousseau* (London: Cambridge University Press, 1974).

Chitty, Andrew, 'Needs in the Philosophy of History: Rousseau to Marx', Ph.D. thesis (Oxford, 1994).

Cohen, Joshua, 'The Natural Goodness of Humanity', in A. Reath, B. Herman, and C. M. Korsgaard (eds.), *Reclaiming the History of Ethics* (Cambridge: Cambridge University Press, 1997).

Cooper, Laurence D., *Rousseau, Nature, and the Problem of the Good Life* (University Park, Penn.: Penn. State University Press, 1999).

Darwall, Stephen, 'Two Kinds of Respect', in R. S. Dillon (ed.), *Dignity, Character, and Self-Respect* (New York: Routledge, 1995).

Dent, N. J. H., *Rousseau* (Oxford: Basil Blackwell, 1988).

Derathé, Robert, 'L'unité de la Pensée de Jean-Jacques Rousseau', in Samuel Baud-Bovy, et al. (eds.), *Jean-Jacques Rousseau* (Neuchâtel: Baconnière, 1962).

Dillon, Robin S. (ed.), *Dignity, Character, and Self-Respect* (New York: Routledge, 1995).

Ferrara, Alessandro, *Modernity and Authenticity: A Study of the Social and Ethical Thought of Jean-Jacques Rousseau* (Albany, N. Y.: State University of New York Press, 1993).

Force, Pierre, *Self-Interest before Adam Smith* (Cambridge: Cambridge University Press, 2003).

Freud, Sigmund, 'On Narcissism', in *The Standard Edition of the Complete Psychological Works of Sigmund Freud*, trans. James Strachey (London: Hogarth Press, 1953–1974), vol. 14, 73–102.

Fuchs, Hans-Jürgen, *Entfremdung und Narzißmus: Semantische Untersuchungen zur Geschichte der 'Selbstbezogenheit' als Vorgeschichte von französisch 'amour-propre'* (Stuttgart: J. B. Metzler, 1977).

Goldschmidt, Victor, *Anthropologie et politque: les principes du système de Rousseau* (Paris: Vrin, 1974).

Habermas, Jürgen, *The Theory of Communicative Action*, trans. Thomas McCarthy, 2 vols. (Boston: Beacon Press, 1981).

Hegel, G. W. F., *Phenomenology of Spirit*, trans. A. V. Miller (Oxford: Oxford University Press, 1977).

Herman, Barbara, 'Rethinking Kant's Hedonism', in A. Byrne, R. Stalnaker, R. Wedgwood (eds.), *Fact and Value* (Cambridge, Mass.: MIT Press, 2001).

Hill, Thomas E., Jr., *Autonomy and Self-Respect* (Cambridge: Cambridge University Press, 1991).

Hobbes, Thomas, *Leviathan*, ed. Edwin Curley (Indianapolis: Hackett, 1994).

Honneth, Axel, *The Struggle for Recognition*, trans. Joel Anderson (Cambridge: Polity Press, 1995).

Hume, David, *A Treatise of Human Nature* (Oxford: Clarendon Press, 1967).

Jaeggi, Rahel, *Entfremdung* (Frankfurt am Main: Campus Verlag, 2005).

Kant, Immanuel, 'Conjectures on the Beginning of Human History', in Hans Reiss (ed.), *Kant: Political Writings* (Cambridge: Cambridge University Press, 1991), 221–34.

—— *The Metaphysics of Morals*, ed. Mary Gregor (Cambridge: Cambridge University Press, 1996).

—— *Critique of Practical Reason*, ed. Mary Gregor (Cambridge: Cambridge University Press, 1997).

—— *Critique of Pure Reason*, trans. Paul Guyer and Allen W. Wood (Cambridge: Cambridge University Press, 1998).

—— *Religion within the Boundaries of Mere Reason*, eds. Allen Wood and George di Giovanni (Cambridge: Cambridge University Press, 1998).

Klein, Melanie, *Envy and Gratitude and Other Works* (New York: Free Press, 1984).

Korsgaard, Christine M., *The Sources of Normativity* (Cambridge: Cambridge University Press, 1996).

Laden, Anthony Simon, *Reasonably Radical: Deliberative Liberalism and the Politics of Identity* (Ithaca, N.Y.: Cornell University Press, 2001).

Levine, Andrew, *The Politics of Autonomy* (Amherst, Mass.: University of Massachusetts Press, 1976).

Locke, John, *Second Treatise of Government*, in Peter Laslett, (ed.), *Two Treatises of Government* (New York: Cambridge University Press, 1963).

Lovejoy, Arthur O., 'The Supposed Primitivism of Rousseau's "Second Discourse"', in A. O. Lovejoy, *Essays in the History of Ideas* (Baltimore: Johns Hopkins Press, 1948).

——— *Reflections on Human Nature* (Baltimore: Johns Hopkins Press, 1961).

Lukács, Georg, *History and Class Consciousness*, trans. Rodney Livingstone (Cambridge, Mass.: MIT Press, 1971).

Manin, Bernard, 'On Legitimacy and Political Deliberation', *Political Theory* 15 (1987), 338–68.

Marcuse, Herbert, *Eros and Civilization* (Boston: Beacon Press, 1974).

Mead, George Herbert, *Mind, Self, and Society* (Chicago: University of Chicago Press, 1934).

Melzer, Arthur M., *The Natural Goodness of Man* (Chicago: University of Chicago Press, 1990).

Neiman, Susan, 'Metaphysics, Philosophy: Rousseau on the Problem of Evil', in A. Reath, B. Herman, and C. M. Korsgaard (eds.), *Reclaiming the History of Ethics* (Cambridge: Cambridge University Press, 1997).

——— *Evil in Modern Thought* (Princeton, N. J.: Princeton University Press, 2004).

Neuhouser, Frederick, 'Freedom, Dependence, and the General Will', *The Philosophical Review* 102 (July 1993), 363–95.

——— *Foundations of Hegel's Social Theory: Actualizing Freedom* (Cambridge, Mass.: Harvard University Press, 2000).

——— 'Rousseau's *Julie*: Passion, Love, and the Price of Virtue' (unpublished manuscript).

Nietzsche, Friedrich, *On the Genealogy of Morals*, trans. Walter Kaufmann and R. J. Hollingdale (New York: Random House, 1967).

——— *Beyond Good and Evil*, trans. Walter Kaufmann (New York: Vintage Books, 1989).

O'Hagan, Timothy, *Rousseau* (London: Routledge, 1999).

Rawls, John, *A Theory of Justice* (Cambridge, Mass.: Harvard University Press, 1971).

——— *Lectures on the History of Moral Philosophy*, ed. Barbara Herman (Cambridge, Mass.: Harvard University Press, 2000).

Rosen, Michael, *On Voluntary Servitude* (Cambridge, Mass.: Harvard University Press, 1996).

Sachs, David, 'How to Distinguish Self-Respect from Self-Esteem', *Philosophy & Public Affairs* 10 (1981), 346–60.

Sandler, Joseph, Alex Holder, and Dale Meers, 'The Ego Ideal and the Ideal Self', *The Psychoanalytic Study of the Child* 18 (1963), 139–58.

Sartre, Jean-Paul, *Being and Nothingness*, trans. Hazel E. Barnes (New York: Washington Square Press, 1956).

Schwartz, Joel, *The Sexual Politics of Jean-Jacques Rousseau* (Chicago: University of Chicago Press, 1984).

Shklar, Judith N., *Men and Citizens: A Study of Rousseau's Social Theory* (Cambridge: Cambridge University Press, 1969).

Smith, Adam, Letter to the *Edinburgh Review*, in *Essays on Philosophical Subjects*, eds. W. P. D. Wightman and J. C. Bryce, *The Glasgow Edition of the Works and Correspondence of Adam Smith* (Oxford: Oxford University Press, 1980), vol. 3, 242–54.

_____ *The Theory of Moral Sentiments*, ed. Knud Haakonssen (Cambridge: Cambridge University Press, 2002).

Starobinski, Jean, *Jean-Jacques Rousseau: Transparency and Obstruction*, trans. Arthur Goldhammer (Chicago: University of Chicago Press, 1988).

_____ *Le remède dans le mal* (Paris: Gallimard, 1989).

Striker, Gisela, *Essays on Hellenistic Epistemology and Ethics* (Cambridge: Cambridge University Press, 1996).

Trachtenberg, Zev M., *Making Citizens* (London: Routledge, 1993).

Velleman, David, 'A Rational Superego', *The Philosophical Review* 108 (1999), 529–58.

Viroli, Maurizio, *Jean-Jacques Rousseau and the 'Well-Ordered Society'*, trans. Derek Hanson (Cambridge: Cambridge University Press, 1988).

Whitebook, Joel, *Perversion and Utopia* (Cambridge, Mass.: MIT Press, 1995).

Wingrove, Elizabeth Rose, *Rousseau's Republican Romance* (Princeton, N. J.: Princeton University Press, 2000).

Wood, Allen W., *Kant's Ethical Thought* (Cambridge: Cambridge University Press, 1999).

Index